WHAT A *Life!*

a memoir

DONALD R. JACOBS

Acknowledgments

Anna Ruth, my wife, pored over the stories, recommending changes that I usually willingly made, and she tried to rid the text of any grammatical errors. She was aided by Twila Leichty, her niece. I am solely responsible, however, for the errors of judgment or interpretation.

I am indebted to Thomas Larson of the University of California, Berkley, who convinced me to tell my story in memoir style and to Omar Eby of Eastern Mennonite University, who pushed me in that direction as well.

In an attempt to be as accurate as possible, I sought the advice of those whom I mentioned in a significant way. I wish to acknowledge their kind suggestions. I think of Galen Burkholder, M. Hershey Leaman, Paul Landis, Malcolm Graham, my own siblings, and others.

I owe a debt of gratitude to Merle and Phyllis Good at Good Books, who felt that my life story might be well worth reading because it is a small window into how the Mennonite Church got serious about planting churches in a bewildering variety of cultures. With the aid of Janet Gehman, they pruned my original longer manuscript to tell that story. Because of their compelling interest in Mennonite World Conference, the Goods saw that my memoir might be a rubric not only to explain the past, but to point toward an even more exciting future, seen through my eyes, a participant.

Finally I acknowledge that I am a happy debtor to the grace of God that shaped and infused my life. My memoir is, in a way, a line in God's eternal narrative.

The book, *Kisare wa Kiseru*, by Joseph Shenk, was published in 1984 by Eastern Mennonite Board of Missions and Charities.

All photos supplied by the author.

Design by Cliff Snyder

WHAT A LIFE!: A MEMOIR
Copyright © 2012 by Good Books, Intercourse, PA 17534
International Standard Book Number: 978-1-56148-758-5
Library of Congress Catalog Card Number: 2012949626

Publisher's Cataloging-in-Publication Data

Jacobs, Donald R.
  What a life! : a memoir / by Donald R. Jacobs.
  p. cm.
  ISBN 9781561487585
  1. Jacobs, Donald R. 2. Mennonites —Tanzania —Bishops —Biography.
  3. Mennonites —Missions —Biography. 4. Mennonites —Africa.
  5. Africa —Church history —Personal narratives. I. Title.

BX8143 J33 2012
289.7/3 –dc23   2012949626

*I dedicate this book to my mother and
father, Trella and Paul Jacobs, whose
influence permeated my entire life.*

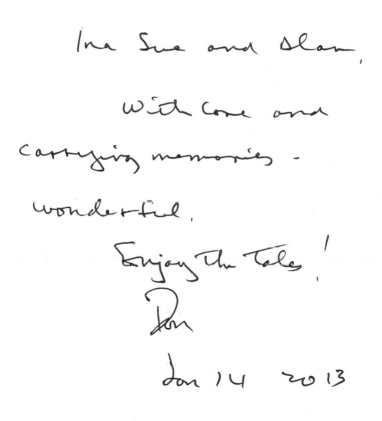

Ina Sue and Alan,

With love and
carrying memories -
wonderful,

Enjoy the Tales!

Don

Jan 14 2013

CONTENTS

FOREWORD

The people who have most effectively advanced God's purposes in the world have almost always been cross-cultural hybrids. They "ride horseback"—in the words of West African poet-politician, Leopold Senghor—with one leg dangling in one cultural context, and the other in another.

The history of God's people is full of such characters. There was Moses who was able to accomplish what he did only because of his total immersion in the realities of both Pharaoh's palace and Hebrew slave quarters. There was the Apostle Paul—and his Hellenistic-Jewish buddies, Barnabas, Silas, Timothy and others—who navigated with effortless ease between the worlds of Greek philosophers and Hebrew prophets.

There was Martin Luther King, Jr., whose boyhood home in Atlanta, Georgia, was situated literally on the dividing line between black and white communities, planting deep within him the early seeds of a vision where both communities might build something new together.

And, of course, there was Jesus of Nazareth, who has modeled for us most clearly of all what it means to be about God's Kingdom purposes—on *earth* as it is *heaven*.

Don Jacobs has been riding horseback his entire life, building cultural bridges between his Mennonite and Lutheran families of origin, between Western and African worldviews, between pastoral passions and academic pursuits, between Lancaster Conference rules and regulations and the East African Revival, between his roots in the Anabaptist story and his simple desire to love and follow Jesus.

Luckily for the rest of us, Don has never wanted to ride alone. He craves traveling companions like few people I have ever met. He stops the horse, warmly reaches out his hand, and gently lifts us into a seat behind him. African church leaders, post-graduate professors, Lancaster bishops—all are welcome to travel along.

I feel like I've been riding with Don for most of my adult life, ever since he modeled for me the clear possibility of being a serious anthropologist and a dedicated missionary, both at the same time. Now *there's* a polarity not always or easily managed!

Thank you, Don—in your life and on these pages—for inviting us on the journey. You have never promised fellow travelers a galloping leap through life on a sleek and handsome stallion. Riding with you is a bit bumpier than that, sometimes plodding along and taking detours to avoid potholes, but always focused on the One you have loved and served—the Suffering Servant who has offered us a donkey for the trek of life.

Ride on, Brother Don, as you ride on with King Jesus! We're hopping on the back and hanging on to your saddle.

"Hosanna to the son of David who comes in the name of the Lord!"

JAMES R. KRABILL
Senior Executive for Global Ministries,
Mennonite Mission Network

Chapter 1

TOUCHING
HERITAGE

LOOKING FOR A PAST

"Twila, look here!" I carefully lifted a rough brick from the dark soil and moved my hand across it with the tender touch of an amazed lover. My fingers explored every nick, every bump, every smooth section, while my eyes welled with yearning and hope. I knew it. "Twila, this brick is from Great-Grandma Susanna's oven!"

What was driving me, a 70-year-old man, as I forced myself into rough brambles covering an area on which an ancient farmhouse once stood? I was consumed by a compelling need to find and embrace a past that I never really knew, yet I hoped that, if I could somehow recover it, touch and feel it, I could better understand who I am.

My sister Twila, scrambling among the sparse, half-buried bits and pieces that lay at her feet, and as excited as I, triumphantly held up what was left of a blue porcelain bucket. Twila, 15 years older than I am, like me, carried a strong desire to embrace a past that we never knew, but one that we could perhaps create and shape with a few shards of pottery that we could lay our hands on. The pot of the past was broken, we knew that, but in our mind's eye we could see how one piece might fit with another piece. Together we dreamed of a past where our grandmother, the infant Almira Blough, saw her first morning, where she drank the milk of cows that grazed the pasture above the house, and how she grew up in that home with four brothers and four sisters.

Twila, my partner detective, had recently discovered an old framed photograph of the Blough farm. Together we pored over this precious picture. We were always asking "Who?" That was what we wanted to know: "Who were these people who produced us? Who was that Mennonite housewife who baked bread in the farm oven, and who was her husband, Samuel, and that little one named Almira, our mom's mother?"

Bishop Samuel and Susanna Blough Farm, near Johnstown, PA

We had examined the dim photograph carefully. Dominating the scene is a two-story farmhouse on a slight rise. Between the house and the sturdy barn, stand several groups of people. My guess is that the picture was taken on a balmy Sunday afternoon soon after Bishop Samuel Blough's death in 1883. I suspect the woman dressed in black was Susanna, his widow, my great-grandmother.

Those trim and substantial buildings were set on a sloping hillside, on the steady, long rise from the Stoney Creek River on which the town of Krings was located, to the plateau of Richland, near Johnstown in Pennsylvania. I was drawn into the setting by the magnet of heritage.

Pictures are good; exploring the site is even better. So Twila and I drove up the hill above Krings, turned into the lane to the left, around rhododendrons, some in full bloom, to the modern home of Attorney Robert Blough, our third cousin, I quickly calculated. I had never met him before, or his wife. Robert had managed to purchase almost all of the acreage of the original Blough farm and built his home on a small rise just opposite the site on which the Blough buildings once stood. Sitting on his porch, we were not too far from where the old picture was taken 120 years earlier.

Twila and I were eager to cross the little brook to walk into history, our history. We were not daunted by inhospitable Appalachian brush. Using the photo, and with a bit of effort, we made out where the barn and house had stood.

We climbed over rocks to locate the kitchen area. Just behind it were the remnants of a spring where the springhouse had been, so evident in the old picture. It was the back section of the house that interested me, where the kitchen no doubt was. It was not easy pushing the briars aside, but there before me lay a few bricks that must have been in the oven. Here was my connection with my past, a ruggedly shaped, red oven brick.

I could see my mother, Trella Jacobs, as she tried to describe her own mother to us. Her reverence for her mother, Almira, was palpable. I was warmed by that thought as I held the brick in my hands. There is a love bond between generations, I do believe. I want to feel the tightening of the bands of love that connect me with my heritage.

It was not that I needed to make that connection to be at peace with myself. That happened when Jesus moved into my life when I was a teenager and, by some inexplicable grace, lives on in me. That is my linkage with God. Without that, I am not "me" at all. However, my determination to link with my meaningful ancestors filled another need, a simple human one. In my missionary days I had focused my attention on being a son of God—certainly the most important—but I had simply brushed aside the fact that I am a son of a line of ancestors as well. In embracing my grandmother and her parents, none of whom I had ever seen, I felt that I was embracing my total human existence.

I needed that connection with my ancestry. I had paid no attention at all to that element as I moved from one culture to another, from the hills of Pennsylvania to the grassy plains stretching to the east of Lake Victoria in Africa, teeming with zebras and gazelles, inhabited by cultures that I never dreamed existed.

My life is a saga of needing to blend into new cultures, new situations, and new demands. Each of those many transitions changed me, some more, some less, but changed me, nevertheless. Now that I am well beyond three score years and 10, who am I? Is it possible to find out? Would finding out make any difference? I am not sure, but I felt that the missing strand in my life was an awareness of my ancestry. I had already pondered my life experiences; now it was time to braid all those strands with the ancestral strand, to produce an updated awareness of "me."

Chapter 2

SHAPED IN HOME AND COMMUNITY

My Family

In the year 1928, my parents, Paul and Trella Jacobs, already had eight children—Willard, Gerald, Twila, Erma, Merle, Dwight, Arnold, and Duane—more than the average at that time. Those eight may have seemed enough, but Dad and Mom went right ahead and had a ninth, me, then two more, girls—Roma and Dorothea. That was it, 11 of us. Dad had dual quips about his large family. The first, "I have five and a half dozen children," and the second, "I wouldn't take a million dollars for any of my children but I wouldn't give a nickel for another one!" What made my family different from the average was not only its large number but the cultural elements that met within it. It was not the typical Johnstown home. Let me explain.

The Blough Line

Some parts of our family culture were carried by the Blough line. My mother, Emma Trella Risch, traced her ancestry through the Bloughs, right back to Christian

Blough, the immigrant during colonial times. He was born in 1710 in Berne, Switzerland. In 1750 he, a widower, and his four children arrived in Philadelphia. They settled in Lebanon County, Pennsylvania. Two of the sons pushed west and settled in Somerset County. One remained Amish; the other, Mennonite. I trace my Blough bloodline to both of them. The Blough family produced a large number of religious and civil leaders, one of whom was Bishop Samuel Blough, the father of my grandmother, Almira. It was his farm in the picture.

The Blough family retained the customs, lifestyle, and language of their ancestors, using both High German for religious purposes, and Low German for everyday communication. Of course, they used English like other Americans as they sold farm produce in neighboring Johnstown.

Bishop Samuel Blough's daughter, our grandmother, Almira Blough, married Joseph Risch, the son of Wilhelm Risch, a Lutheran immigrant from Germany. Wilhelm and his wife, Margaret, bought a farm among the Mennonites, just south of Johnstown, where lay the best land out of the reach of the floods for which the city was noted. So a Mennonite Blough married a Lutheran Risch. Both families, the Bloughs and the Rischs, spoke German. Language seemed to be more important than denomination. My mother, Emma Trella Risch, was the youngest of three children born to this farm couple.

The Risch family. Joseph, my grandfather, is second from left.

After Almira died of throat cancer at age 51, my grandfather, Joseph Risch, came to live with our family. He had a great impact on my older brothers, but I never knew him. He died two years before I was born.

RELIGION, LANGUAGE AND CULTURE

Samuel and Susanna Blough raised their nine children on a farm located only two miles from the dynamic, expanding, steel-producing city, Johnstown. The Blough family felt the pull of urbanity just at the time when the Mennonites in the area were switching to English. Consequently, of the nine Blough children, only one remained Mennonite, John Henry. My grandmother, Almira, as already noted, married a Lutheran, Joe Risch, but she was never baptized into the Lutheran church. According to my mother, even though Almira married a Lutheran, she did not become a Lutheran herself. In fact, she considered

*Samuel and Susanna Blough family about 1890. Susanna,
now widowed, is in the front row, second from right.
My grandmother, Almira, is just above her.*

herself a Mennonite and insisted that she be buried in the Kaufman Mennonite Cemetery. None of her three children received Lutheran baptism as infants, nor were they baptized as Mennonites.

THE JACOBS LINE

My Dad's side was also German. About 1873, a young German couple, Ludwig and Elizabeth (Koch) Jacobs, emigrated from near Frankfurt. Ludwig was about 23 years old; Elizabeth was 20. In America they settled in the burgeoning steel city, Johnstown, Pennsylvania, where

Elizabeth and Ludwig Jacobs' wedding picture in Germany

Ludwig was employed as a steel worker. The steel company provided a house for them not far from the factory gates in the borough of Johnstown, in an area called Cambria City.

Sixteen years later, on Thursday, May 29, 1889, Ludwig just had to be among friends to enjoy the Memorial Day parade in Johnstown. Sloshing through the water was no issue for him; he loved marching bands. It seemed like the rain would never stop. It had rained for days. On Friday, May 30, a rare day off for him, he trudged the streets again, this time to purchase a dog license. Having pocketed it, he joined his buddies in the bar along the river. Suddenly, the violent waters from the broken earthen dam 12 miles upstream struck with deadly force. His body was discovered three days later, down river, identified by a dog license that he had in his pocket.

As the dam broke, his wife, Elizabeth, then at home, managed to take her three-month-old baby, Mary, and the five older children and run to the hill behind their house. Darkness fell as the raging flood destroyed the city. As

Recent picture of the stone railway bridge that figured prominently in the Johnstown Flood of 1889.

buildings and debris piled up behind the heavy stone railway bridge, fire broke out. The eerie light from the fires cast a hellish light across the scenes of destruction. It was a night of terror for the Jacobs family.

Fortunately their house was not destroyed, but almost everything in it was, except for Elizabeth's prized White sewing machine. It was a long three days until it was confirmed that Ludwig's body was recovered, downriver.

Elizabeth, then 38, had to remake her life; there was no other way. She would need to depend heavily on her oldest son, Lewis, then 12, and on Lena, 10, to help her to get on with life. My own father, Paul, five years old, had no idea what was going on. It is a mystery to this day how she managed to raise her family without a marketable

The Jacobs children a few months after the Great Flood. My father, Paul, is second from left.

skill, without a steady job, in a "foreign land." She certainly relied on prayer and hard work, along with some charity from her German friends who shared membership with her at the Zion Lutheran Church in Johnstown.

Life must have been bitter for Elizabeth, far from relatives and the embrace of the German culture that shaped her in her childhood village of Langd, near Frankfurt. That was another world, one she loved but now a hazy memory. Shaken by tragedy, she moved into the future. She not only survived but managed to send her children to the Lutheran school. Eventually, she was able to move out of the company house into one that she purchased with money earned through custom sewing, cleaning, taking in laundry, and that sort of thing. She lived until 1948, age 96. We called her Grossmom. She was the only grandparent that I knew. My dad grew up without a father but with an extraordinarily resourceful mother.

I remember Grossmom. Always slim and fit, and always dressed in black, she never learned English nor did she become an American citizen. The center of her life was God, her church, and her children. She must have had a strong faith to take her through the many hardships that she endured, a litany of pain. First of all, she left family, friends, and motherland to make a new life in America, and then buried her two firstborn daughters in American soil. In addition, she lost her breadwinning husband in the Great Flood. Then she experienced the tragic loss of her 11-year-old American-born daughter one year after the flood, a victim of what was then called diphtheria. On top of it all, her second son, Otto, was sufficiently crippled in his legs that he could not work as others did. As she grew older, she lived in her German Bible and prayed a lot. I think that her constancy in prayer bore fruit through the years. The world could do with more like Grossmom.

That was the home that shaped Paul Jacobs, my father. He was the youngest of the three boys, all of whom were expected to pitch in and help support the family. The major bread-winner in the family, Lewis, the oldest boy, married and moved to Universal near Pittsburgh just about the time Paul, my dad, finished his elementary education. Paul, as expected, worked in the steel mill not far from the family house. He later supplemented his meager pay by opening a sandwich shop near the mill entrance. He was a born entrepreneur.

As Paul grew older, he and his Lutheran friends formed a singing group which became quite popular, singing hymns and Christian songs. Riding the newly-built streetcars that fanned out from the city to the rural villages, Paul and his friends got into the Mennonite and Lutheran communities up on the high plateau south of Johnstown. There he met Trella Risch, a young farmer's daughter whose ambition was to be a schoolteacher. They were married in 1909, 20 years after the Great Flood in which Dad's father, Ludwig, drowned.

Mom had been raised as a farmer's daughter in a rural Germanic community. She married my dad, the son of an urbanized German. Their cultures were miles apart.

Mom got nostalgic when she talked about life on the farm. Her own mother, the daughter of a prominent Mennonite bishop, had tried to keep one foot in the Mennonite community and the other in the more Americanized Lutheran community. My mother experienced the same dilemma. Even though she idealized her rural upbringing, the strongest urges in her life pulled her away from typical farm life to teaching school. Her hero was Lloy Kniss, a neighbor and her first cousin, who left the farm to pursue higher education. Her eyes welled when she told me of how wonderful it was to teach school like Lloy Kniss. When Lloy and his wife, Elizabeth, answered the call to be among the earliest Mennonite missionaries in India, Mom was thrilled.

When Mom and Dad were married in 1909, they set up housekeeping on the Risch farm, where they stayed until Mom's mother, Almira, died in 1912. Willard and Gerald, my oldest brothers, were born there. My parents tried life in Johnstown for a while but moved within a couple of years to the familiar Mennonite and Lutheran community, about seven miles south of Johnstown.

Because she was busy raising her family, Mom could not continue teaching school, but she did teach piano at home later on. She became a housewife. But she could not content herself with that role only. One of her gifts was financial management. As Dad's business ventures progressed, Mom served as his treasurer in both business and land transactions.

CHOOSING A FAITH COMMUNITY

When Mom and Dad married, they, presumably, did not take religious matters very seriously. In fact, for more than a decade after they were married, they did not make any congregation their church home but attended both Lutheran and Mennonite churches. Dad was baptized as a baby in the Lutheran church. Since he was an accomplished singer and song leader, he had a wide-open door among the Mennonites who, at that time, were moving from Amish-style chant singing to full four-part harmony.

Dad was right at home with that. He was born with music in his blood, a Jacobs trademark.

Neither Dad nor Mom ever told us how they came to know Christ, or how they felt about being Mennonites. They did tell us that they decided to wait to join a local church until their two oldest sons, Willard and Gerald, requested baptism. When the boys were about 10 and 12, Dad and Mom left it up to them to choose which church they wished to join. The boys decided to join Kaufman Mennonite Church because the singing there was much better than in the Lutheran church. There may have been other more significant reasons, but I never heard them. Anyway, I liked the story! When the boys made their decision, Mom decided to be baptized with them at the Kaufman Mennonite Church. She was 33 years old at the time. Hence, our family became Mennonite!

Fitting in at Kaufman Mennonite

The Mennonite community represented by the Kaufman Mennonite Church extended a most gracious hand to our family. We were outsiders. Their welcome was a gift and a great comfort to Mom and Dad. I never heard a critical word about the church from either of them.

Later, their older children—Willard, Gerald, Twila, and Erma—all baptized Mennonites, married non-Mennonites, one after the other. This must have puzzled the Mennonite community that Mom desperately wanted to be part of.

Yet through it all, Mom retained a dignity and a faith that baffled me. She kept on teaching the Bible, writing her notes, never missing a Sunday at church, always reaching out and helping others. Admittedly, our home did not

Paul Jacobs, my father and a business executive

resemble a typical rural Mennonite home, not at all. Paul was a car dealer, an urbanite and unmistakably so. His work outfit was a full suit with vest. Mom was not comfortable in that world. She felt more at home, culturally, among her Mennonite "sisters." She organized the Kaufman Mennonite Church Sewing Circle. When the women gathered to quilt, they switched into Pennsylvania Dutch, and Mom was right in there laughing at all the quirks and quips, enjoying it all.

I suppose being a Mennonite was not a stretch for Mom. As I noted earlier, she admired her own mother, Almira. She also had great admiration for her grandfather, Bishop Samuel Blough. She told us often of how he gave himself so completely to shepherding the flocks of believers around Johnstown that he actually worked himself to death, so to speak. She told us, in holy awe, of the time that he rode horseback through the mountains in freezing weather to officiate at a service. When he arrived, they had to remove him from his horse and thaw him out before he could minister to them. Mom was profoundly proud of her Mennonite grandfather.

It was a different story for Dad when it came to things Mennonite. He had a romantic attraction to rural people and their way of life, but he had no capacity at all to be part of the Germanic Mennonite rural culture. But he was loyal to and attended the Kaufman Mennonite Church. It must have been difficult for the church to fully accept Paul.

For beginners, he was a Jacobs. The Mennonites had been in that community for six generations but had not opened their doors very much to people who were not born Mennonites. The saving factor, I suppose, was that Dad married a modified version of a Pennsylvania Dutch woman whose grandfather was a noted Mennonite bishop. It also helped that Dad loved the music that Mennonites did.

The Kaufman Mennonite Church never gave Dad a leadership role. They surely knew that he was a leader; after all, he ran a business that probably had more capital and employees than any of the members there could imagine. I think the reason was that even though they knew that he was a leader, he was not one of their own culture. He accepted his role as a song leader and did well. I never heard him complain. He did not hanker after acceptance. He knew who he was, and he was content. I chuckle when I think of how hard it must have been for the Yoders, the Shetlers, the Esches, the Holsopples, and the others, all descendants of cultural Mennonites, to absorb a Paul Jacobs. That they succeeded at all is a miracle of God's grace.

Evidently, none of this squelched Dad's commitment to do his part as a member of the church. For example, when he installed an electrical system in his own house, he decided to do one for the church, too. That is how the Kaufman Church got its "Delco plant."

In the 1920s when Dad was prospering in his business, a plea went out to the American Mennonite community to supply funds to purchase tractors for Mennonites struggling in Russia. This struck Dad as a fine idea. He decided not to make a small donation but to contribute enough to buy one Fordson tractor all on his own. That fit his style.

I believe Dad respected the local Mennonite leaders. I do not think that he admired them, however. The Mennonite leaders that he did actually admire were C. F. Derstine, a very gifted evangelist from Ontario; John L. Stauffer, the principal of Eastern Mennonite School in Harrisonburg, Virginia; and C. F. Yake and A. J. Metzler from the Mennonite Publishing House in Scottdale, Pennsylvania. Somehow Dad could understand these people, and they befriended him.

In the late '20s, when the Mennonite Church in North America was becoming more mission-minded, the call went out for every congregation to develop an outreach. That was good news for the Jacobs family who had attended the Kaufman Church Sunday after Sunday. Mom and Dad jumped at the opportunity and focused on "their field," a community just two miles away called Carpenter's Park, or Cambria Fuel, a company-owned coal town which drew immigrants mostly from eastern and southern Europe. Their cultures were so alien that rural Germanic communities like the Mennonites or the Lutherans were baffled by the thought of trying to relate to them.

That did not deter Dad one bit. As the son of an immigrant himself, he had a soft spot in his heart for immigrants, regardless of their culture. He wanted to evangelize them. He invited a noted Canadian Mennonite evangelist, Clayton Derstine, to come and preach to these people. I recall distinctly that Dad rented the newly-opened community center in Carpenter Park for the event. I sat on the porch with my legs dangling. This was new!

Quite a few young people were eager to attend a Sunday School, so Dad and Mom teamed with another couple, Lloyd Croyle and his wife, to operate one in the two-room public school. Lloyd officiated, Dad sang, and Mom taught. That's where I grew up, surrounded by Ponacos, Kaltenbaughs, Santorums, and other strange family names.

Apart from the Sunday school, we had no social contact with these recent immigrants. They had their school and we had ours. We were Mennonites, whatever that meant. We may not have known what we were, but we knew exactly who *they* were — "The Cambria Fuel Kids." I learned prejudice by osmosis, or like one gets the mumps, by human contact. Being a Mennonite made it a little easier to know who the "foreigners" were since Mennonites were outsiders of a sort, too.

I was slowly becoming aware of the fact that cultures can bind people together, but they can also divide people. Later I faced these issues in my missionary career. I think this was my initial introduction to what a tribe is. We were in one, they were in another, whoever the "they" were.

LIFE IN THE JACOBS HOME

At home Dad and Mom created an atmosphere of openness, fun, and excitement that we as a family enjoyed and which, I believe, blessed the community.

I was two years old when a financial shockwave hit, the Great Depression. It marked a watershed in the life of our family, changing us from being well off to scrambling to press on with a life with no frills. Prior to 1930, we were considered wealthy. We had a large, fancy, electrified, Sears Roebuck house with indoor plumbing and a fenced tennis court, all quite modern. Dad had a prosperous car business in Johnstown; we also owned the farm across the road which Dad had purchased to develop as a middle-class housing project. He was a recognized business leader in Johnstown. The future looked bright, indeed.

When the banks foreclosed, Dad had about 300 cars out, only partially paid for. Two hundred of these he had to repossess and bear the outstanding indebtedness on each one. Willard and Gerald, then in college in Goshen, Indiana, came home to help to rescue the business. They ran the parts department that grew and grew since people had to maintain the cars and trucks that they had. That helped to keep the company from failing.

Our family had to tighten our belts again 10 years later as World War II clouds gathered. When the government initiated rationing to help the war effort, I saw Mom at her best, stretching everything to amazing limits. The challenge to live lean was good for us. Our little farm took on added significance. It became our source of supply for much of our food, from milk to potatoes. Since I grew up in that lean period I had no idea that life could or should be different. I was a happy boy.

Chapter 3

SCHOOL –
A NEW CULTURE

TIRE HILL SCHOOL

I attended Kaufman Elementary School for five years,
all with the same teacher. All of us students were from
the same basic culture—white, Germanic, mostly Mennonite. All the parents knew one another and probably even
knew one another's grandparents. Not so in the Tire Hill
School where I was sent for sixth grade. It was only three
miles away but 1,000 miles away culturally. I found myself
seated among perfect strangers. I hadn't the slightest idea
who they were, and Mom and Dad knew absolutely nothing about their families. I was lost and a bit small because
I was a year ahead of my age, having completed grade
one before I was six, a fact that I was reminded of every
school year.

I soon discovered that the guys spent almost all of their
recesses playing marbles. I decided to practice so that I
could compete. I collected a few marbles and practiced
until I could pretty much hit what I was aiming at. I was
allowed to join in. Surprisingly enough, I won some marbles, and some more, until I had pockets full of marbles.

I was quizzed about those marbles at the supper table at home. "Donald, do you mean to tell us that you are playing 'for keeps'?" I was about to be educated! "That is gambling," Mom said. "Those kids that you are playing with are gamblers. They do not know any better. We do not gamble! The Bible forbids it." Next time that I played I won as usual, but then returned all the marbles I had gained. At first they were surprised. But they let me play with them, each time allowing me to return my rightly earned booty.

That year at Tire Hill School introduced me to another world. Many of the students were children of miners and day laborers, mostly with immigrant parents. I was the first of our family to get thrown into a cultural mixed salad that early in life. All eight before me finished all eight grades at monocultural Kaufman School, and then plunged into the "world" as high-schoolers. For the first time in my life I was uncomfortable and confused. At home I knew who I was, but at school in that strange cultural mix, I was a nobody and it hurt.

After grade six I entered the new consolidated school, Conemaugh Township High School, about five miles from our home. My older brother Arnold had transferred there from Moxham High School, and another brother Duane was a couple grades ahead of me. I entered as a seventh-grader. "Oh, you are Arnold's brother." I soon learned that Arnold was a "somebody" around school. He excelled in sports and was the best sports reporter and journalist that the school had. That mantle was passed on to Duane. He, too, wrote well. They were also both good students. I was condemned to be like my two older brothers. I knew I could never live up to those expectations. But I tried.

I was a bit too slight for most competitive sports, but I could write some and, like my brothers, became the sports editor for the school paper. That meant attending football and basketball games, writing up the results and sending in the story to the local newspaper. I rather liked that. It gave me a little feeling of self-worth, but I knew that it was a very temporary sort of thing. For the first time in my life I began to wonder what would ever become of me because I was shaping my life around how I thought others viewed me, not around who I actually was. I could never be like my brothers. But who, then, was I? I lacked the courage to ask!

A CLASH OF VALUES

I had a hunch that I carried some deep and abiding structure in my inner person—good, substantial virtues— but it was impossible for me to articulate what that was and, even more troublesome, live up to those virtues. I knew that my home shaped me. There I was content and grew. In this new world where I found friends that I never knew and where I was never quite sure how I fit in, I was being pulled apart. I found that I was becoming two persons, "me" at home and "me" out in society, where I tried to figure out what people thought of me. The two seldom met. During that time I did not even think of myself as a Kaufman Church Mennonite. I cared little what the Mennonite community thought anyway.

In my junior year, because I was on the staff of the school paper, I found myself in a clique where I began to truly interact with peers outside my own family. I discovered that some of the best writers among my peers had no morals at all. They spurned any restraints. I was living a disjointed life. The values that drove that little, tight, elite writers' group bore no resemblance to the values of our home. No matter how I tried, I could not find any meaningful connection. That junior year I began to ponder whether I should run with the crowd, which meant my writers' clique, or whether I should break out and espouse the values which shaped me. Peer pressure and the desire to be with the avant garde decided the issue for me. I was going to try my best to be a liberated guy and move with them.

None of my classes in high school appealed to me very much. I was there because, like almost everyone else, I had to be. It was not considered cool to get excited about anything academic. So, I cloaked my admiration for Latin class, for example, the best I could. I thrived on Latin because it provided a key to English vocabulary. I began to dismantle many words to find their Latin roots. I still find myself doing that. But I did not let my enthusiasm show. It was the same in my science classes. For moments I could get carried away by the wonder of our natural world, but since that was not a good way to feel in our group, I throttled my enthusiasm and imagination about most everything except the trivial and frivolous.

A Family in Upheaval

When I was a junior in high school, all my brothers were in some sort of national service. It was the fourth year of America's involvement in World War II. Along with what was happening at school, my emotions had to deal with what was going on in our family. Two of my brothers, Arnold and Duane, entered the Marine Corps, two joined the Army, Willard and Gerald, and two entered

Duane and Arnold, Marine Corps, on   Willard, Army
a chance meeting in the Pacific area

Gerald, Army,   Merle, CPS   Dwight, CPS
retired as colonel

Civilian Public Service (CPS) as conscientious objectors
to war, Merle and Dwight. I am not sure how all that
impacted me, but I was sure of one thing. I had no incli-
nation, not one iota, to enter the military. I am not sure
what would have happened if the peer group that I was
in at school had swarmed into the military. My compul-
sions to belong may have trumped other virtues in my
inner structure.

Let me digress for a moment. I was raised in a Mennonite family. That is, all my siblings were Mennonites by
baptism. It occurred to me only later that our family had
no close blood relations in the Mennonite Church. The
blood relatives that we had and with whom we spent most
of our time were not in the least Mennonites. Somewhere
along the line I got bitten by the nonviolence bug. That
meant that I was out of step with my relatives.

I grew up straddling two cultures, that of my home and that of the group that I ran with. Our home, which was large enough to be a subculture, tried to blend the best of both. I think we were somewhat successful. I always felt safe and happy in the culture that our family had cobbled together. We were at home in both cultures yet not completely comfortable in either.

The cultural diversity in our family widened because of the choices my siblings and our peers made. We children were probably not as aware of this as our parents, because Dad and Mom had to live under the scrutiny of the Mennonite community. I could not verbalize all of this at the time, but I felt it. I internalized my feelings. The tensions had the potential to tear us apart as a family. I felt for Mom and Dad. I felt for my brothers. I determined to make peace. I hurt for both sides. I found myself in a spot that was to be repeated time and again in my life, a person "between." I was between our family and our relatives, between pacifists and soldiers, between Mennonites and the whole wide world! I was destined to be a person "between."

Paul and Trella Jacobs after the Depression

I observed Dad and Mom as they tried to maintain good relationships with their children on one hand and the church on the other. All I could do was observe, because they never breathed a word of resentment against the church, and I knew that their commitment to everyone in the family was unsullied. What truly amazed me was that Mom was so committed to her children, all of them, that she wrote to each one every week, whether they were in the military or in alternate service. That commitment that I saw in my own parents to love all equally, regardless of the decisions that they made, impressed me.

As I moved into responsible positions in my life, I found myself wanting to emulate Dad and Mom in that regard. I must love all! Their example served me well, not only in my life work but in my personal life. True love is unconditional. And true Christian love is even stronger because it is based on forgiveness and hope. I must admit, however, that I felt the pain of the split that was happening in our family, probably more than I should have.

Chapter 4

MEETING JESUS
AT EASTERN
MENNONITE

1944

A Surprising Question

Dad and Mom were well aware of my wandering ways in the local high school. But I was not prepared for Mom's question: "Donald, would you consider going to Eastern Mennonite School (EMS) for your senior year?" At first

I was shocked, but the idea began to stir me. That might be a way to get out of my problems at school, I thought. It might relieve some of the tensions that I felt getting tighter and tighter within me. Within a few days I brought myself to say, "Yes, I will try it."

Don, high school
graduate, 1945

I did not ask Dad or Mom why they suggested that I transfer to the school in

Virginia. I knew that Dad was called in for a friendly chat about me with the high school principal at the end of my junior year. I knew I was on a slippery slope that I was unable to halt. If I ever had a sense of direction in my life, I had lost it. If my parents had not been aware of that, Dad's chat with the principal must have done it. That put Dad on the spot, because he never spoke harsh words to me. The solution? Send me off to a Mennonite boarding school in Virginia! In any case, Mom and Dad were silent on the "why" and loud on the offer.

When September came, I was on my way to an entirely new setting, the Shenandoah Valley of Virginia. On arrival, I never felt stranger in my life. My room was not ready, so I spent the first few days in the home of the legendary J. L. Stauffer, the principal. I have no idea what he thought. Maybe he knew that my two oldest brothers, Willard and Gerald, were asked to leave that very school when they clashed with authority years earlier. Twila, who followed them, was just fine. She spent four years there and graduated. I took a liking to J. L. He was homespun. I liked that.

It was 1944. School opened. There I met people so unlike those at my home high school that I could hardly believe I was on the same planet. They were Mennonites, but not like the ones at Kaufman Church. I dismissed this new lot as unreal and searched out a few friends whom I thought I could relate to, guys and girls. I found a few, a very few, and soon I was partying just like before.

A New Sense of Direction

Thoughts of God did not concern me. I stuck out my chin and dared anyone to challenge my independence. Whatever that meant. Suddenly, on October 10, 1944,

I was arrested by the Lord. I can take you to the spot between the Administration Building and the Chapel where I was overwhelmed with a Presence. I knew at once that this was God. Before that evening was over, I had declared to God my personal bankruptcy, received forgiveness for my sins and my sinful nature, and determined to follow Jesus to the best of my knowledge and ability. J. Lester Eshleman, who was to become a missionary medical doctor and lifelong friend, prayed with me that night when I gave my life to God.

That was, for me, an end and a beginning, the end of self-sufficiency and the beginning of a life as a wobbly but determined follower of Jesus. I was given the power to be me, a person who could shape a life and not just be carried along by what others were thinking or what I thought would bring me some short-term benefit. Following that commitment to Christ, I became a person with a center of my own. Upon reflection, I believe I had a growing compulsion to be radical, to break out and be different. But to be different in that direction never entered my mind. When Dad and Mom got my letter describing, in the best way I could, what had happened to me, they were absolutely elated.

For the first time in my life I knew who I was—a follower of Jesus, with a self-realization that went far beyond human experience of any kind. I am not now sure how much theology I knew or perceived, but one thing was certain. My inner being with all the emotional freight I was carrying was overcome by the feeling of being one in spirit with Jesus. That startled and delighted me. I probably had intellectual reservations about the church, Christianity, and all that, but my spirit contacted the Spirit of Jesus and we clicked. My head would need to catch up later. I had entered an entirely new world, a new existence.

At last I was free to feel things deeply, things that mattered. Music provided me with abiding beauty and joy. EMS was the place for that. And literature came alive, especially British and American poets, and for the first time I experienced the hand of God in nature. While on a field hike in biology class, for example, I knelt beside a meadow pool and saw in the shadows and shifting lights the darting of a water beetle, the water as clear as crystal. The entire world was in the pool, all for me to see and ponder. I was a child again, a child of wonder.

MOVING ON AS A BELIEVER

What I just described was the beginning of a journey with twists and turns. That final year of high school was a period of playing peek-a-boo with Jesus. Sometimes he dominated my thinking; at times I felt much alone. But I knew I had encountered God, and that was the bedrock event. I would never be the same again. I had touched God through Jesus, and I had felt his love. Life was simply a way of building on that fact in the best way I knew how.

I read the Bible a lot, prayed much, and tried to discover how to please God. This all happened to me in a Mennonite setting, at a Mennonite school, and, since I wanted to be a good Christian, I assumed that meant being a model Mennonite. I found out how the "best" Mennonites behaved and dressed and all that and sought to

Don with a Virginia Mennonite elder, while at EMU

equal or outdo them. This resulted in a bit of potential legalism, I suppose, but at that time I determined that simply being a lackadaisical Christian was not enough. The school's dress codes and its behavior codes and social codes, all well established, posed no threat to me. I never asked myself whether I wanted to be a Mennonite or not; I was one and that settled my heart.

As the year progressed, I became fascinated by the teachers. I owe much to J. Mark Stauffer, Professor of Music, who taught a Sunday school class for senior high boys. He personified a new option for me—a professional musician, a great outdoors man who loved horses and was totally committed to Christ. I loved that package. Other faculty members combined the best of academia and the arts with a love for God. That impressed me. It was a combination that I did not know existed. I think of D. Ralph Hostetter in biology and M.T. Brackbill in physics as examples. I never knew that there were people like this in the world. And they were Mennonite! They even dressed and acted like Mennonites.

That year a group of us who wanted to share our walk with God gathered regularly in the Upper Room in the Administration Building. That little furnished garret room became a sacred place for us. In the quietness of our prayer times in that room, I knew that God was speaking into my heart and life. I owe much to those deep times of prayer with other fellows.

It was there that I got to know on a deeper level people such as Paul Swarr, later a missionary to Israel; John Miller, a future New Testament scholar; Harold Housman, who became a missionary doctor in Tanzania; Eugene Souder, a future noted editor; and my roommate, Carl Miller of Mississippi. That was my initiation into open, honest, and challenging sharing at a rich spiritual level. I never interacted like that with anyone before. It was a new way to live. I grew by leaps and bounds.

I found an outlet in singing. How I loved to sing in choir and especially in male quartets. We went to jails, street corners, and churches, singing those charming men's quartet songs.

When I graduated in 1945, I was a Mennonite! Of Virginia vintage. My dad and mom said little, as usual, about my faith walk, but I knew they were overjoyed about the change that they could surely see. I gave them full credit for making that change in my life possible.

I graduated from high school a different person, in many ways, from the fumbling young man that entered the class nine months earlier. Having restructured my life around Jesus in the company of an entirely new community, I felt safe and ready to return home without the support of those friends.

RETURN TO VIRGINIA

I had a great summer. My dear dad lined up a good job for me. It was not long before the young adult groups in the area's churches got in touch with me, and I had a delightful time of sharing with them. I could have stayed right there, I thought, and worked with the young people of the district. But that was not to be. The siren of more education lured me, once again, back to Harrisonburg. This time it was not to high school but to Eastern Mennonite College, on the same campus.

My first year of college confirmed me in my faith and gave me the opportunity to observe real live Mennonite teachers. As I've said, I knew of no Mennonite in our home community that I considered a role model. EMS was chock-full of them. I named some earlier. To those I add Dorothy Kemrer, J. L. Stauffer, John Mumaw, C. K. Lehman, and Daniel Lehman. I admired these people and aspired to be something like them. And I had good student friends like my roommates who shared an off-campus apartment, Gordon Shantz and Paul Kniss.

A NEW BLESSING — ANNA RUTH

The singular most wonderful thing that happened to me in my first year in college, however, was learning to know Anna Ruth Charles of Lancaster. She first appealed to me as a winsome young lady. She had a primness and

radiance about her that I found attractive. Her pulled-back hair, tied in a bun, gave her eyes a clarity that stunned me. And through those eyes she gave me glimpses of what was in her heart and mind.

I also saw in Anna Ruth a stability and commitment to a way of life which drew me to her more than I realized at the time. I knew that if we should get to know one another, I wanted to be more like her than she like me. She exuded a meaningful tradition, a context,

Anna Ruth at the College fountain with the Administration Building in the background

and I wanted that. I knew that my own exuberance and dynamism had to be tempered by wisdom and tradition. Furthermore, I knew that she was a person that I could truly love with all my heart. I had never dated seriously before, but I felt that I could elbow all others away, hoping that she would have me. We talked, prayed, and got at least somewhat comfortable with one another. I just had a deep, warm, settled feeling that it would be more than I could ever dream of if I could shape life around her. We could be a Mennonite Christian couple. I shivered when I thought of the prospect.

As I learned to know Anna Ruth during that first year of college, I felt in my spirit that we would live this life together. That firm assurance enabled me to concentrate on what I was doing in the months and years ahead. Later I realized that Anna Ruth and I were as perfect a fit as I could possibly imagine for what God would lead us into in our lifetime of service.

That year, my first in college, was a sorting out time for me, so I didn't exactly excel in academics. I made two D's, one in Old Testament History and one in Biology. Horrors! I'll never forget how that felt. By the way, Anna Ruth excelled in all her courses, including New Testament Greek. She dazzled me. And she was so unassuming.

MORE GROWING, SERVING, THINKING

Grades aside, it was a year in which I grew spiritually. The college sponsored Gospel Teams that went here and there sharing their faith. Their programs always included music. Since I could sing baritone in male quartets, I was invited to join in. That put me side by side with some of the more senior men like Paul Landis, Joe Bear, Nevin

Miller, Don Augsburger, and Richard Detweiler. That kind of ministry really excited me.

About that time I discovered that I was not bad as a speaker. I could communicate fairly well with people. I enjoyed public appearances, even though I felt wobbly-kneed. Both my father and mother were good at speaking on their feet before people. I was not totally surprised when I found myself up front trying to explain something, but I had not the faintest idea that I would have a life of speaking before people.

Above all, I was discovering who I really was inside. My new identity revolved around my new-found relationship with God through Jesus, energized all the while by the Holy Spirit. I was at peace with myself, and I found that the rules and stipulations of our rather strict college suited me just fine. The intellectual and spiritual setting in college inspired me and helped me to shape an identity built around the values espoused by staff and students alike. This emerging identity found an echo in my own inner person, fostered by virtues I unknowingly learned as I grew up in our family.

I felt closer to Jesus than to anyone I had ever known. As I sidled up to him, I felt protected and affirmed and loved. It would require a lifetime to begin to understand how a bewildered young man could profoundly love a person called Jesus Christ. I speak not of an imaginary Jesus, but a Jesus more real than teachers or friends. I live in the glow of that mystery.

Being a Mennonite, or determining to be one, has always been with me since I was converted at age 16. But it did not begin there. I believe that God, in his providence, placed in my heart, probably through family nurture, some core values that constituted my inner self.

These fundamental, primal constants in my life include my understanding of who I am in my own eyes, in the eyes of those around me, and in the eyes of God. This triune cluster forms my spiritual spine and has hardly changed at all. Conversion served to make them central.

Being a Mennonite was not just a trivial issue with me; it was important because that identity had both a spiritual and a sociological meaning. Sociologically, I came from a long line of Mennonite Bloughs. My great-grandfather was a beloved Mennonite bishop. It dawned on me that I had a heritage that I could relate to, even though I did not pursue that line of thought at all. I knew that the Bloughs were a distinct subculture in the sea of American cultures. Because I embraced a Mennonite identity for myself, I was able to affirm my heritage. Be that as it may, I was a committed Christian. Of that I had no doubt.

Chapter 5

TEACHING IN KENTUCKY

1946 – 1948

A SUMMER CHALLENGE

In my freshman year, I met Richard Detweiler. God sent a bona fide hero to befriend me. He was as spiritual as Saint Paul, I thought, but could play ball like Joe DiMaggio. He told jokes, sang, and preached with elegance. And, to top it off, he was a Mennonite. He had no idea how he shaped me to be a contented, eager disciple of Jesus Christ.

Richard Detweiler, a prominent person in my life

This was the kind of Christian I wished to be, a Mennonite one as nearly like Richard as possible!

During the spring term of 1946, he told me that the Virginia Mennonite Mission Board was inviting him to spend about a month of the coming summer in Kentucky. The Board, which already had three mission posts in Kentucky—Lost Creek, Relief, and Crocket—asked Richard to survey a community west of Lost Creek as a possible area for expansion.

He sat me down and asked, "Will you go with me? We can do this together." Me? I knew nothing about missions and even less about doing a community survey. I did a lot of praying those days, asking for discernment. It occurred to me that God was answering my prayer. On the lighter side, I thought that if Richard and the Virginia Mission Board had enough confidence in me to feed me for a few weeks in the summer, I was more than ready for the adventure. Summer came, and Richard and I pitched our tent beside the Weaver house in Kentucky. We learned to know these amazing people. Melvin was from Iowa; Miriam, his wife, was the daughter of C.K. Lehman of EMS; and Esther, Miriam's sister, was there as a teacher at Lost Creek.

Richard and I spent several enjoyable days just roaming around Coffee Creek and some other "hollers" whose names I forget.

An Invitation to Teach

As I look back on that summer, I realize that the purpose of it all, for me, was to be in a mentoring relationship with Richard Detweiler. I held him in high regard as a man who truly wanted to serve the Lord and who loved me dearly. I think that I would have done anything for him if he had asked. But I was not prepared to hear what he did ask of me as we, having finished our survey, began to write our findings about Coffee Creek for the Mission Board.

In our report we noted, incidentally, that the Coffee Creek School would probably not open that fall. That was because it was desperately hard to get a teacher to take a job in that far-off, rather difficult situation. The students were not an easy bunch to keep in line, largely because of the culture of the place and because of family rivalries. In almost every home we visited, we heard frustration over the fact that no one had been able to run a good school. They had had two or three teachers in the past year, none of whom liked it on Coffee Creek. There was not enough unity in the community to even establish a school board to look after the school.

Then Richard caught me off guard. He suggested an outlandish thing—that I should apply for the job! Me? I had just turned 18 in July, and now it was August. I was much too young. Furthermore, I had but one year of college. I had no training or experience as a teacher. But, urged on by Richard, I showed up in West Liberty, the county seat, applied for the job, and got it. If I hadn't offered to teach the school, they would have had yet another school in the high valleys of Appalachia without a teacher.

My mother, who had always kept up a lively correspondence with me, informed me by letter that she was not at all happy about this decision, nor was Dad. She included comments from family members asking me to come home. The family and church youth needed me, she pleaded.

I read Mom's letter carefully, prayed about it, and then responded, thanking her and all the family for their concern for my welfare, but explained that I felt I must stay and teach this school in Kentucky. What made this decision so difficult for me was that, since I made my commitment to Christ at age 16, I deliberately placed myself under the authority of my parents. I enjoyed sharing with them how I was feeling about things and welcomed their advice, which I usually followed. When I had to decide about whether to teach in Kentucky, I felt a call to do so. This was my first big decision against my parents' counsel. I had no idea how this was going to affect my relationship with Dad and Mom, but I had a deep-seated assurance that they would love me, nevertheless. My sail was set. I might add that Mom and Dad, along with Roma and Dorothea, my younger sisters, visited me in Kentucky during my stay there. Slowly Mom and Dad, as usual, got reconciled to what they could not change!

Diving into Teaching

We hastily made arrangements so that I could open the Coffee Creek School on time, and I moved in with Melvin and Miriam Weaver as a boarder. I registered 57 students in eight grades, and almost all of them showed up. Most of the families had records of birth dates. In one case, however, they simply did not know the year. When I asked when a particular child was born, the mother said, "I forget the year, but it was in 'baka strippen.'"

Teaching all grades kept me stepping. I still remember teaching history in one class, while reading from a geography book held in the other hand, and at the same time

On the way to teach school on Coffee Creek, Kentucky

Coffee Creek School at recess time. I taught all eight grades with over 50 students for two years.

getting ready for the next class. I was always running to catch up. How I managed, I will never know. But the weeks passed and we were still having school. I wanted to get to know the parents of my students, but that was not easy because I lived at the Weaver house across the mountain, and I spent my weekends with them.

Teaching at Coffee Creek taxed everything in me. Looking back, I realize it was audacious of me to think that I would not only survive a year of teaching there but actually enjoy it. It did my self-image a heap of good just to know that I could do something that seemed impossible.

A SUMMER AT GOSHEN COLLEGE

After my first year of teaching, I went to Goshen College for summer school. The drawing card was that I could live in the 8th Street House with Merle, my brother, whom I admired hugely. He had spent several years in Civilian Public Service (CPS) and was just then finishing his first degree. That summer Merle and I bonded in a remarkable way. We had many great walks together, checking out the birds and wildlife. I wanted to be more like Merle. I thought, "Merle is a Blough. I am mostly Jacobs." But that did not mean that I could not develop the little Blough that must surely be within me.

That summer I was introduced to classical music, one of Merle's passions as well. I knew that music would become an increasingly important part of my life. I took Music Appreciation, taught by Dwight Weldy. I could have filled my whole summer with courses like that! It was not true of an ex-GI in the class who had absolutely no ear for music. He managed to identify enough of the pieces to pass the course. I asked him how he did it. He said, "I memorized the scratchy places on the records."

I also got into philosophy, taught by J. C. Wenger. I did a paper on Immanuel Kant which opened doors into the world of philosophy. I also had a class with John Mosemann, the former missionary to Tanganyika. He taught a course on Paul's letters to the Corinthians. What fun, studying the Bible like that.

A SECOND YEAR ON COFFEE CREEK

Then back to Kentucky, to Coffee Creek. During my first year of teaching at the school, I lived with Mennonite missionaries and rode a horse named Dixie. She carried me the three miles to school, up across a mountain and down the other side. During my second year, the one I was now entering, I felt I should live right in the Coffee Creek community. I boarded with Sanford and Becky Hamilton, true mountain folks. Sanford could spit tobacco a mile, buy and sell horses in the twinkling of an eye,

A recent picture of the Hamilton home where I boarded in Kentucky

usually losing money in the process, and he rode upright in the saddle with billowy pants and lace-up shoes. What a man. Becky was a bit on the plump side with a ready smile, always with an apron that had straight pins stuck in a row, just in case she would need them. She managed her way around her rather demanding husband, often saving the last word until he left her presence and it was just me.

A highlight of that school year was Anna Ruth's visit. She had several days off over Christmas, so she took the train to Paintsville, where I met her and introduced her to the Weavers. She spent a few days with me at the Hamiltons. At that time she was a junior at Millersville State Teachers College, training to be a teacher. She helped me for at least one day at school. Becky was enthusiastic about Anna Ruth. She didn't point her finger at me very often, but when Anna Ruth left, she did so and said, "Marry her!" Becky was not known for her subtlety. Sanford offered his advice as he shifted his wad of tobacco to his other cheek, "The morning after the honeymoon, you may be tempted to make the fire. Don't! That might spoil her."

My greatest delight was spending time in the homes of the students. The parents valued visits from the teacher. The more I did it, the more I enjoyed it. Now and again I had meetings with parents when they came to the school, often for a concert of some kind. It was something to see those rugged, large adults squeeze into the wee desks designed for less ample bodies. The parents kept telling me, "Woop'em good if they mis bahayve. When they git 'ome, they'll git'nuther'n."

Since there was no church on the upper reaches of Coffee Creek, I decided to have Sunday morning Sunday School and a worship service in the schoolhouse when the weather was nice. A couple dozen adults came, as I remember. I taught the Gospel of John, my first opportunity to probe the depth of that marvelous Gospel. That was my little, feeble attempt at forming a fellowship on Coffee Creek. As long as I was there we had Sunday worship. It did not continue after I left.

I was not trying to plant a church on Coffee Creek. Had that been my assignment, I would have had to dive into the culture and sink or swim. As it was, I could stand outside the culture and observe it with compelling interest, but not as a true participant. I was a schoolteacher from Pennsylvania, from a strange culture. I found that, as a teacher, it was fine to be a little different. That was expected. I think I succeeded in meeting that expectation. I tried not to be aloof. I even took to wearing local togs, like a leather jacket, and now and again slipping into their dialect, but that was about as deep as I went. I was an observer, not a participant. I was teaching their children, but I did not really belong. I wonder that it worked at all.

Signs of Discomfort with Cultural Religion

While living in Kentucky I began to think about how one might go about planting churches in other cultures. I admired the missionary families there, the Weavers, the Landises, and the Horsts. I never doubted their integrity or calling. What did concern me was whether they could actually plant their kind of a Mennonite church in the local Kentucky culture. I might add that all the missionaries were shaped by the same Virginia influences that shaped me.

As I pondered this, I began to see the Germanic Mennonite dilemma. Through the years Mennonites had wrapped themselves in a cultural cocoon that set them apart from society, so to speak. That mutually submissive, uniform community clearly expressed the people's interpretation of their own history and the Scriptures. They believed that they had found the answer to living as a God-fearing community in American society. They held themselves together by stressing those aspects of biblical teaching that served to strengthen community, such as limiting communion only to those who embraced their discipline.

Mennonites brought this subculture to near perfection in several sections of North America. Having managed to do that, they now faced a new, powerful, and unsettling theme — what to do with Christ's mandate to take the gospel to the whole world.

Living two years among Appalachian mountain people of mostly Anglo ancestry, I began to wonder if the desire to forge a uniform Mennonite subculture could possibly be turned into a worldwide missionary movement. I had my doubts, reinforced by my life among people in Kentucky who looked upon the Mennonites who lived among them as sincere but quaint.

They inhabited a Baptist world, with a few Methodists here and there, all reflecting the values held by the mountain culture. I recall asking a local person, years later, why no one seemed interested in being Mennonite. Her response was simply, "We never could figure out what kind of Baptists you people were!"

KENTUCKY REVISITED, 1991

To close out the Kentucky chapter of my life, Anna Ruth and I decided to drive to Coffee Creek in 1991, 43 years after I taught school there. We found our way to a house with which we were familiar. As I knocked, Nora Wright burst out, looked at me with those penetrating eyes of hers, and said, "You are Mr. Jacobs. You left here in 1947. I remember the year because I was carrying my youngest then." What a time we had, catching up! Her daughter Wilma was away teaching at the time. Wilma was the only one of my students who went on to high school and then college. Since that visit in 1991, we have visited there several times, and people from Coffee Creek visited us. We were especially close to Wilma and Carol Wright, Nora's daughters, and Belva, their cousin, who helped me teach the "lit luns" at school.

In 2005 the Wright family invited to their family reunion anyone who attended the school during the years I taught there. Unable to resist, I went to it. My heart leaped as I felt the embrace of those whom I taught many years ago, now with grandchildren. One asked me, "Are you the real Mr. Jacobs?" I could hardly believe my ears. The legend of "Mr. Jacobs" lived on, in spite of my blunderings and fumbling. Memory is a blessed thing; it can forget the unpleasant!

Recent picture of Carol and Wilma
Wright who flank their mother, Nora

Chapter 6

FEELING
UNSETTLED

A Non-Mennonite Campus Experience

In my second year of teaching, it was possible for me to leave the school a few weeks early so that I could get in a semester at Kentucky Wesleyan College in Winchester. As the first Mennonite to attend that particular college, I was a bit of a mystery on campus. I was getting used to that and was not uncomfortable with it. My kind was unknown there. They did not even ask if I was related to the Amish. One teacher stuck out, the philosophy professor, who owned a Churchillian bulldog face, as gruff as can be. He was a strange blend of gritty, no-nonsense, penetrating philosophy, and a star tennis player. He taught the Sunday school class that impressed me. I have often thanked God for that fellow because he used his brain yet exercised his faith. I liked the mix. It reminded me of what John and Charles Wesley were like. I treasure Wesley hymns, a blend of head and heart.

I entered the college as a practicing school teacher. I had that under my belt, so I was determined to be a no-nonsense student. And so I was. What two years of

teaching can do for one's self-worth is astounding. I did
not realize how much I had changed in two years. Now,
I was a man. Albeit a 19-year-old one. I was developing a
spark of audacity. In any case, I hit my stride academically
at Kentucky Wesleyan. I was excited about learning. The
only obstacle that stood in my way was funding.

A Seller of Books

That semester drained my meager savings. Now what?
I needed to make some money to continue my education.
My opportunity came when a recruiter showed up at college, encouraging us to think about selling his company's
line of Bibles, cookbooks, and Bible storybooks. It was a
program designed for college students who were working
their way through school. I welcomed the challenge.

I did well with my bookselling. Some days it was hard
to walk up to the first house and introduce myself. In our
training they taught us some set "openers." I abandoned
all that early on and introduced myself as a young Christian, working my way through college. From there on,
I played it by ear. It was a successful summer, as far as
money is concerned, enough so that I could trade in my
beloved, bright red, Cushman Scooter for a black Model A
Ford Roadster, the kind with a rumble seat. I piled all my
stuff into that and headed to Johnstown. I was exhilarated
to be with Mom, Dad, Roma, and Dorothea again. It felt
so good to be at home after many months away.

Dad could not bear to see me driving a small Ford,
so he obtained a Chrysler of the same year, 1929, in
good condition, which I proudly drove to college. It was
a stately automobile in the real sense of the word, with

upholstered seats and wooden-spoked wheels. Old, but heavy with character. Quite unlike me.

A SEMESTER AT EMC

I had only a few days at home before packing the hefty Chrysler with my stuff and then heading off to Harrisonburg, Virginia. The fall semester of 1948 at EMC is a blur. So much had happened to me in the two years that I was away from the Mennonite college community that I could not figure out who I really was when I returned. I thought I could slip back in the same way I left. That was an illusion.

I had changed; the college had changed. I began to wonder who I had become. I was still a Mennonite, a good one, but not the one who left there two years prior. I did not feel settled there. A restlessness stirred in my spirit. I should have asked, "What is happening to me?" But I was so mixed up that I could not even formulate the question. I did not realize how life experiences can bend and reshape a person. For me it was two years of teaching school in Appalachia, college at Goshen and Kentucky Wesleyan, a summer among the mountain folk selling books. I **had** changed.

I slowly realized that I had changed much more than the culture at EMU had. The cozy culture that I left may have still been there, but for some reason it was no longer cozy to me. For the first time in my life I faced the question, "Are you **you** or are you a reflection of a culture?" Little did I know that that very question would become a lifelong refrain for me.

I had to now learn how to have an internal set of values and beliefs that would serve my self-identity wherever I was. That meant that the Mennonite culture which protected me originally could not and should not shape who I was. That did not mean that I could discount culture in my self-awareness, but I began to see it as a husk protecting the live kernel. That understanding would make it possible for me to move within cultures because it relativizes culture as a factor in identity.

I found the issue of culture and faith to be a bit beyond me, so that semester I decided to help organize a Philosophy Club where we would read and expostulate on the major philosophers, ancient and modern. I enjoyed that because it was neither culture nor religion. One day a favorite teacher asked me if I still loved Jesus. I assured him that my philosophizing did not diminish my commitment to Christ. That seemed to satisfy him. To be sure, my faith was not as simple or as keen as it had been when I left there two years earlier. I was not sure why. I had the feeling of being between things, detached from one reality but not yet embracing a new one.

All that came to a screeching halt when I faced the fact that I did not have enough money for another semester of college. I decided to go home to Johnstown where I was always able to get a job of one kind or another.

BACK TO JOHNSTOWN

It happened that my oldest brother, Willard, had a job opening for me. He was in charge of a regional area for the Jewel T Company, a house-to-house retail business. He needed someone to fill in for salesmen who were sick or on vacation. It suited me just fine. It was also a good time to learn to know my brother and his wife, Dolly.

I could bond again with Dad and Mom and have some good adult times with them. Dad was selling cars but had time to chat and go to ball games. Both of them encouraged me to live a clean life and be a witness to Jesus Christ in the community and the church. Dad had experienced a religious awakening in his own life just before that. Home felt like home at its best.

I sensed, however, that my days in my ancestral home in western Pennsylvania were drawing to a close. I delighted in selling my wares up and down the streets of the little coal-mining towns that dotted the valleys in the Johnstown area, but I knew I could not stay. I nursed a melancholy feeling in my spirit, saddened by the need to move on, but buoyed by the thought that I must move closer to Anna Ruth and get on with pursuing a career.

Twenty-One Years of Age — What Is Happening?

"Don, who are you, now that you are 21?" No one asked me that question, but it kept popping up in my subconscious. I could make very little sense out of what was happening to me. I was a novice teacher, an eager student, a salesman, a writer, a speaker of sorts, and a jumble of other things. During the five years following my conversion, I found myself in one demanding situation after another. I was learning that in my weakness I was not helpless, that God was there to get me through. I discovered that my faith, though shaky at times, never collapsed. I knew who I was in my relationship to God. To be sure, the cultural aspects of being a Mennonite that I appreciated earlier definitely dimmed in importance. Life in Kentucky and in Johnstown served to make that happen.

I was also discovering that God did not mean for me to be alone. I was not strong enough for that. I saw a bright light in Lancaster that beckoned me. I knew that the next step in my life was not vocational but personal. Anna Ruth and I had written to one another regularly for three long years. I valued our relationship and held it dearly, even though we lived at a distance from each other. However, I realized that I could not live like that very much longer. I needed a good wife who could keep me from frittering my life away. In short, I could not trust myself to make life decisions alone. I could never have survived as a hermit.

When I first began to relate to Anna Ruth in 1945 — it was now 1949 — I realized I was attracted to her for many reasons. For one, where I saw weakness in my personality, that is precisely where she was strong. I was impulsive; she was thoughtful. Together we could move forward with confidence. The more I thought and prayed about it, the more I was drawn to find out if Anna Ruth could possibly agree to be that heart-partner that I longed for desperately.

Chapter 7

LIFE IN LANCASTER

1949 – 1952

A New Challenge — Teaching at Lancaster Mennonite High School

During the summer of 1949, when I paid a brief visit to Anna Ruth, I got bold and made an appointment with Noah Good, Dean of Lancaster Mennonite High School (LMHS). I wanted to ask if there was a remote chance that there might be a slot at the school for a young fellow like me. That was brave of me because, even though I had taught elementary school for two years, I did not have a degree of any kind. In fact, I was barely a junior in college. Noah Good impressed me right away. I told him my story. He admired Anna Ruth, of course, a star student of his when she took her final years at LMHS. Noah knew her family very well also. I don't know what he thought of me. Perhaps he was impressed by my audacity and my sincerity. He assured me that the school board would take my request seriously but did not offer much hope. He told me later that he was impressed by my quick stride.

To my amazement, the school agreed to hire me to teach industrial arts, boys' physical education, a Bible course, and a few other classes that did not require a degree. That was better than being a hall manager or a maintenance worker, two slots that were open. So I felt extremely grateful and agreed to join the staff without once asking what they might pay me. I was just happy to get a job.

Lancaster Mennonite School landmark building used as a gym and an auditorium

STAFF RELATIONSHIPS

J. Paul Graybill was the principal. I tried to figure him out. He was as plain as a fence post in dress and in discipline. If it hadn't been for that sparkle in his eye, I may have just avoided him entirely, but he intrigued me. A time came when I got to know him better. One morning before the compulsory, daily chapel service, another young teacher, John Weaver, and I were playing either chess or checkers and were so engrossed in our contest that we simply missed chapel, an unheard of thing, I learned. Principal J. Paul called me into his office where he deplored my setting a horrid example. I knew he was serious because his dark eyes sank deeper into his head and his brows knotted. It was like he was looking at me from inside a dark cave. I apologized and told him how I got carried away by my need to win that game. Then he smiled an authentic smile, unlike his official one, and asked, "Who won?" I knew from that moment on we could get along. He had done his duty by reprimanding me but then extended a hand of friendship. He acted out the bishop role; he lowered the boom, and then reached out a hand of friendship. I ached for his unenviable dilemma.

PREPARING FOR A WEDDING

The best part of teaching at LMHS was that I could drive out to Silver Spring, a distance of about 10 miles, to spend the evenings with Anna Ruth. My mind went back to when I was living in Kentucky and dating Anna Ruth by mail. My mother did not know Anna Ruth very well. One day I got a no-nonsense letter from my mother, insisting that I reconsider the relationship because, she wrote, with emphasis, "You should marry one of our kind." I suppose Mom thought I did not know what I was getting into if I married the daughter of a Lancaster Mennonite preacher. I forget how I answered Mom, but I tried to be nice to her as

Anna Ruth and I pose for our wedding picture.

I closed my ears completely to her concern. Anna Ruth was my kind, and I knew it!

A word about Anna Ruth. She completed two years at Eastern Mennonite College, then transferred to Millersville State College, located near Lancaster. She went there because it was near home, so she could help on her family's small farm, and the state school was also less expensive. She graduated with a teaching degree and began teaching at the new Kraybill Mennonite School at the same time that I began at LMHS. She taught all of the students in the first six grades, a huge challenge for a new teacher.

Every day my shiny, two-tone, green Frazer found its way to the Charles' residence at Silver Spring. That was the first time that we ever had an extended time together. The relationship deepened. We enjoyed many things together, including ping-pong, music, books, bird-watching, hiking, or just walking around exploring things. Even though we came from radically different backgrounds, we found we had many interests in common. Joy, joy.

The Charles family absorbed me very graciously. That included Anna Ruth's parents, Cora and Jacob, and Raymond, her brother, with his wife, Anna Lois. Maybe they, too, wondered at first if I was of "their kind." If so, they did not dwell on that and, to their credit, they did their best to make a place for me. They just accepted me for who I was. I admired their openness and their love. Adjusting to life in the Charles family circle presented no challenge at all. I kept changing, in their direction. I was an eager learner among them. I could see myself slowly—and I emphasize "slowly"—becoming a happy member of the Lancaster Mennonite community. I had already become a happy "Charles."

The Charles family. Left to right: Raymond, Jacob, Cora, Anna Ruth.

The wedding party after our marriage in the Charles home front room, on December 24, 1949. Left to right: my brother Duane, me, Anna Ruth, and Barbara Keener.

By then we knew that we would get married, so, skipping a formal engagement, we agreed that it would be nonsense to wait until school was out for the summer. Why not during the coming Christmas break, a matter of weeks away? We thrilled at the thought. Since the year was one of huge changes already, why not have another big one? So, we did. It was a family affair in the Charles' front room, presided over by Bishop Henry Lutz. That was the common way to do it among the Mennonites. The Charles side and the Jacobs side enjoyed a most marvelous time celebrating our love and our marriage.

OUR FIRST HOME

Following a wonderful honeymoon in Florida, we stayed with Anna Ruth's parents for several weeks. That was nice, but I was soon looking to purchase a mobile home. We found one that suited us—a large one for the time, 8 × 33 feet, a Shultz. With Anna Ruth's parents' permission, we placed it beside their four-car garage. We dug a hole and lined it with cement blocks for our septic system. And we just hooked into their water and electricity lines. I do not recall that we ever paid a cent for being there and often filled our car with gasoline from their farm tank, free. What marvelous people, Cora and Jacob Charles!

The firm where I bought the mobile home asked me to serve as a part-time salesperson, which I did gladly, and the following summer I sold trailers for several months. It paid much better than teaching. But that was not my calling, and I knew it. It sometimes seemed unfair that I could so easily get someone to buy from me. I realized later in life that the talent for selling was a key to getting on as a missionary. I think I inherited that trait from my father. It was a Jacobs thing and not at all like the Bloughs.

Fitting into Lancaster Mennonite Conference

How was I, a culturally marginal Mennonite, able to fit into the Lancaster Mennonite Conference, which was well-known as one of the strictest Mennonite conferences in North America?

Fortunately, I met the Lord at Eastern Mennonite School in Virginia, where many values, similar to those of Lancaster Mennonite Conference, were upheld. I not only had a spiritual conversion at EMS, but, as I already explained, I also embraced the new culture in which I began my walk with Christ. I was happy to be enfolded into a culture in which I had a place, a culture that enabled me to grow. My forays into Kentucky and beyond tested if I was still enthusiastic about that culture. There were times when I doubted whether the Mennonite culture that I experienced in Harrisonburg could be transplanted to another cultural context. But I didn't have time to dwell on that. That question was now moot as I wondered if I could thrive in this new setting.

I learned that the entire Conference had its eye on LMHS where I was teaching. That was where the rules and discipline of the Lancaster Mennonite Conference would be put into practice and tested in an institutional setting among the young people. Many in Lancaster Conference considered higher education a slippery slope. The Conference determined to embrace higher education and, at the same time, to make LMHS a lighthouse of Mennonite decorum. To assure this, they appointed as Principal J. Paul Graybill, who was both an advocate for the school and a strong bishop. It was his job to apply in an academic setting the rules and discipline of Lancaster Conference. I determined to fit right in. After all, I married a young woman of this Conference, and I considered it a privilege to adhere to her culture as much as possible. I was happy to be among people who lived with a purpose. I saw so much good in what they had achieved that I happily went along.

For example, in school, when the Principal announced in an assembly that on a certain Monday in October all men would wear hats, I bought my first felt hat, a brown one, not the typical black. I rather enjoyed wearing it because it was my sign of submission to the shepherds of the Lancaster flock. Aside from the hat, the fact that I did not kick over the traces was appreciated, I presume, because I was soon conducting music schools in the congregations of the Conference. My brown hat, a slightly saucy one, seemed to fit my stance, if I might say so.

Because of my obvious desire to fit in, people learned they could trust me. It also helped that I married Anna Ruth, the daughter of Preacher Jacob and sister of Raymond Charles. Raymond was highly regarded in the Conference. That may have been one reason that the Conference was able to swallow the strange name "Jacobs."

My challenge was to swallow Lancaster Mennonite Conference. That was a slow process, indeed. I chewed it slowly and with discernment, without actually swallowing very much. I became aware of the fact that as the Conference tightened the rules, such as disallowing radios and neckties, people my age simply walked away. I had agreed when I taught at LMHS to submit to the Rules and Discipline of the Conference. That was part of the deal. So I just bowed my head, closed my ears, and hoped for the best. I began to see how enforcing a cultural agenda could lead to unhealthy parochialism. My naiveté saved me from raising unsettling questions in my own mind, and I was certainly not going to express my uneasiness in public.

The Joy of Teaching at LMHS

My life at LMHS was idyllic. From the beginning, I was aware of the fact that I should not have been hired at all because I had yet to obtain my first degree. So I accepted with gratitude any responsibility that came my way. I found joy in teaching subjects that did not require a degree.

At LMHS I got serious about birding. The campus straddled the Mill Stream and bordered a wooded area beyond the stream. It was a marvelous habitat for many kinds of birds. I had always assumed that I would pick up that hobby but kept putting it off until LMHS. Birdwatching served Anna Ruth and me marvelously through the years.

While teaching, I was diligent about adding credit hours to obtain a B.A. from Franklin and Marshall College. It was there that I completed several science courses. The college had just installed a computer that operated with vacuum tubes, so it filled a room. It had large fans to keep the place cool. That was my introduction to computers. I was fascinated. I could see the demise of the slide rule that we all used for calculating.

During my days at LMHS I agreed to serve on the first denomination-wide youth cabinet of the Mennonite Church. It was called Mennonite Youth Fellowship (MYF). This put me in touch with leaders of Mennonite youth across the nation. It was a fledgling movement, the first of its kind. I was excited about the future of Mennonite young people.

Lancaster Mennonite High School was definitely not Coffee Creek School in Kentucky. I welcomed the change! My teaching days at the one-room Coffee Creek School in Kentucky had demanded everything I had and more. It was a venture into the unknown, and it bent me more than I could have imagined. I was constantly pressing my limits, not only as a teacher but as an administrator, always making sure that I had things under control, which never really happened, by the way!

Not so at Lancaster Mennonite High School. It was well run, had a base in Christian values, and was on the cutting edge of high school education in the state. All I had to do was teach. And that I did with my whole heart. I loved it. I recall coming home after school one time and exclaiming to Anna Ruth, "I don't know why they are paying me for this. I am having so much fun." It dawned on me that God wired me to be a teacher. I appreciated the administrators in the school, but I never hankered after being an administrator. I was a teacher and that was that.

Culture and Faith in Community

Allow me to muse on faith and culture in Lancaster Mennonite Conference as I saw it. I soon became aware of the fact that the Conference was serious about enforcing its rules. Some of its rules seemed a bit trivial, like the length of women's hair. I found that the Conference did not have two lists, one essential and the other trivial. A breech of any rule precluded one from taking communion. I began to wonder how specific a denomination should be in defining and enforcing a code of behavior and whether using communion to enforce the rules was biblical.

In my more sullen moments I pondered some of the rules regarding female dress. I wondered, why pay so much attention to that? The typical answer at the time was, "Because it is in the Bible." Indeed there are a few verses in the writings of Paul and Peter that stress the need for modesty in dress and behavior. But why make so much of that?

I found a reason that satisfied me. As I thought about it, I realized that in American culture, women were acting more and more like men. That would not work in a Mennonite culture where gender roles were important. I began to realize that the Conference rules served a cultural purpose. I could see nothing wrong with that. Rules set boundaries between the church and the world on the one hand, and on the other, they bound the members of the church together. That could not be gainsaid. I did wonder, however, about the amount of detail that went into the rules and the scriptural justification for those rules. I decided to think about that at some more appropriate time.

Such thoughts were not swirling around in my head all the time. In fact, I and my fellow teachers at LMHS spoke little about them. I liked it that way. I was among

good models. I think of Lester Brubaker, for example.
He pursued higher education without moving away from
his spiritual and cultural community. He and his wife,
Lois, stole my heart. He was bright, well-groomed, and
stately. It was not difficult to admire him. We became close
friends, sharing quite deeply. He saw the ambiguities that
plagued Lancaster Conference, but he was prepared to live
with the situation. And Clyde Stoner, the business manager of the school, helped me to do what he was doing—
go along with things that were trivial in order to maintain
unity around what was essential. I decided to take the
same approach, with the assumption that I was the one
to decide what was trivial.

That was similar to how I felt at the Chestnut Hill
Mennonite Church that we attended. The congregation
had roots in the 1740s when Mennonites moved into the
area. They built their first meetinghouse of logs in 1799.
That served them for 50 years, when they built a nice brick
meetinghouse. Not long after this new church was built,
Anna Ruth's grandfather, Christian F. Charles, bought a
farm in the area, attended the church, and in 1898 was
ordained deacon. Only one of his children continued at
Chestnut Hill, Jacob L. Charles, Anna Ruth's father. The
congregation selected him to be their pastor, a ministry
that he and his wife, Cora, pursued with love and compassion. So Chestnut Hill was Mennonite through and
through—all members were of the same Mennonite stock.
How they absorbed a whimsical young fellow named
Jacobs is still a mystery, but they did. I felt free there and
developed friendships that lasted throughout my life.

I was perfectly content to be a submissive member of
that Lancaster religious culture. How could I turn against
the Conference? It gave me a place to belong. I left it at

that. I did not even think of asking the question: will it be able to achieve the uniformity that it is seeking? Nor did I ask of myself, could I be happy as a lifelong member of this Conference? Along with these questions was another: will the uniformity that the Conference is pressing for among its members stymie their desire to plant churches in other cultures?

Chapter 8

FROM LANCASTER
INTO ACADEMIA

1952

❖

A PLACE TO STUDY

As I completed three years of teaching at LMHS, I had also managed to accumulate enough credit hours to earn a B. A. in American History at Franklin and Marshall College in Lancaster. Now what? The military draft was nipping at my heels. One way of staying ahead of that was to become a full-time graduate student.

Anna Ruth's close friend, Mary Jane Rudy, then a teacher near Baltimore, said, "Anna Ruth, I think I can get a job for you where I am teaching in Glen Burnie, and Don can study at the University of Maryland. Think about it." I had already decided to study the history of the Renaissance and Reformation no matter where I went. I found that U of M had a good European History department. Before long, Mary Jane landed a job for Anna Ruth, so off we went with our house trailer on a new adventure—Anna

Ruth to a public elementary school, while I made my way into the History of the Reformation.

I was ready for some serious study. I knew that the day would come for me to delve into the historical and theological context of the 16th century Anabaptist movement, so why not now! It did not take me long to realize that I was in a secular university. I must have been a quaint student as a Mennonite. For my professors, Anabaptism was little more than a footnote in the great Reformation story. Poor me. I thought of my Mennonite peers who were swimming in Anabaptist studies, specifically Church History, being shaped by believing teachers. Not me. It was sink or swim.

Anna Ruth and I outside our trailer home in Glen Burnie, Maryland. Anna Ruth is a teacher; I am a student.

ENJOYING A SUPPORT GROUP

While living in Glen Burnie, we found ourselves in a spiritual support group with Mary Jane Rudy, her brother Clarence, who was a high school teacher, and Marion, his wife. We met on a regular basis to help one another on our pilgrim ways. That was the first time since we were married that we were in a meaningful, serious, small group of keen believers.

During the course of the year, we invited them to pray with us about our future.

At some point in the year, it became clear that we could not stay ahead of the draft much longer. Now what? We felt the next thing was to fulfill the draft requirements. So we approached the Mennonite Central Committee (MCC). They wasted no time in offering us a job as spiritual counselors for their many volunteers serving in Europe in Post-War reconstruction.

I realized that the MCC assignment in Europe would be a natural next step for me because of my focus on the Reformation, especially Anabaptist history. I was aware of the work that John Howard Yoder and others were doing in the area of Anabaptist studies. They were rereading the sources in order to address the issue of nonviolence as an alternative to war.

That was the era of the Concern Group, a small circle of Anabaptist thinkers who were concerned that Mennonites remain faithful to their calling and history. I liked their blend of history, theology, and contemporary living. I saw myself as a "concerned" Anabaptist Mennonite. A few years in Europe would place me in the vortex of these issues, and I welcomed the prospect. I knew that I had to learn German if I was to dive into Anabaptist sources. No problem. Life in Germany appealed to me.

A New Option — Africa

We were moving in that direction when another possibility presented itself. I had been working on my M.A. dissertation, a requirement at the University of Maryland. I decided to examine how the Anabaptists who came to eastern Pennsylvania established schools for their children and how that developed into the educational system that the Lancaster Conference Mennonites enjoyed. My research led me to the roots of the movement in Europe and then through the early years of the Mennonite experience in Pennsylvania, right up to the present, which was marked by a new vision for Christian education. The title of my dissertation was "A Study of the Religious Life of the Mennonites in Lancaster Conference, in Pennsylvania, 1890–1952."

While doing research, I discovered that the Lancaster Conference mission board, Eastern Mennonite Board of Missions and Charities (now known as Eastern Mennonite Missions, or EMM), was looking for a couple to send to Tanganyika to train teachers. Anna Ruth and I both pricked up our ears. Anna Ruth divulged the fact that she had a stirring in her heart since she was a girl to be a missionary. I had never given it a thought. Furthermore, Africa was not even on my map. Yet the challenge stirred a latent longing to serve somewhere, or was it a hankering to move on to something new and demanding? Who knew? I was not unfamiliar with the work of EMM, since I had lived in Lancaster for three years, right next door to Raymond Charles, Anna Ruth's brother, who was missions head to toe.

As the possibility began to take shape in our minds, ever so dimly, we took it to our small support group. They encouraged us to think and pray about it and not to be bound by our informal commitment to MCC to go to Europe. We worked some with our families in making this decision, especially Raymond. All the while we had the assurance that God was pushing us toward an unknown place. We offered ourselves to EMM, if they would take us, as educationists in Tanganyika. They did. Little did we know how that would set the course of our lives from then on.

REFLECTIONS ON LIFE IN MARYLAND

Had I taken the time to reflect on how my Maryland experiences helped shape me, I would have certainly noted my growing enthusiasm for Anabaptist studies. I suppose I needed historical connections with my heritage to add to my present desire to know how to fit into the denomination. I also learned the importance of a small accountability group. On the side, I found that I was intensely interested in American politics. Since I did much of my studying at the Library of Congress in Washington, D.C., I often slipped over to the houses of Congress where I sat in the visitors' gallery with eyes wide open as I listened to the debates. I had a nose for politics. As far as spiritual development was concerned, I probably did not grow much, but I survived as a Mennonite in a secular history department. Anna Ruth learned that she could do well in a public school system like her dear friend, Mary Jane Rudy, a princess if there ever was one. Anna Ruth was our breadwinner for an entire year. I owe that year to her.

Chapter 9

LAUNCHING OUT
INTO THE DEEP

1953

ORDINATION AND PREPARATION

Summer 1953 was a flurry of activity. The high point was my ordination to the ministry. I had never imagined myself as an ordained person. However, the Mission Board had a policy at that time which they were not in the mood to break: all male missionaries would be ordained as pastors unless there was some compelling reason not to. The little Chestnut Hill Mennonite Church, the congregation that shaped Anna Ruth's family and which I inherited, laid hands on me that August day. In an instant, behold, I was ordained as a pastor for life! I might note that a few weeks prior to that we were commissioned for one term as missionaries to Tanganyika. That was for a term. My ordination was for life!

I knew that in my brain, my heart, and in every sinew of my body, I was being called into a lifetime ministry that would strain every nerve and bring me to a place of brokenness and usefulness as never before.

Our parents were supportive. They were committed to Christ and loved him dearly; nevertheless their joy in seeing us go off to Africa was tinged with a note of sadness. It must have been especially painful for Anna Ruth's mother, whose only daughter was on her way to the far unknown and might begin a family there. Knowing all that, she wished us well and promised to pray for us. Our leaving moved Anna Ruth's father as well. He loved his daughter, but he had a heart for missions which made it a bit easier to see her go.

My brothers bought me a newfangled watch which wound itself. I treasured that until it gave up the ghost in Africa. Dad, in closing his hunting career, gave me his Winchester 12-gauge pump shotgun. In addition, I purchased a used 30-06 for large animals. Africa, here I come!

It was a high moment for us spiritually. For Anna Ruth, who had felt a tug for years to be a missionary to Africa, it was a dream come true. She confided, "I did feel a call to be a missionary ever since I was a girl when we read the letters that the earliest Lancaster missionaries circulated. Later on I wondered if it was but a girlhood fantasy or a real call by God." Her faith was strengthened by the fact that the Lord had laid his hand on us for this ministry. I had mixed feelings. I realized that I was at the beginning of an adventure which would take me into a host of new things. I had a profound realization that I was taking a step which would require more dependence on God than anything I had ever known.

NEW IDENTITY

During that summer I had to deal with a new identity. I felt no more like a missionary or a pastor than I had a year before my community placed me into those new categories. The label "pastor" humbled me, as expected, but this new label, "missionary" was absolutely daunting. To begin with, missionaries are supported by the churches. That went across my grain. I grew up nurturing my inner person to take responsibility and not be dependent on anyone, but instead to help others. I had learned to make my way, and I derived a certain pride in attaining the lofty age of 25 years with no debt and some savings.

I recall that shortly after we were commissioned as missionaries, I was greeting people as they left a church where I had spoken. One dear older sister shook my hand with considerable vigor and left a 20 dollar bill in my hand. My fear of needing to depend on anyone other than myself came crashing down on me. Instead of thanking God for the gift, I mourned the passing of my independence.

For a long time I pondered what effect living on the generosity of others would have on me. The only way I could handle it was to see myself as a paid employee of the Mission Board, doing a job just as though I was being sent to establish a business or another institution. To counterbalance that, I felt elated that the Lancaster Mennonite Conference and Mission Board trusted us enough to present us to the world as their missionaries.

"Don, my brother," a dear Mennonite bishop said as he looked into my eyes and shook my hand, "please return just like you are now. Do not change." I assured him that I would do my best to stay unchanged. I think he was referring to some of the distinctive cultural practices. Bless him. I had not the slightest idea if I would change or the direction such changes might take. And I may have even thought that I could return after five years, unchanged. I should have known that within a year or so he might hardly recognize me, if he could look within! That is where authentic change occurs, within.

FAREWELL TO THE USA

Anna Ruth and I waving good-bye from the railing of the Queen Mary at departure from New York.

"Can you see our people?" I asked Anna Ruth. We stood on the deck waving to the crowd on the pier as the Queen Mary moved ever so slowly away from the wharf. "There they are. See them waving?" Down there were Anna Ruth's parents and mine, together with Raymond's family and church friends. I am sure it was much easier for us to do our farewell waving than for them. We were heading out on an adventure that excited us. They had to deal with the hole that would be there after we left. The ship's loud haunting departure horn set the mood. "Let the journey begin."

We found on our bedside stand in our little stateroom a lovely bouquet of flowers from my brother Willard and his wife, Dolly, wishing us God's blessing. Willard and I did not talk very much about faith. The differences in our ages, our lifestyle, and our personal priorities made that difficult. I like to think that those flowers spoke what words could not express.

The New York skyline slips by as the ship begins its Atlantic crossing.

On board was another Mennonite missionary

couple, Roy and Florence Kreider, who were assigned to Israel. We knew the Kreiders quite well. It gave us a little consolation to know that they were aboard.

I already mentioned that when teaching at Lancaster Mennonite School, I bought a brown felt hat because the rules there required men and boys to have their heads covered when outside from October to spring. That hat reminded me of the importance of conforming to the expectations of others. I wore it proudly! To be honest, I never liked it at all. But I took it along and wore it on the Queen Mary. On one of our walks around the deck, a gust of wind lifted my dear brown hat off my head. It sailed like a fluttering bird, then touched the water, settled, circled a bit, and disappeared. My days at Lancaster Mennonite School were over, really and truly over. An era ended as my brown felt hat was swallowed by the "briny deep."

On board we read, prayed, and thanked the Lord for his mercy and his grace. We also prayed that we might find favor with the British people, particularly those with whom we would be living, and with our teachers in London. Way down in our souls, we realized that we were facing new situations which would demand some changes in us. We knew that we were going to be challenged to grow.

The famed Queen Mary

Chapter 10

A YEAR IN
EUROPE

1953 – 1954

AT HOME IN LONDON

The Queen Mary docked at Southampton where we boarded the train to London. Yes, LONDON! We would call this fabled city our home for an academic year. It was the land of Shakespeare, Kipling, Dickens, Wordsworth, and many others. Our literary roots were in English soil. This was going to be an adventure.

The Mission Board arranged for us to stay at the Foreign Missions Club, an inexpensive place for missionaries while training in London, or passing through. Nothing fancy but very, very British.

We had many reminders that it was only eight years since the end of World War II, when

At the door of the Foreign Missions Club, London, 1953

Germany had bombed London to smithereens. Things had been cleaned up, but shells of buildings still stood, waiting to be rebuilt. We were reminded of wartime scarcities, not yet entirely over. For instance, on Sunday mornings we each had our weekly egg—in an egg cup. Not eggs, egg. We learned how to do it right. Set the egg upright in the egg cup. Scalp the thing with a swift pass of the knife. Then dip strips of buttered toast into the soft-boiled yolk until it runs over a bit, down the side of the porcelain cup. A work of art. It required many tries to even begin to look like an Englishman.

To be honest, Anna Ruth and I had a nice cache of food which we bought at the local store, as a backup when meals in the dining room left one wanting. I recall saying once, when the bell rang for a meal, "Let's go down and supplement our diet." We assumed that all the other residents were doing the same.

One of our first purchases was bikes. For the first time in our adult lives, we were without a car. Those bikes served us well, not only in England but in Africa, too. The University of London was about 20 minutes away by bike. We enjoyed moving along with the biking throng. In post-war England, cars were a scarcity. One of the delights of our stay in England was to put our bikes on the train and head out to spend the day cycling through the idyllic countryside. But our major joy was studying at the University of London!

STUDENTS AT THE UNIVERSITY OF LONDON

We were not in England just to enjoy ourselves but to get educated. Anna Ruth took a course in Swahili, taught by a recognized expert on the language. I enrolled in the Faculty of Education in the University of London to be trained as a British teacher, since we were headed to Tanganyika, then a British Protectorate. It was my good fortune to be assigned to a fabulous tutor, Mr. Evans. He was a Welshman and a committed Christian. He had served in Kenya as an Education Officer in the British Colonial Service before joining the university faculty. Because he had lived and worked in Kenya, he knew our needs and did his best to make sure that we succeeded. He arranged that I take some of my courses in the University of London School of Oriental and African Studies, the faculty that trained British Colonial Servants. It emphasized area studies and insisted that every graduate have an in-depth understanding of the nation or culture in which he or she would serve.

Mr. Evans arranged for me to spend three weeks in rural Northern Wales where education was bilingual, as it is in East Africa. He also arranged for me to do my practice teaching of 11- and 12-year-olds at a rather challenged school in a working-class section of London. In the teachers' common room at that school, I discovered what it took to succeed. These teachers were determined to keep control of the unruly youngsters no matter what. They had their own very British ways of doing that and were largely successful.

When it came to teaching, I decided to wax bold and use the project method

Dr. Paul and Marie Yates of Canada, with little David, became our friends at the club.

in teaching my class of restless youngsters. I decided to make the life of Dr. David Livingston the centerpiece of the unit. As an English lesson, for example, we read of his encounters with lions. For geography, we studied the countries of Central Africa. I decided that the only way I could possibly keep order was to make it so interesting that they would stop bullying one another and pestering me. Mr. Evans liked what I was doing and so entered my name to be tested for an advanced teaching honor, called Distinction. When the inspectors came to watch me teach, I was sure that I had failed Mr. Evans. But probably out of respect for Mr. Evans, they passed me, and on my degree I have those magic words, "With Distinction." Upon our arrival in Tanganyika, eyebrows were raised because I was not only an American missionary with a British teaching qualification, but also "With Distinction!"

During our stay in London, we were challenged spiritually. James and Ruth Shank, who had been in London the year before we were, preparing for educational work in Tanganyika also, encouraged us to attend the Westminster Chapel where Dr. Martyn Lloyd-Jones ministered. It was located a few blocks from Westminster Abbey. We had intended to shop around a bit, but we went along to hear Lloyd-Jones the first Sunday morning and found ourselves devotees from then on. He was preaching a series on Psalm 73 the entire time we were there. My faith deepened at Westminster Chapel.

I recall another moving event which strengthened my faith. During the Christmas season we crossed the Thames River to the Royal Albert Hall where the London Symphony Orchestra and the Westminster Choir presented Handel's "Messiah." When they got to the chorus, "King of kings and Lord of lords," I found myself crying, something that seldom happens to me. I saw Jesus clearly as above all in majesty and grace. I was convinced all over again that Jesus is King of Kings forever.

During our few weeks in Wales, my classmates spent their evenings in the local pubs. I stayed in my room and read Butterworth's classic, *Christianity in World History*. Butterworth's book was the first serious book I read that looked at world history from a Christian point of view. That provided me with a new grid through which I could view the history of the world. This was but a seed at the time, but it grew, and I relied on it heavily in my life in Africa. It put colonialism and many other aspects of world history into perspective. Over time as a missionary, I developed a strong aversion to colonialism, but I began to understand how God can and does use flawed systems, such as that, to enable the gospel to spread. I began to look for signs in world history which pointed to the fact that God's central focus is the spread of the gospel of Jesus Christ into the whole world.

SPRING BREAK IN EUROPE

While Anna Ruth and I were in London we thought about visiting Europe, but it was only when we received an invitation to attend a meeting of the Mennonite Concern Group on an island in the North Sea during spring break that we turned our mind in that direction.

They asked me to present the findings of my M.A. thesis. This group was made up mostly of Anabaptist scholars who were intent on redefining the Anabaptist stance with regard to theology and sociology, based on the challenges of the WW II years when the Christian voice in Germany was silent as the Nazi party built a war machine. John

Howard Yoder and Paul Peachey, friends of ours from college days, were to give primary leadership to the group.

Spring break came, and we were off to Europe. How we enjoyed those days of cycling through Switzerland and then down along the Rhine River toward Holland. One day we put on 125 miles, a long day. In Holland we determined to visit Friesland, the home of Menno Simons. That was a spiritual journey for us. We had to remind ourselves that we were in the very village where Menno did much of his writing, Witmarsum.

Our spring break concluded with the meeting of the Concern Group. I had a strong affinity to this group. Their concerns were part of my spiritual pilgrimage. I tried to make sense of my own study of Anabaptist sources at the University of Maryland. Now we were sitting with a group of academic Anabaptists trying to update the Anabaptist understanding of the Kingdom of God in the world. I loved it. Little did I understand what was going to happen to me as God was taking me away from academia, into the trenches of battle as a missionary in Tanganyika, away from formal Anabaptist studies.

After this meeting near the North Sea, I continued to read the publications of the Concern Group, but I found that my world was moving in a different direction. I truly enjoyed relating to the Group. It was a connection to a meaningful part of who I was and what I felt was important. As I think of it now, I suppose that deep in my heart I carried a longing to some day actually see a spiritual upheaval like that of 1520–1560.

Boarding the ferry from Belgium to England was like going home. We had clocked 1,200 miles on our British bikes and lived for three weeks in a kaleidoscope of images and experiences that we enjoyed. But we also knew that we would need time and living to put into perspective all that we had seen and experienced.

OUR LONDON EXPERIENCE

During our stay in London, the General Mennonite Mission Board purchased property at Shepherd's Hill in Highgate to develop as a Mennonite center. They asked us to move into the huge house, just so someone would be there. We were the first Mennonites to inhabit the place. In due time Quintus and Miriam Leatherman appeared and moved quickly to organize the place as a church fellowship hall and center for Anabaptist outreach. At that time, Britain was not on the Anabaptist map at all. In my reading, I found a reference to a small Mennonite church in the 16th century when the British textile industry hired experts from Flanders, among whom were some Mennonites. They met as a congregation for a while and even produced a few martyrs, but then petered out. I found myself asking, are any British people interested in Anabaptism?

After an academic year in England, I was still an idealistic Anabaptist. I held the Anabaptist movement high as a golden moment in the history of the church, certainly of the Mennonite church. The only problem was, I had not met very many people who were living like the Anabaptists of the 16th century. Including myself.

Our visit to Europe had presented a "Y" in the road. I realized that I had to walk away from my deep involvement in rethinking Anabaptist renewal in Western culture. I was going to Africa. Instead of learning German and French, Anna Ruth and I were destined to be submerged in Swahili, a language that represented a large and ancient culture that had no linkage, whatsoever, to our Germanic heritage. It was African. Having studied Anabaptism in the West, we were moving out of the familiar world into an entirely new one. I did not turn my back on Europe; I just pushed it to the periphery of my thinking. I knew in my soul that I was about to leave that particular engagement with Anabaptism, not forget it, but leave it where it was, as ballast in my ship, and sail into another culture altogether.

On the spiritual front, while in England, sitting under the preaching of Dr. Martyn Lloyd-Jones, I could see the cross once again as the epicenter of all revelation. I saw clearly that the cross of Jesus was not the cross of a martyr fighting for justice, but the cross on which God's own Lamb, Jesus Christ, gave himself willingly as a sacrifice for the sins of all humankind. As I pondered that, my spiritual compass became fixed more than ever on the cross and resurrection of Jesus.

Since I had met Jesus 10 years earlier, I had tried to follow him faithfully. Now I discovered that alongside my love for Jesus and my Anabaptist heritage, I had a new longing in my heart to pursue a deeper understanding of the cross of Christ. That desire was to find its fruition later in Africa, but the yearning began in earnest in England.

How did participating in a British world impact me? Things were moving so quickly that I did not take the time to muse on that. One thing for sure, Anna Ruth and I confirmed that, even though we had German ancestral roots, we felt absolutely at home in England. Had we thought about it, we would have realized that the English language opened the door through which British influences poured into our lives. Nevertheless, Anna Ruth and I were

German, English, and American, if that can be viewed as a culture.

I began to understand that human beings live their lives in the ebb and flow of cultures. As pragmatists, they select what they want and reject what they do not want. That's what we were doing without giving it a thought. That insight helped set the stage for our next cultural adjustment, Africa, whose cultures bear little resemblance to those of Europe or America. We left England and Europe to enter a new world. We knew no more than that. It was good that we were in our mid-twenties, when life is still pliable.

For some reason I did not feel threatened by the whirlwind of cultures. In fact, I wanted to dive into something quite new. Was that the work of the Spirit of God? I think so.

Chapter 11

INTRODUCTION TO TANGANYIKA

1954

From London to Italy to Kenya

Our minds began to focus on moving on to Tanganyika, but first we wanted to tour northern Italy. We checked with our travel agent who agreed that we could load our things on a British ship named the Dunnottar Castle. It was scheduled to leave from England and call at Genoa,

Italy, on its way to Mombasa, Kenya. We found that we could spend a week or so exploring northern Italy, and then board the ship in Genoa, the birthplace of Christopher Columbus. By bus we explored the Po Valley, home of the Leaning Tower of Pisa, Michelangelo's famous statue of David, and hosts

The Dunnottar Castle, headed for Africa

of other reminders of the Renaissance era. I could have stayed there for weeks, trying to figure out what happened to Western culture when the Renaissance permeated the atmosphere. But we had to hurry to catch up with our ship and our baggage in Genoa, Italy.

Heavy Indian Ocean waves

Approaching Africa

All went smoothly. As we made our way through the Suez Canal, I had the sense that we had entered Africa. On one side walked a string of camels, swaying and braying. Real camels! Some sights I will never forget. After two weeks on board ship we finally entered the palm-studded harbor of Mombasa on Kenya's coast. From there we took the train to Nairobi, where we had to wait for a few days to catch the lake steamer at Kisumu and sail to Musoma, our final destination.

A SHORT STAY IN KENYA

We had planned to stay at the African Inland Mission Guest House in Nairobi for a few days before continuing our journey to Tanganyika. There we met an American missionary couple who took us out to their station, called

Kijabe, 20 or so miles from Nairobi, and introduced us to the world of that huge mission compound.

On the way to Kijabe we passed a concentration camp where the British were protecting loyal Kenyans. We had heard a bit of the Mau Mau uprising, but here it was. The movement grew out of the discontent of the Kikuyu tribe, who felt that their land had been taken away from them and given to white settlers. Our hosts pointed out places where the road cut through deep forests, perfect places for Mau Mau fighters to pounce on any vehicles they wished.

New Understandings of Nonviolence

We thought little of it at the time, but that insurrection was to have long-range consequences for Christianity in Kenya in the years to follow. At Kijabe, we heard stories of how Christians in the Rift Valley suffered terribly at the hands of their fellow tribesmen. They welcomed their enemies into their homes and befriended Kenyans of all tribes. Central to their actions was their insistence on obeying only Jesus, who gave them love for their enemies as well as their friends. Their tribal leaders forced them to swear, using an ancient oath, to obey their tribal ancestors. That they could not do. Nor could they take up arms to defend the interests of the British. Kenyan martyrs were killed one after the other by their own people. What I heard from the mouths of Kenyan witnesses, then and later, convinced me that the great Revival that swept over the East Africa nations, beginning in Rwanda and Uganda in the early 1930s, had produced a great number of martyrs in Kenya by 1954.

LEARNING ABOUT THE EAST AFRICAN REVIVAL

I had heard about this movement that began among nominal Anglican Christians in Uganda, but I did not realize its extent or influence, nor was I all that interested. But when I became aware of their determination to remain loyal to Christ there in Kenya, even to the point of martyrdom, I could not dismiss it as a passing fancy. In fact, it reminded me of my own Anabaptist roots.

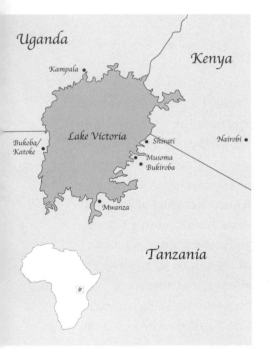

This movement that spread rapidly in Uganda was an invitation to be saved. That meant coming to God as forgiven sinners, and then living in light with others who were also fully committed to following Jesus. Believers emphasized loving one another in spite of tribal, gender, racial, or class differences. Not every Christian was willing to live like that; in fact, most were content to remain nominal believers. But almost everyone became aware of the invitation to be cleansed and renewed by the sacrificial blood of Jesus. The movement's signature song touches on the heart of the movement: "Glory to the Lamb, for the cleansing blood has reached me."

I had heard from returned missionaries how, in 1942, less than 10 years after the Stauffers and the Mosemanns pitched their tents on the Shirati hill, this wave swept over that area and both upset and settled the church there. I had not realized how widespread or how influential the movement had been. Now I found that there were martyrs among Presbyterians and Anglicans and other denominations on the slopes of Mount Kenya. These were people who were ready to die rather than to take up arms to defend themselves or their groups.

Parenthetically, as months passed and I could see things a bit more dispassionately, I wrote to a few Mennonite theologians whom I regarded highly, such as John Howard Yoder. I wondered why we tend to consider the Anabaptists unique when other Christians have also suffered for their faith. (I exposed my naiveté.) Yoder explained that the Anabaptists were unique in that they congealed as a subculture where mutual accountability and discipline were practiced. That is, they became a denomination, not just a spiritual movement.

I saw Yoder's point but was not totally convinced that the difference was that significant. The Revival brothers and sisters felt led to stay in their own denominations unless elbowed out. No "Revival" denomination resulted. Instead, the saved ones in all the churches maintained a powerful, though ad hoc, structure that enabled them to speak into the lives of any denomination and into the world, pointing to Jesus as the one to follow. More on this later.

WELCOMED TO TANGANYIKA

The slow train ride from Nairobi to Kisumu took us up into the highlands of Kenya where we could see volcanic peaks. At Kisumu on the lake, we boarded a ship to Musoma, our final leg. It was August 1, 1954. Missionary friends were there to meet us at the dock. They whisked us off to Buki-roba, seven miles away. We were finally there, on the shores of Lake Victoria, just south of the equator. This area was to be our home. We welcomed the opportunity to settle down a bit and relax in a culture unlike any we had ever known and among a breed new to us—Mennonite missionaries!

Our first home at Bumangi, where we lived for a year and a half

Our first home for 18 months was at Bumangi, about 22 miles southeast of the lakeside port and government center, Musoma. As missionaries almost always do, I remember in great detail our first place "on the field." Our cozy little house was set among the picturesque granite boulders. It was built of plastered, whitewashed, sun-dried brick with a metal roof and spouting which kept the water tank replenished. The little living room had an open fireplace, a rarity in mission houses. We loved the entire setup and even got used to the outhouse. At night when we made our necessary trips out there, we always carried a flashlight to make sure we did not tread on vipers or scorpions. Next to us was the big house where the Clyde and Alta Shenk family lived. They eased our entry into Africa. What a family!

LEARNING TO KNOW THE MISSIONARIES

Anna Ruth and I enjoyed getting to know this new "tribe," Mennonite missionaries. We found them generally energetic, interesting, and highly motivated. All were from the North American culture except a Swiss nurse, Hedwig Nacht. They had one thing in common, a genuine desire to relate to the people and to walk with their Tanganyika friends who were incorporating Christ into their lives. What they may have lacked in formal training, they made up for by, what I perceived, was a genuine love for the people.

We had several assignments during the 18 months that we lived at Bumangi—administer the school, learn Swahili, and develop some familiarity with both the local culture and that of the missionaries. Administering the school was not terribly difficult because I had an efficient Tanganyikan vice-principal who knew all the ropes. I more or less let him run things, while I concentrated on curriculum and relating to the government, and keeping a firm grip on the school's finances. The government insisted that all schools of this level must be conducted in English. I soon realized that the minute students walked out of class they naturally used either their tribal languages or Swahili. I knew I had to learn Swahili.

As we were moving onto the station, Clyde and Alta Shenk, with their family, were in the process of moving out to start a new station at Kisaka, up the Mara River in a mixed tribal area. Mahlon and Mabel Hess moved into the house that the Shenks vacated. Mahlon was Educational Secretary with the assignment of upgrading many of the former bush schools to full primary school status and of establishing new schools. To describe Mahlon as a hard worker would be an understatement. I don't know when he slept. He was responsible for the placement of teachers, building programs, and a host of other things. He was the appointed director of education for the mission, which meant he was my superior. He did not act the part. On his regular visits to our little house, we enjoyed eating local roasted peanuts together and just chatting. That was my introduction to the hopes and dreams that the people had for education.

Prior to his coming to Tanganyika, Mahlon was a prototypical Lancaster Conference pastor, held in high regard by the more conservative bishops. I believe they expected him to help the other missionaries follow Lancaster Conference guidelines more faithfully. When Mahlon arrived in Tanzania, the hope that he would straighten out the Leathermans, Stauffers, Smokers, Phebe Yoder, Rhoda Wenger, and the rest did not materialize. Mahlon, though not caught up as much as they in the ways of the East Africa Revival just then, had little time to make sure that all the missionaries toed the Lancaster Conference line.

Because Mahlon traveled so much, Rhoda Wenger was assigned the responsibility of running the station. We had the great joy of usually having Rhoda as our guest for meals. Rhoda had been through it all, and her spirit was open and eager to learn. Rhoda was happy to go along with things and fulfill her calling to love the people and uphold the gospel of Christ. Lancaster Conference, as far as I know, had no official role for women then. Rhoda knew that but paid it little heed. She was from Virginia! I slowly became aware of the powerful role people like Rhoda played in the planting of churches in Africa. Her insights and vision were remarkable.

I think also of Phebe Yoder from Kansas. She came to Tanganyika as a nurse but was soon out doing literacy work, starting schools, setting up clinics, and generally running ahead of what one would expect of a single Mennonite woman. A mission career offered people like Rhoda and Phebe an almost limitless vista for exercising their gifts. The contribution of single missionary women was outstanding. The mission set-up did not make room for the single women to voice their usually good advice. In fact, the governing Council contained only ordained men. I squirmed at this, probably more than the women themselves. I might add that this did not daunt all of them, especially Phebe. Such women had learned to catch, in their own way, the ears of those who could take action.

Phebe was the very first of the Mennonite missionaries to experience the refreshing revival winds of the Holy Spirit. She bonded with Rebeka, a typical Tanganyikan woman who had led Phebe to the place of spiritual freedom in Christ. Together these two women, a gifted missionary nurse and a Tanganyikan housewife, traveled as a team to invite all who would join them at Calvary to receive forgiveness for sins and a new life together. Through their influence, the Spirit of God touched several prominent church leaders and eventually the missionaries.

The Bumangi thatch-roofed church

THE VAGARIES OF LANGUAGE LEARNING

My Swahili improved slowly as I used it more and more. I could have gotten by with only English in administering the school, I suppose. It is a great temptation for a missionary, with a shrug of the shoulder, to put off the challenging task of learning the local language, saying, "I don't really need it. Everyone wants to practice his or her English on me." In my missionary career I have found that there is a positive correlation between feeling at home in a culture and knowing the language well. I will admit that there is another blessing, in disguise. It keeps one humble! For example, after six months in Tanganyika I took the plunge and preached my first sermon in Swahili. I used for my text the sin of Adam and Eve. In Swahili, fruit is "tunda"; hole is "tundu." Horrors. I had Eve looking at the hole, tasting the hole, and then passing the hole on to Adam. I gather it was hilarious—to my listeners, but not to me!

PIONEERS

I was impressed with Elam Stauffer, the mission director and bishop. Elam and his first wife, Elizabeth, together with John and Ruth Mosemann, first lived in tents under a sprawling tree on a hill overlooking Lake Victoria in 1934. Elam fathered all of us on the missionary team. Languages seemed to come easily for him, and he was held in high regard by the local people. He was a true pioneer, the first foreign missionary sent out by Lancaster Mennonite Conference. He carried himself with humility and grace. I watched him with my eyes wide open to get some understanding of what was expected of me. Fortunately, since I was ordained, I was eligible to sit in on all mission meetings and all church meetings. Elam led them all. I saw in Elam a spirit that I deeply desired.

MISSIONARY FELLOWSHIP

Each month the missionaries in that region met at Bukiroba, near Musoma, for a Saturday of fellowship and sharing. We combined shopping in Musoma with attending these very worthwhile meetings. A good deal of the talk concerned the revival through which quite a few people, locals and expatriates, were being blessed. A Lutheran named Emmanuel Kibira, then the headmaster of one of the best boarding schools in the nation, located in Musoma, was deeply involved with the awakening movement. He met with us missionaries quite often. He was one of the first of the revival people to astound me with his penetrating insights, not only into the Bible but also into people's lives. I wanted to get to know him better.

JANE IS BORN

While we were adapting to a new culture, we also faced a wonderful change in our family. We were married on December 24, 1949, but it was not until July 5, 1955, that we were blessed with our first precious child, Jane Elizabeth. When school closed for the summer months, Anna Ruth and I moved to Shirati, the hospital station, into a small house for parents-in-waiting, like us.

Those were happy days, three weeks of just enjoying the abundant birds and flowers of Shirati and the hospitality of some of the world's nicest people, including Dr. Lester and Lois Eshleman. Lester had walked with me way back in 1944 at Eastern Mennonite School when I took my first steps following Jesus. Our paths parted for many years but met again in the most unlikely of places—on a hill overlooking Lake Victoria. Life with God is full of surprises.

Anna Ruth and I found that something profound happens when a couple, married for five years, receives the marvelous gift of a beautiful baby girl. Our cup ran over with thanks for Jane, a flaxen-headed bundle of life and beauty. Not only did Jane's coming mark a huge step in our family life, but our African friends were overjoyed. From then on Anna Ruth had a new name, "Mama Jane." That said volumes. She was now a productive member of the family and a mother. No such name change came my way. I was simply the husband of "Mama Jane."

The missionary family took on new meaning as Jane appeared and grew. All missionary women became aunts, and all of the men became uncles. So Jane had aunts and uncles who were not in the blood family, but they did serve as good, surrogate relatives.

Interacting with Neighbors

As we got settled, I began to interact more with the local people. For example, each morning I rode my bike to school, up a rather steep hill. I always needed to get off and push the bike the last few yards up the hill. Several times at just this spot, I met an old man with draped clothing and a walking stick. Invariably when we greeted with the usual "habari gani," which is a generic form of "How are you?" he never seemed to be satisfied with that. He wanted to know how the Mama was. How the child was. If we slept well. How things were with us. Were we suffering from any sickness? Sometimes it went on and on. He was, to me, just an old man.

One day, part way into our little exchange, he asked how it was going with two school boys that he named. I knew the boys and could assure him that things were going well with them. Then I asked, "Do you know them?" He then let me know that they were his grandchildren. He knew that their welfare was somehow tied up with my own welfare, because if negative things began happening to me, it would diminish the chances of his descendants passing the exams. Several years later when I began to study culture seriously, I knew why he was concerned. I was slowly beginning to make some connections with at least the obvious things in the local culture.

I tried to learn something of the challenges which faced believers in their cultures and was surprised at the vitality of faith that I found in this place. In that culture, witchcraft was prevalent. This became an acute issue for the believers because, as followers of Christ, they did not do everything their culture expected of them. So the culture employed witchcraft to bring them back into line. Stories abounded about that. I stood amazed at the courage of these new followers of Christ who refused to use local potions to avert witchcraft but relied entirely on the power of Christ to defeat Satan.

I learned to know the attractive young farmer, Elisha Meso, who, together with his wife, Susanna, was determined to live the life of Christ in a typical rural setting. I enjoyed visiting their village with the traditional cattle kraals made of twisted branches and sisal stalks. And there was Stephano Tingayi, a man with a real heart for God. He was bright, a good manager, and a friend in Christ who was not timid about giving his testimony. I marveled often at the grace and persistence that I saw in those believers.

PERSONAL SPIRITUAL STRUGGLES AT BUMANGI

The revival that began in Rwanda and Uganda about 20 years earlier impacted Bumangi as it did many communities across East Africa. Meso and Tingayi, with their spouses, together with a few dozen others, reflected the new life that they received by giving their hearts completely to Jesus Christ. The themes of the revival were unconditional belief in Jesus Christ, submission to his will, readiness to confess personal sin, freedom in giving testimony, and deep, open fellowship with those who shared the walk together.

I had been trained to analyze Christian movements to some degree, so I mused over this revival. I was indeed impressed with the fact that those who were walking in revival had a radiance about them that could not be denied. But I was annoyed by some of my students who point-blank asked me, "Are you saved?" Who were they to question my salvation? Hey, I am a missionary! What they meant by "salvation" did not square with my definition of the word. For them, being "saved" meant a radical break with the past and switching loyalty to Jesus Christ whom they sought to obey. That was too simplistic for me. I concluded that the themes of the revival might be right for Africans but not for me.

I do remember a dream I had at Bumangi, a dream that I shrugged off at the time. I am usually not impressed with dreams, but I could not easily dismiss the meaning of this one. In it I came in from working on our little vegetable garden, hot and tired, ready for a nice bath. Throwing a towel around my neck, I headed toward the river. As the path opened up to where I could see the river, I saw Africans bathing. I was not going to lower myself to bathe with them! Noting the direction of the flow of the river, I started upstream, looking for a secluded spot among the rushes where a white missionary could have a nice private bath in clean water. Suddenly I heard a voice, "There is only one place to bathe in this river, Don." I awoke with a start. Only later did I discover the meaning of that dream.

While I was enjoying the adventure of living in a culture not my own, there were some things that definitely annoyed me. For example, having made it known that no one should bother me at our house at siesta time, between noon and two o'clock, my anger rose when yet another schoolboy knocked on the door during my off-hours. I could not remember ever being annoyed by small things like that before. It seemed that all the weak-

Recent picture of the slate of headmasters at the Bumangi Middle School. Don Jacobs appears as the first.

nesses that I had suppressed through the years were being exposed, often by people that I did not respect very much. I found myself getting critical and cynical and hard. I concluded, "It must be Africa's heat!"

FACING THE TRAUMA OF FINDING A NEW IDENTITY

I was very well aware that the local people were not a bit interested in finding out who I really was. Why should they? And to be sure, I was not driven by a desire to know who they were. Had I stopped to think, it would have been obvious that part of my problem was that I did not know who I was. I was trying to get used to a new identity. I believed that people were watching me carefully to see how I would react to challenges. I was not only like an exposed fish in a fishbowl, but I was being defined, I believed, by their expectations of me. I did not like that at all! I hated being evaluated by the people I came to help.

I was acutely uncomfortable and often wished for a place to hide, or to forget about the whole thing and go home where I had a clear identity. I felt that I was being victimized because they were not seeing the true me. On the other hand, if they were to see the true me, what would that be? I was not sure that even I knew who I was. The markers that identified me for 25 years had little meaning on the hills of Bumangi. That I had three degrees, attended school for over 18 years, and was an obedient Mennonite with an illustrious ancestry that included many men and women of God did not impress them one bit.

To balance some of the anxiety of not knowing who I was, I welcomed, with open arms, my new identity as a father. My role as a missionary perplexed me, but being a father did not. I had been a husband. That was not new; being Jane's father was. It was a role that I understood and embraced, heart and soul. When the three of us were together in our cozy white bungalow, we made our own world. I think that helped me weather the storms of not knowing who I was on the outside. Being a father was a life-changer for me, as though a small seed that was there in my inner person all along sprang into life and became a living reality. "I am Jane's father! Glory be! And the husband of Mama Jane."

Let me try to explain what was happening on the outside, as I understood it. During those 18 months at Bumangi I had to bend in order to survive. For instance, as the school's principal, I was expected to direct my staff, all of whom were older than I. A good principal must know the staff. I soon discovered that if I was to give any leadership, I had to crawl into the skins of people on staff. This was hard to do because their world was a mystery to me. As they poured out their dreams, frustrations, and hurts, I was baffled. My first reaction was to think, "But you should not feel like that!" It slowly dawned on me that in order to understand my friends, I had to stop judging them and just listen and enter into their joys and pathos. As I did that, I found myself facing realities that I knew would not sit well with me. "I am a Westerner, not an African." I must have said that to myself a hundred times.

And another issue. Who was I among the white Mennonite missionaries? They were all older than I and had thrust roots into the local culture. Furthermore, they were either responsible for mission stations or were Bible teachers. Not me. I came on the scene to train primary school teachers. That was a new kind of mission work. My fellow missionaries had to get involved in culture because their effectiveness depended on that. I found myself out of step with what they might have expected of me.

Missionary Spirituality

The powerful revival which had spread across the area the decade before we arrived was still very strong among missionaries and the local people. As I sat in on their meetings where they had open fellowship together, I did not understand what was going on. Their determination to walk in newness of life in Christ brought them to repent of those sins that separated them from God and from one another. That they had meaningful fellowship was undeniable, but I did not see a need for constantly analyzing relationships and confessing sin. I left it at that and went into the fields with my 12-gauge shotgun to hunt guinea fowl.

Even though I was uneasy, I still clung to Jesus Christ. The Bible spoke to me with familiar power. I could not imagine life without Christ. My faith did not waver, but I was beginning to wonder if Jesus was going to ask more of me. He was.

Before closing out the Bumangi story, I want to mention that I got acquainted with the Chief of the Zanaki Tribe, Edmund Wenzagi. He held court on a hill just opposite Bumangi, maybe two miles away. This delightful man introduced me to his brother named Julius Nyerere Wenzagi. Little did I know that brother of his would be the first president of the new Tanzania, nor that I would have the privilege of knowing him personally after he became President. I might add that Tanganyika and Zanzibar joined after independence to become Tanzania, a combination of the two names.

Chapter 12

KATOKE
DAYS

1955 – 1957

Mission Schools

After a year and a half at Bumangi, it was time to move on to the assignment that brought us to Tanganyika in the first place, to assist in training teachers for the growing number of primary schools which were administered by the Protestant churches of the Lake Area. The Mennonites, the African Inland Mission, the Lutheran Mission, the Anglican Mission, and the Swedish Free Mission cooperated in education. The Roman Catholics had their own system.

At first, missions were somewhat reluctant to get involved in formal

On our way to Katoke, on the western shore of Lake Victoria

education, since they considered their primary goal the planting of churches and nurturing believers into strong communities of faith. However, the pressure became so strong, both from the people and the government, that one mission after another began to establish and administer schools. The place designated to train teachers was Katoke Teacher Training College, located several miles south of Bukoba on the western shore of Lake Victoria. The college was quite new, probably in its third or fourth year, when the Mennonite mission sent us there.

Our mission, bless them, provided us with a sturdy, American-made, Ford V8 pickup, recently overhauled by Sam Troyer, the mission mechanic. We felt fortunate because this little truck just fit our needs. It was old enough and built simply enough that I could work on it, and it took the rough roads in stride.

OFF TO KATOKE

After school closed at Bumangi, sometime in December 1955, we started our trip that took us around the bottom of the lake, through Mwanza, then on a ferry to Geita. We learned that an African Inland Mission family lived in Geita on the road to the western side of the lake. They graciously took us in and showed us genuine missionary hospitality.

A single sister lived on that station with a missionary couple. She and the man who ran the station had just had a hurtful misunderstanding. They got into a heated tiff at the table. I forget what it was all about, but I found myself disturbed that neither was repenting and asking the other for forgiveness. Mutual, heartfelt forgiveness marked the way the Mennonite missionaries that we had lived with for a year and a half related to each other. In that way, even though inevitable frictions occurred, they did live in peace.

At this time I had been holding the revival at arms' length, but when I saw these two people at one another, I wished that they knew how to repent like the Leathermans and the Smokers, the Shenks and Phebe. I thought how nice it would be if these two dear people could both repent, get cleansed, and live together in peace. That was a small but not insignificant step for me in the direction of a deepening spiritual awareness.

That road journey from Bukiroba to Bukoba was one of the transition trips that Anna Ruth and I took in our lifetimes. We were leaving the Mennonite missionary family, a colorful, loving group, people with whom we were somewhat familiar, a station and school where we felt at home. And we were leaving an African community in which we had developed substantial friendships. Now what? Travel times offered a good opportunity for the two of us to reflect, dream, and pray. We had no idea whatsoever what our new assignment would be like, but we were ready, now a family with our Jane. Our little green pickup became a house of sharing and praise as we churned up dust on our way.

From Mennonite Neighbors to Interdenominational Neighbors

I forget whom we first met at the Katoke Teacher Training College. I do, however, remember the slightly inclined lane, lined with huge trees, leading up to the College. We were amazed by those huge trees, unlike any we had seen east of the lake. That was not all. Huge, chicken-sized, black and white hornbill birds flew among the tall trees,

Jane in front of the College building at Katoke

splitting the air with their weird, raucous call. We were impressed! Under my breath I found myself saying, "We are going to like this." Katoke (the Swahili word for small banana) lay before us. Our house was a thatch-covered rondavel.

Anna Ruth and I met the challenges of a new place, a new culture, a new set of colleagues, with a certain excitement. Captain Jack and Ethel Bennet clearly ran the place. Jack was 20 years my elder, a Captain in the Church Army, something like the Salvation Army but in the Church of England. Jack's task was to establish this college. He did so in line with his philosophy of strict discipline. I tended to be much more American in my approach to students and the classroom. I thanked God for those months in England where I had met many "Captain Jack Bennets." But we truly admired Jack and Ethel and were enriched by a deep and abiding relationship. Jack personified for me what an authentic missionary should be like.

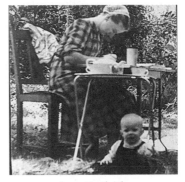

Anna Ruth, the faithful letter writer

His strict nature, I hasten to say, did not alienate him from the local African community. They expected it. Jack identified with the people, and they knew it. I believe that they were truly pleased when the British Colonial government appointed Jack to represent the local Bukoba region in the Legislative Council, established to prepare the nation for independence, a responsibility Jack took seriously. His extended trips to Dar es Salaam, 1,000 miles to the east, to sit in the Coun-

Jane with her Tanzanian friends and doll

cil often took him away from the school. As his young sidekick, I found myself stretched to the limit to run the college and to maintain the Bennet discipline when he was gone. I tried to administer like he did. That was hard because it was not me, not a bit of it. However, after a while I developed a style that did not compromise who I was, yet enabled me to do things in a modified "Bennet fashion."

I was put in charge of teaching students how to teach children to read Swahili, among other things. By then I had become very fond of the language and was quite excited about putting materials into the hands of my students, which they could use to good effect when they found themselves in a classroom situation. Many of the materials that I developed were picked up by other colleges. That pleased me immensely.

Jane straddles the equator

ELIEZER MUGIMBA

In addition to the British and American teachers at the school, we were privileged to have African staff of the highest caliber. Among them was a Ugandan who was to play a large role in my life, Eliezer Mugimba. Mugimba came into a saving relationship with Jesus Christ through the witness of the revival in Uganda while he was a seminary student at Bishop Tucker

Eliezer Mugimba with Don later in life

College near Kampala in the 1930s. He and his "revived" classmates were expelled because they were questioning almost everything that was being taught by the British missionary teachers, who had been influenced by a liberal school of theology.

The experience sent Mugimba on the path to becoming a teacher, not a pastor. He received a scholarship to study English at Oxford, where he earned a B.A. in English. Upon his return, he taught school in Uganda, but when the Anglican Church in Uganda asked for missionaries to teach in Tanganyika, Mugimba and his wife, Frieda, offered to go.

My relationship with Eliezer Mugimba opened a new chapter in my spiritual journey. He was tall, tender, and kind, like a caring family member. He opened his heart to me, encouraging me to come out of my spiritual shell and be willing to walk in light with another person. His love overwhelmed me, and at last, my reserve broken, I poured out all my frustrations and fear, my cynicism and critical spirit and a host of other sins that I was pampering in my life. The dam broke, in an instant my resistance to the revival collapsed, and I knew that I had found a truly human context in which to learn of Jesus.

Many years later, I visited Mugimba, then an old man, almost blind, in his village in Uganda. As we reviewed those early days, he said, "When you came to Katoke, the Holy Spirit said, 'That young American missionary is your mission field!'" That explained it all. I was sent to the mission field, not knowing that I was that "field." I surely was. God turns things upside down often.

THE BIRTH OF DAVID

During the second year at Katoke, our second child was born. David's birth on August 6, 1957, was unique in that he was born of American parents in Tanganyika, a British protectorate. His birth was attended by a Swedish midwife and a German nurse, attended by Tanganikan nurses. The doctor in charge of the Swedish-run hospital was also Swedish. It was something of a mini-United Nations experience.

FASCINATED BY CULTURES

At both Bumangi and Katoke I was becoming increasingly fascinated by East African cultures. That fascination was not always to my liking. In fact, I worked hard at times to try to change some of the ancient ways of these cultures. For example, I was taken aback when a student requested permission to return home to attend the funeral of his "mother." Not that it was a strange request, but it was the third time in two years that his mother had died. He explained laboriously that those three did indeed die, but none of them was his biological mother. They were aunts of some description. I was curious that the students felt that they were duty-bound to attend the funerals in their families. It dawned on me later that attendance at funerals meant that you had no part in wishing the death of the person. In their terms, that meant that you did not help to "bewitch" the person. I wasn't sure about all of this, so I just tried to connect the dots, realizing that I may have been missing the truth entirely.

In my first assignment at the Bumangi Middle School, I had only a superficial understanding of the tribal makeup of the student body. In my second assignment at Katoke Teachers' College, my eyes were opened. I began to see that if I was to understand what was going on among the students, I had to pay attention to tribal loyalties. The college drew students from many of the tribes around Lake Victoria, maybe 25 or more tribes, each with its own hearth language and as many traditional sets of practices. Not only was I introduced to tribal loyalty, but I also learned that it was woven into the psyche of the students. They were consistently loyal to those of their tribe, it seemed to me. I suppose they thought we outsiders should catch on to that. The truth of the matter was, I had not the slightest idea of what it meant to be a trustworthy member of a family, an extended family, and a tribe.

Understanding gaps plagued all of us, I suppose, because we came from a great variety of cultures. As for the students, they had to submit to the rules and ethos of the school; otherwise they would be on their way home. But they had their own integrity to protect. When rules and requirements did not threaten their integrity, they could go along. Now and again, however, this tension between the rules of the school and their own general sense of what was right and fair was so great that the students simply went on strike as a group. I had heard of student strikes in other schools, often over food. We had no such problem. Yet.

FACING CRUCIAL LEADERSHIP ISSUES

I remember the day. It was our second year at the college, and I was the acting Principal. I was in charge. The Bennetts were on home leave in the UK. On that day, when I returned to the college from lunch, I found one of the missionary teachers in a dither. Before him was the entire student body, sitting down in front of the college, glum. In the morning work detail, a daily ritual, he had set a punishment for one or more students to gather a specific number of bundles of grass, a normal thing. The students thought his order, however, was unjust for some reason, so they all refused to obey. No one fetched grass.

That was in the morning and now it was noon, after morning classes. The teacher ordered the students to get out and stand in ranks in front of the college so that he could talk to them. He berated them for their insolence in not following his morning orders. They said not a word, but all sat down, as one, on the ground. This enraged the teacher. He ordered the students to stay out there in the hot sun until his orders were obeyed. Then he walked off the scene.

That is when I appeared. He was adamant. "They must obey my orders! They'll stay there till they do." I saw at once that this was not going to work. Their resistance was solid. At that moment the students were not different tribes with different languages; no, they were one force against what they thought was unjust treatment. I dismissed the teacher who left in a huff.

"Oh, Jesus, help!" In situations like this, one prays quickly but desperately. I called a handful of the student leaders to come sit with me on the grass. We chatted. I heard the story. I then addressed the striking students, not in the usual English, but in Swahili. I assured them that I would forget the entire incident if they carried no grudge against the teacher. They agreed to that and were soon in the classrooms. Later, after the teacher reflected on it all, he did the most gracious thing that a person can possibly do. He humbly made an apology to everyone.

What did I learn through this crisis? Right up front I learned that when the group agrees, as one, that an injustice has been meted out on them, they suppress their own tribal loyalties and stand strong and immovable like a granite outcropping. It is profoundly important for a leader to discern when he is about to push a group off a cliff, or when he is in immediate danger of getting pushed off himself!

I also learned that leaders should, if at all possible, allow for a way out, both for themselves and for the protesting group. Because of this crisis I began to discover that God had given me a gift of being able to discern the mood of a person or a group. I hasten to admit that I did not always follow my best instincts because I am basically, aside from God's grace, a self-serving person.

Nevertheless, as I look back, I see that this sixth sense helped me as I interacted with people, not only of my own culture, but also with people in other cultures as well. I discovered that if I sit where people are for a while and find out how they are feeling, my attitudes are softened and I can slowly move them towards a more positive stance. I discovered I must withhold judgment and accept what comes as meaningful, even if not true. If I stand in judgment while the process continues, I hinder rather than help the healing or reconciling.

I might also add that the Lord gave me facility in the Swahili language. In that crisis, English was useless. The cultural authority of Swahili carried the day. I was often amazed at how I was enabled to express in Swahili precisely what I wanted to say and in a way that could be understood. I believe that I learned more about this at Katoke than at any other place. When things got tight, I switched into Swahili, and the ice melted a bit. Proper use of a local language can do wonders, for it touches the heart.

One of my learnings came because I was dealing honestly with God about my sinful nature and my unrepentant spirit. For some reason a flash of anger came over me one day as I was dispensing a discipline in the college. I suppose I showed my irritation, even though I tried to hide it.

That night I had one of those heart-wrenching, maybe even life-changing, struggles. The Holy Spirit made it plain to me that I got angry because I felt personally assaulted. My authority was being threatened. As the students were lined up in parade the next morning, I did one of the hardest things ever. Knowing that what I was about to do could erode my authority, I confessed my sin of anger and asked for forgiveness from the students. I feared that my leadership could never be put back on track again. To my utter surprise, they sang a little song which was used on such occasions to acknowledge the sincerity of a confession. I discovered that if I try to protect myself and my authority, I am in fact eroding it. If I simply obey the Holy Spirit and take the risks that a disciple of Jesus must take, God looks after the consequences.

A New Spiritual Family

Anna Ruth and I were warmed at the same spiritual fire. That blessed us as a couple. But we soon discovered that there were others just like us on the campus who had a profound experience of the grace of God. We heartily joined them in their life-changing meetings. They enabled us to be real as we brought things that we knew were not pleasing to Jesus to the light and cleansing of the cross. Eliezer Mugimba gave leadership to our meetings. We found this little fellowship group which met on a regular basis to be a safe place where we experienced a most intimate touch with the Spirit of the Lord Jesus. This little group listened to our frustrations, our disappointments, and our joys, and held us to the highest standard of walking with Christ.

Sometimes we attended area-wide conventions that included a broad span of missionaries and Africans. The Holy Spirit hovered over these meetings in a profound way, bringing people to the cross of Christ where sins were forgiven and life in Christ was restored. Invariably people left these conventions with renewed joy and freedom. Singing filled the air. These meetings brought together all tribes, cultures, denominations, and races in a most remarkable experience of Christ-centered spiritual fellowship. Those were exciting days. I was experiencing a new freedom in my own soul, to be sure. Seeing the Spirit of God at work like that seemed to make all things possible. I found a new sense of complete dependence on God and a new freedom from depending on myself. Had someone asked me in those days who I was, I would not have thought twice. "I am a saved sinner." How about that for simplicity and heart honesty? No sham. I got more complicated later.

A CROSSROADS — EDUCATION OR LEADERSHIP TRAINING

Sometime during our second year at Katoke, our own mission asked us to make a radical shift, from training teachers to teaching in the Mennonite Bible school at Bukiroba, filling in while John and Catharine Leatherman were on furlough. With mixed feelings we agreed to the change.

As the day approached to leave Katoke, we did so with great reluctance. Within a short span of two years we had fit in, done a significant bit of work on curriculum development and administration, and had come to feel at home there. It was scary to move from one place where we felt, humanly speaking, successful and pick up another assignment which offered no prospect of success at all. In fact, failure was a distinct possibility. I did not see myself as cut out to be a Bible teacher and certainly not to give leadership to a Bible school. I was not trained for that and could not envision myself doing it. However, we felt that God was leading through the directors of the Mission. At the end of the term we packed up our things, and off we went to Musoma where our sojourn in Tanganyika had begun almost four years earlier.

Off to church

Chapter 13

FROM
EDUCATION TO
THEOLOGY

1957

AMONG MENNONITE MISSIONARIES AGAIN

With our trusty Ford loaded with stuff, we said our
final farewells to our Katoke friends and, after a few days
of travel, arrived in Musoma. It was 1957. In a way, it
seemed like returning home because that was where we
began our missionary journey in 1954. When we left there
in 1955, our Jane was an infant. She was now two and a
half and, of course, we had our newborn, David.

We were rather apprehensive about how we were going
to fit among the Mennonite missionaries and the Mennonite Church in that region. During our two years at
Katoke Teachers College, we seldom thought of ourselves
as Mennonites. Now we were heading for the Mennonite
Bible School at Bukiroba where church leaders had been

In 1959, the large group of Tanzanian missionaries gathered at the time of the deputation visit of Bishop Amos Horst, Paul Kraybill, and Orie O. Miller, who appear in the center of the first row.

trained since 1936. It had its ups and downs in its 20-year history. John Leatherman was usually the principal, while George and Dorothy Smoker, along with Phebe Yoder, were the primary staffpersons. The teaching was in Swahili with a sprinkling of English instruction.

We had little time to overlap with the Leatherman family, but we fell in love with them all over again. One thing was for certain. John and Catharine were renewed in their faith within the revival which was moving and producing new life in much of East Africa. Likewise, George and Dorothy Smoker, who also beamed with the joy of newfound peace and profound spiritual fellowship, were among the keen believers. George was good at teaching church history; Dorothy could teach anything. She reminded me of my

Our home at the Bible School, with Jane and David

own mother. We had another powerful woman on staff, Phebe Yoder. Thankfully I had no problem with women taking the lead. I saw how it worked in my own family. I had a very strong mother.

I was made principal almost as soon as I arrived at Bukiroba. John Leatherman was eager to get rid of those responsibilities and prepared to leave. So those burdens fell on my shoulders. I did not see that as a hardship. We moved in with the Leathermans as they set their faces toward a furlough.

I remember the scene in Musoma as the Leathermans were boarding the lake steamer on the first leg of their trip back to the States. A huge group who loved them gathered and sang as the Leathermans boarded. Soon the ship slipped the moorings and headed out onto the calm lake into the glow of the setting sun, a breathtaking sight.

The Lake Steamer that docked in Musoma weekly

As we were leaving with a group of well-wishers, a British colonial officer who was there asked, "Do you know that white man?" My Tanganyikan friend said, "That is John; he is our brother." I never heard a more profound testimony to God's grace. Truly, John and Catharine were loved dearly. The Leathermans had opened the doors of their lives to all, with a special welcome to their African brothers and sisters in Christ. I was learning slowly.

A NEW TEACHING CONTEXT

"I have to learn how to teach all over again," I admitted to Anna Ruth during a tea break at our place. There was a night and day difference between Teachers College and the Bible School. To begin with, in the Bible School the students were all older than I was. I had just turned 29.

Bible School students in 1959. My first attempt to teach Christian leaders.

In Africa, age is an advantage. I was supremely impaired in that regard. Furthermore, all of them were deep into their local cultures, witnessing to the gospel of Jesus Christ and doing battle with Satan in their communities. I knew almost nothing about the settings in which they lived and served. It was my job as teacher to better equip them to be effective leaders within their communities. How was I to do that?

As I thought of it, I became aware of the fact that at the Teachers College at Katoke I was teaching teachers how to teach subjects. Of course, I had to learn something of the culture, because learning must be culturally relevant, but I did not actually delve into the worldview issues. Now I had to address the profound ambiguities and challenges which African church leaders faced every day in actual life situations within the stream of their own cultures. Quite often I considered just sitting in the back of the room somewhere. At least then I would not show my ignorance, my prejudices, and my shallowness.

It is one thing to teach teachers how to teach math, for example, and quite another to walk alongside pastors of the flock of Jesus Christ. I was forced to enter an entirely new and unexplored field—African religion and philosophy—not as social science, but as a real place in which I was called upon to help develop effective leaders. Those years, 1958 and 1959, were watershed years for me. I shifted from being a teacher of a subject to being a willing learner myself, eager to go deeper into the realities and mysteries of African cultures.

Chapter 14

READING SCRIPTURE WITH NEW EYES

THE BIBLE, OUR TEXT

Our primary text was the Bible. In fact, most of the students had not read one full-length book other than the Swahili Bible. Their entire world was lived in the knowledge that was handed down to them through their elders, now enlightened by the Gospel. They were not acquainted with the great moments of Western culture, including the Greek and Roman eras, the Middle Ages, the Reformation, the Renaissance, the Enlightenment, and the growth of industry, trade, and empires of the present world. Those periods had shaped me. Not them.

Instead, these people were shaped by fierce raids from enemy tribes, by periods of uncontrolled witchcraft, by long-remembered periods of famine, by the coming of colonists, by the shock waves of modernity, and now life in what was called a "nation." I kept wondering if there was any way that I could even remotely connect with life as they were experiencing it.

I discovered, to my amazement, that our meeting place was the Bible—the Swahili Bible, the second language of all the students—and the teacher! So, I concluded, let's swim in the Bible together. And so we did. How should I go about studying the Bible with these men? I decided to start with the Trinity. I carefully defined God the Father, Jesus the Son, and the Holy Spirit. I went to great lengths to make sure that each was treated as a separate personality and that each served a distinct role. While I was trying to divide them, the men seemed to be much more interested in how Father, Son, and Holy Spirit lived and worked together without strife between them. They were more interested in relationships than they were in identifying individual identities.

I was uneasy. I had lessons to teach according to the syllabus that I was acquainted with. I felt safe doing that. But I had the distinct feeling that I was too often scratching where they did not itch. Were they making any connections at all between my Western-style teaching, which is basically analytical, and the real life questions from the world in which they lived? They were used to narrative-style teaching. I was used to rational, propositional teaching. Could we possibly communicate?

ISSUES OF WORLDVIEW

I was the teacher and they were the students. The role of the teacher is to teach. But how was I going to do that? If I had gone home with one of those pastors for a weekend and followed him around, I was sure that I would not have understood half of what he was asked to do—pray for the demonized, bless a barren woman who wanted a child, make sure his few cows were kept safe

*Leaders in church, determined to improve their
education, make wonderful students.*

from pestilence, pray for a young man who was about to write an exam, look for work for an unemployed nephew, pray for protection from witchcraft. I could go on. On top of all that he was expected to preach the gospel.

My initial response was to suggest that they change their way of thinking to perhaps become more scientific. For example, I was well aware of the prevailing belief that persistent, unrelenting, life-threatening fevers are caused by malevolent spirits, maybe a dead ancestor who wished the person harm. In my zeal to challenge this false notion, I got a public health chart which depicted the life cycle of the malaria parasite. There it was for all to see, the anopheles mosquito which was the carrier of the parasite, biting a person and so depositing the parasite in the person's body. The parasite found the liver of the person and there reproduced a brood of parasites, which got into the person's blood. When the infected one was bitten by a mosquito, the insect spread the parasite that produced the fever.

It was all very scientific, cyclical, and unambiguous. I made sure that everyone understood that malaria fever is caused by a parasite. No one contested that. "So," I said, "that proves that fever is just that—fever—caused by the parasites that mosquitoes carry."

Then one of the men asked, "Why did that mosquito bite that person?" My jaw dropped. He had no problem understanding what happened after the infection took place—even a child could understand that. His problem was trying to figure out why that mosquito decided to bite that person. Living in a universe where animals, even insects, have some degree of freedom and power, that simple question made great sense to him, if not to me. Can spirits employ something as simple as insects to do their will? Now we were getting into a world where I was absolutely clueless.

The Bible, our Meeting Place

The men were fascinated by the Old Testament. They related to almost everything they read, including sacrifices, both blood and cereal sacrifices. The book of Proverbs made sense because they had their own proverbs which expressed many of their values and concerns. They understood completely the polygamy of the Old Testament. They were cautious about Christians adding wives, but they had to think through why they felt that way. In discussion, I found that they resisted polygamy because it was based on male superiority, which was contrary to the life and teachings of Jesus, and because they observed that more witchcraft took place in polygamous households than in monogamous ones. That is what they thought of polygamy. Hardly anything in the Old Testament was strange to them, including the mystery that bound heaven and earth.

My tolerance for mystery was growing, slowly and begrudgingly. I had taken great pride in my objective reasoning. To me, that was what a liberal, scientific education was all about. I found that I was so conditioned against subjective reasoning that I was unable to think that way at all. The men who sat before me could think objectively and subjectively without knowing the difference! Another dilemma! How would I resolve this one? Would trying to think subjectively do violence to who I was? Would tolerance for mystery bring my scientific bent into jeopardy? I feared for who I was if I changed on that point.

NEW APPROACH TO MEANINGFUL FELLOWSHIP

Those were exciting days, because all of us who were touched by the winds of God's Spirit blowing across the land felt the need to gather on a regular basis, outside the school setting, to gain strength from one another and to help each other on the way. So as the late afternoon sun began to settle for the night over the expansive Lake Victoria, lying to our west, we gathered in the village church. We arranged the benches in a circle, not like a normal service where all the benches faced forward where the preacher held forth. There were usually 15 or 20 of us—men, women, missionaries, local believers of several tribes, wealthy, poor, some with no formal schooling, those with degrees, ordained, and ordinary people. All had one thing in common, an uncommon hunger for the things of God—things which change lives and make people whole.

Men and women usually sat separately in formal services, but not during fellowship meetings. And the informal leadership of the group just happened. As the group gathered and settled, someone suggested that we pray. That meant that frivolous things ended, that we were meeting in the name of Jesus before our Father, enabled by the Holy Spirit. Then someone opened the Scripture and read a portion that had an impact on him or her. There followed a time for honest, open sharing about walking with the Lord.

These people were finding a new identity. My friend, Zedekiah Kisare, of whom you will hear more later, kept referring to this new experience as people living in the same village where Jesus is the head. In this new village, all are close to Jesus and all have distinct roles to fulfill. They all have a foot in the old village still, but their hearts are completely committed to Jesus who is head of the new village. Life in the new village is blind to any cultural achievements or failures. It is a village of sinners being saved.

People such as Kisare responded instinctively, "I am born again and I love Jesus. He has given me a new name." I hadn't thought of it before, but most of the people that I baptized selected new names, mostly biblical, to denote their new identity. For them, moving into the new village, the Kingdom of Jesus Christ, gave them a new and eternal identity, a new name in glory.

CALLED TO MISSIONARY SERVICE

Our missionary team included all sorts, but the common feature among them all was a determination to make a difference where they were. In order to do that, they knew that they had to master the language and become well acquainted with the culture. This is the missionary culture that welcomed me. Even though those early Mennonite missionaries with whom we lived in Tanganyika had limited formal training in understanding culture, several of them were quite good cultural anthropologists. I had heard of missionaries who lashed out against local culture, calling it demonic. Those that I had the pleasure of working closely with were not like that. For that I was well pleased.

It was during this time at Bukiroba, after we had been in Tanganyika for roughly four years, that I knew that I was called to missionary service in Africa. Here is what I wrote in my book, *Consider Jesus.*

> Heb. 1:1 "God spoke...at many times and in various ways." I had gone to Tanganyika in my mid-twenties because it seemed a good thing to do, and it was. However, I saw my future, not in Africa, but on a lush green college campus in America, teaching my beloved subject, history. I was definitely a "one-termer" in Africa. That all changed when one evening, when I was bathing in the golden glow of the African sun setting over Lake Victoria, I heard the voice of the Lord, "This is your place, Don. Learn of me through these people." God spoke! I knew, without a shadow of a doubt, that I was where God wanted me to be and that he was getting me ready to hear even more things from him through the brothers and sisters in the Lord there.

EVERYDAY JOYS

While at Bukiroba I found great relaxation in doing quite ordinary things—building a nice stone wall, constructing a mud-dried, brick, two-hole outhouse with

storage space, rebuilding the engine on my 125cc Enfield
motorcycle, swinging the hoe with the Bible School students to make terraces in order to stop erosion at the Bible
School. I was beginning to see how important it is to break
the stress and strain of always dealing with an alien culture by slipping into what was to me the familiar. Since I
was not convinced that I was making any progress in my
teaching, it was especially gratifying to build something or
make something work that was broken. And it was great
fun to add new birds to our growing list of Tanganyikan
birds that we had seen.

To be sure, there were moments of joy and even exhilaration. Here I refer to the throb of the heartbeat of Africa's
phenomenally varied natural beauty. Sunsets and sunrises
lifted my spirit, and the smell of the first rains after a long
dry spell sent me into ecstasy. When the long-awaited rains
finally came to the parched earth, it felt surprisingly like
springtime in Johnstown. Up sprang monkey flowers and
amaryllis lilies instead of crocuses, but the impact on the
senses was the same. Nature comforted me. I found deep
and meaningful delight in nature; birds became icons of
God's love. I melted in wonder as I saw the sparkling iri-
descent sheen off the back of a superb starling, for example. My heart burst in instant joy when I saw a handsome
klipspringer, a small antelope, standing tall on a granite
boulder behind our house. I had never seen one on our
hill before. I was surprised by nature, inspired by nature,
and taught by nature. I praised God heartily for the joys
of natural beauty and mystery.

Nature has a settling quality for me. But that cannot
compare with the solace of the love-bond between Anna
Ruth and me. It is inexplicable. Living out and experiencing that love was foundational. Married for more than

seven years, I found that I had taken our love too much for granted. I found that Anna Ruth had her own way of dealing with the same stuff that I was going through. She, too, was moving through change, but she seemed to move more easily than I. In some marvelous way, our separate ways of adjusting did not do any damage to our relationship, but rather strengthened it.

Introduce our dear Jane and David into the picture and another certainty was revealed—I was a father and Anna Ruth was a mother and together we were a family! I loved being a father. When I held Jane, then David, then both, I had no doubt who I was. Being a husband and a father began to re-identify me. That was consolation beyond measure. In Africa, having children is an identity-maker! That ties cultures together. A father is a father in Lancaster, and a father is a father at Bukiroba. That was a pleasant thought.

Scenes on Lake Victoria were a constant delight.

RELAXING AS IDENTITY CHANGES

As the cool winds of the evening swept across Lake Victoria to bring relief from the daytime heat, so the Spirit of God brought peace and assurance to my feverish life. Something changed deep inside me. I recalled that when I was a high school senior, I cast myself upon God, live or die. The flood of peace came when I believed that Jesus could forgive me and remake me. That had happened almost 15 years ago. My passion for Christ was not always as high as it should have been. But I knew that it was restored, that I was now alive in Christ as much as or more than ever before.

"Who am I in Christ?" I asked myself that question with unclouded eyes, not because I wanted to update my self-identity, but because I wanted nothing to stand in the way of walking with my newfound Jesus. Like Paul of old, I peeled off one layer of self-awareness after another and deliberately put them on a pile labeled, "Good but without ultimate meaning." My heritage, my achievements, my abilities, and a lot more went on that pile. What a relief.

What happened next surprised me. God gave me back everything on that pile. I was still white. I was still educated. I was still a teacher, a communicator, and a student of cultures, a lover of nature. And I was still a Mennonite. I found that what I gave up, I got back again—but without the prideful edge. I hasten to admit that I was not cured of my pride entirely, certainly not, but I had gone through the process of knowing that God loves me, not because of who I am, but because of who Jesus is, and Jesus is my friend. He loves me though stripped of all the "good" things that went into my self-identity.

In some remarkable way, that spiritual metamorphosis of shedding and renewing my self-image enabled me to sit where others sit, to feel like they feel, to rejoice like they rejoice. I believe that many things that I clung to, cultural things, actually impeded my journey into the depth of the souls of others. All kinds of possibilities opened up to me, if I could just let the process of releasing, cleansing, and sorting go on.

Chapter 15

BEING A
LANCASTER
MENNONITE IN
TANGANYIKA

LAW AND GRACE, LOCKED IN CONTEST

Word came from Eastern Board. "The Jacobs family should plan to stay for about six months longer because we are running into difficulty processing the Leathermans." We had been called away from Katoke Teachers College to fill in at the Bible School while John and Catharine Leatherman were on furlough in the United States. The plan was that when they returned, we would leave.

It seemed ages since we left home in 1953. We had spent an academic year in London, a year and a half at Bumangi Boys' Boarding School, and then two years at Katoke Teachers College. And now a year at the Bible School. The normal missionary term was five years, but duty demanded a bit more. We agreed to stay another half year to allow time for the Leathermans to be reappointed.

That half year extended to an entire year. That was because the Leathermans found themselves crosswise with the bishops of the Lancaster Mennonite Conference over many issues, but particularly whether people who did not subscribe to the Rules and Discipline of Lancaster Mennonite Conference could take communion with those who did subscribe, even in Tanganyika!

Like most of the missionaries, the Leathermans believed that they should be able to commune with sincere believers of other denominations. That undercut a basic tenet of Lancaster Conference at the time, which was that the best way to help people to live holy lives, distinct from the world, was to ask each person to submit to prescribed rules and discipline determined by Conference bishops. Before taking communion, a person had to openly express a determination to keep all the rules and submit to the discipline. Without that statement of obedience — no communion. So communion became a gate by which holiness was protected, and, by the way, the bishops tended the gate. The whole thing became, in my eyes, a bit ridiculous.

Missionaries returning from Africa freely admitted that they took communion with other denominations in East Africa and that they had served communion to people of other denominations. That had to stop, ordered the bishops. Otherwise, they protested, how can we encourage holy living among our people if any Tom, Dick, and Harry can take communion with us? This bone of contention delayed the return of the Leatherman family. It proved to be a big bone among many smaller bones. The news we received through the Mennonite grapevine was that the Leathermans might not be reappointed. So what about us? Who knew?

"Tell John and Catharine to make peace quickly with the elders there so that they can come back and be with us again." That was the view from the keen believers in Africa who loved John and Catharine and desired their fellowship. I shared their feelings.

MISSIONARIES DEALING WITH CULTURE AND RELIGION

What role did revival play in the development of the Mennonite Church in Tanganyika? Let's look at that question against the backdrop that I just discussed, that before missionaries could be appointed they had to agree to obey and teach Lancaster Conference Rules and Discipline. No exceptions.

Switch the scene to Tanganyika where missionaries were trying to plant churches. They did their best to apply the "culturally specific" requirements contained in the Rules and Discipline of Lancaster Conference, but they soon came to the conclusion they were forcing the impossible, not just the undesirable. For example, the rules stated that women should not cut their hair. In Tanganyika, women who did not trim their hair were morally suspect. Another example was the holy kiss. Male kissing was abhorrent there. And the style of dress prescribed in the Rules was obviously not designed for Africa.

I give the early missionaries credit for not pressing on Tanganyikans the dress requirements and other culturally specific items. But now the rub comes. The Lancaster Conference bishops made no allowance for the fact that the Tanganyikan culture was quite unlike their own. They expected the missionaries to guard the communion table and not allow anyone to participate who was not in agreement with the Rules.

In Tanganyika, the great movement of the Spirit touched people of many denominations. At huge revival conventions where Christ was preached and many were saved and blessed, it seemed only natural to close these events with massive communion services, administered by a variety of clergy present. Lancaster Conference did not like that one bit. To open communion to all who love Jesus, regardless of denominational affiliation, would in effect, the Conference believed, weaken the whole idea of a disciplined church, a focus of Lancaster Mennonites for a half century or longer.

What kind of church would emerge in Tanganyika, birthed, in a sense, by missionaries from Lancaster Mennonite Conference? Who knew? Certainly not the missionaries. The central theme of the East Africa Revival was that true fellowship with God the Father was through the merits of Jesus Christ and not because of denominational affiliation, certainly not in obeying a common set of culturally-specific rules. In fact, the message of revival was a strong declaration that people of a variety of denominations, a variety of cultures, a variety of races are, in fact, one in Jesus. This was a tremendously liberating word with profound consequence for a part of the world torn apart by all sorts of divisions, notably tribal ones.

It was hard for Lancaster Conference to work into one braid the need for firm discipline on the one hand and taking seriously the atoning, reconciling work of Jesus on the other. They struggled with that. They knew the power of divine grace, for they were themselves debtors to that grace. Otherwise they were not saved. Their path led them to a question that dominated their thinking: "If there is not a common set of rules and discipline, how else can you preserve and foster the holy life among a people?"

Up to that time, Anna Ruth and I had been blessedly outside the orbit of such hot discussions. In our idyllic multi-denominational setting at Katoke, we almost forgot we were Mennonites. It was there at the college that the Lord did a deepening work in our hearts. I think it was there that I tumbled onto the realization that nothing with the stamp "made on earth" would have eternal consequences, and "denominations" had that stamp. We left that multi-denominational setting in order to fill in at the Mennonite Bible School at Bukiroba.

After about a year's delay, the Mission Board and the Bishop Board managed to clear the Leathermans to return to Tanganyika. I think the bishops just gave up—not *in*, but *up*. The Mission Board was obviously the "liberalizing" influence in the Conference. Not liberal in the theological sense of the word, but liberal when it came to encouraging the local cultures to decide what was best for them. As far as I knew, none of the missionaries questioned whether the church, anywhere in the world, should conform to the world or not. That was settled. The question was along what cultural lines were the spiritual battles to be waged.

We missionaries began to speak of this process of having the local believers sink their roots deeply into the local soil as "contextualization." It became a theme for us. We read and reread the Bible, especially the New Testament, to find out how it was done as Jewish and non-Jewish people lived together in one loving church. The book of Acts became our foundational text.

REASONS FOR A DISCIPLINED CHURCH

It was about this time that I began to unpack Germanic Mennonite life to see why we are like we are. I reread the classic Mennonite theological book, *Doctrines of the Bible*, written by Daniel Kauffman in 1932. I realized that huge changes had taken place in the first quarter of the 1900s. English replaced German dialects, revival meetings became commonplace, Sunday schools flourished, as did youth groups. In a sense, the Mennonite church was becoming Americanized at a rapid rate. Many features of the Mennonite community that marked it as different from the dominant society fell away as the sociological orientation of many Mennonites changed. So what was a Mennonite?

As I pondered this, I noted that Kauffman made a strong case for both nonconformity to the world and nonresistance in relationships. He then proceeded to list the great sacraments like baptism, communion, and holy marriage, to which most believers in the world subscribe, and quite surprisingly, at least to me, added anointing with oil. In all my growing up years, I never saw that being practiced in a Mennonite congregation. That confounded me.

I noticed that baptism, communion, and marriage are bonding rituals. He added an additional bonding one, foot-washing. Then among the ordinances, he listed prayer head coverings for women, which assured that gender roles would be preserved, an important community glue, and the practice of the holy kiss in greeting one's own gender. It dawned on me that the covering and the holy kiss get little mention in the body of the New Testament, yet Kauffman lifted them to the level of ordinances. As I pondered Kauffman's powerful writing, I became aware of the fact that the emphasis was on community, not evangelism and church planting or missions.

His concern for community based on Christ and held together by love made sense to me. I also believed that going to war was fraught with all sorts of biblical difficulties, especially Jesus' clear teaching on the matter. I also believed that a church anywhere in the world must see itself as a called-out separate community, even while it engages in evangelism and getting on with the larger world.

While I was at peace with the virtues expressed by Kauffman, I knew that when East Africa believers became serious about formulating their stance in society, they would likely come up with a different set of so-called "ordinances." The solid sacraments would certainly remain.

As Lancaster Conference and its Mission Board engaged more and more cultures at home and abroad, they slowly, sometimes rather begrudgingly, agreed that Holy Spirit-directed contextualization was a good thing. It was better, certainly, than for believers of one culture to direct how people of another culture should live, in culturally specific terms. I leave it at that.

Chapter 16

FIRST
FURLOUGH —
RETOOLING

1959 – 1961

LOOKING AHEAD

As the time drew near for our furlough, after six years that had slipped by much too quickly, the Mission Board wanted to know our future intent. We indicated that we were prepared to return to Tanganyika in any role that the Tanganyikan church and the Mission Board considered appropriate. We assumed that it would be in the area of leadership development, no doubt by improving the Bible School. We all recognized that the future welfare of the church and community hinged on the effectiveness of leaders.

I did struggle with the idea of training leaders. I believed that leaders should be trained by leaders. I did not consider myself to be a gifted leader. Upon reflection, God reminded me that I had administered schools in Kentucky, Bumangi, Katoke, and Bukiroba. "That may be true," I argued, "but I did that because I was pushed to do it by circumstances, not because of a leadership talent." With these reservations buzzing about my head, I knew that God was calling me to get involved in leadership development and that my base would be at the now-familiar Bukiroba Bible School.

As I peered into the future, I felt I needed to become immersed in the local view of life so completely and meaningfully that I could, to some extent, look at things through the locals' eyes. I became increasingly aware of the fact that life as they were living it every day was miles away from the world that I was living in. It was even further away from teachers of theology in Western seminaries and universities who were, rightfully so, addressing the questions of a culture that was profoundly impacted by the Enlightenment and modernity. The questions that my Tanganyikan friends were asking addressed a different worldview.

This line of thought led me to suggest to the Mission Board that, on furlough, I wanted to study how to understand culture. I believed that as part of a community of faith in Tanganyika, we could find biblical answers only if we knew what the most basic questions were and if we could see the answers in light of the Tanganyikans' view of the world. My job, I felt, was to discover with the people what questions they were facing every day in their ministry of God's grace. I believed that any culture could bring its deepest questions to the Scriptures where the Holy Spirit, who is the Spirit of revelation, would lead to the answers. The upshot of the matter was that I was being drawn to spend some quality time studying, of all things, cultural anthropology. I wanted to study culture as linked to theology and Christian faith.

A little experience helped push me in the direction of examining worldviews and value systems. One Sunday in Africa, shortly before leaving for furlough, I heard a powerful message on the Luke 8 passage that tells of Jesus casting out demons from a man who was sorely possessed. The demons begged Jesus to send them into nearby pigs. He did so, and the pigs rushed into the water and drowned. That was marvelous good news for our maturing congregation in Tanganyika. They had similar experiences in their own neighborhoods as Jesus liberated those who were bound by demonic forces. They were excited all over again to read how it happened when Jesus ministered in Palestine. It was a "hallelujah moment," as they say in Tanganyika.

Not long after that, on furlough, I was in the United States, sitting in a normal Sunday school class of people my age. Interestingly enough, they were dealing with the same Luke 8 text. It produced a heated discussion. No one, as I recall, rejoiced in the great good news that Jesus Christ had power to cast out demons, as was the case in Tanganyika. No, they got into an argument about whether Jesus was punishing the Jews for doing something that the Law prohibited, raising pigs, or whether the people who were raising pigs were, in fact, pagans.

It struck me once again that people read their Bibles wearing their own cultural spectacles. They see only what makes sense in the worldview that shaped them. It surprised me that in that text, I could see sense in both responses to that biblical passage.

The decision was made. I would study cultural anthropology, always remembering why I was doing that, which was to better comprehend the worldview of the people that God was calling me to live with.

HOME AGAIN IN PENNSYLVANIA

After six amazing years away, 1953–1959, we had a marvelous homecoming. In 1953, we had boarded the Queen Mary that sailed to England. In 1959 we landed in New York on a DC-8! Not only had the mode of transportation changed, but we had as well. Further, we had become a small family with Jane, four, and David, two. Of minor significance, but just as real, was that we returned with "Africa" written indelibly on our minds and hearts.

At the airport to meet us were our children's grandparents, plus Raymond and Anna Lois and their family. We tasted the delights of reunion with family. My mom and

Jane, 4, and David, 2, meet their grandparents, both Jacobs and Charles, and other family on the way home from the New York airport.

dad hugged Jane and David heartily, even though they already had a quiver full of grandchildren. They were, of course, overjoyed. For Anna Ruth's parents, and especially her mother, it was a holy moment. I think grandmas have a special love for their grandchildren to start with, but to have your one and only daughter present you with two wide-eyed children, after six long years away, was pure delight! I quivered with joy.

Anna Ruth's parents opened their home to us, just as they did when we were first married. Once again, we luxuriated in being in the hands of those marvelous people, Jacob and Cora Charles. All sorts of summer vegetables and fruits found their way to our table. Jane seemed to like crunchy American apples just as much as she liked sweet African mangoes.

Soon we were in churches, telling our stories. People responded warmly to our tales of danger, elephant charges, poisonous snakes, and how fast the church was growing in Tanganyika. Often what I really wanted to talk about was what happened to me, about how I needed Jesus so much, time after time, that I almost despaired. I blended stories with my witness. Over time, I believe that I succeeded, to a limited degree, in weaving things together into a tapestry of experiences that made sense to our friends at home.

OFF TO NEW YORK CITY

The summer months sped by quickly. Change for us was on the horizon, one that was about as scary as any change we had made up until then—diving into the very heart of American culture, New York City, to study. That culture was so different from the cultures of Tanganyika that it was like two planets. The university in which I enrolled, New York University (NYU), was located in Greenwich Village in lower Manhattan, noted for its bohemian, secular character, as unlike African cultures as one can imagine. How was I going to juggle the worlds that I moved in and out of? I did not bother to answer that or even to ask the question.

I enrolled at NYU but took some courses at the New York Biblical Seminary, which qualified us for residential housing there, on E. 50th Street near the United Nations building. On weekends we usually drove to Lancaster where we spoke in churches and, upon return, jammed our green Ford station wagon with food that we gladly carried up the six floors to our walk-up apartment. One such time I counted 12 trips up those stairs. We bought very little in New York City. The largess of the generous Charles family sustained us. And gave me needed exercise.

Studying Cultural Anthropology

The Faculty of Education in which I was enrolled had a few courses in sociology and anthropology, but I wanted more. So I put one foot into the Faculty of Anthropology where I took advanced courses in cultural anthropology. There I found the help that I was looking for. I began to get an understanding of how cultures work and how to plumb their worldviews.

I was asked more than once, "You're a what? A 'missionary'?" "Yep," was my answer. A missionary among students of anthropology was an anomaly. I was probably the only person of that species that they had ever met. Everything they had read and imagined painted missionaries in the worst possible light—as those who had no cultural sensitivity at all. My colleagues could hardly believe that there was a real live missionary sitting among them.

They were convinced that missionaries perpetuated the worst parts of the Victorian Era, including male dominance. I found it amusing that my fellow students, most of whom were somewhat cloistered by having heard the same presuppositions year after year, had no way to stop for a minute and question their ideas about missionaries.

When Dr. Alpenfels asked me one day, "Mr. Jacobs, would you be willing to address our entire department?" I accepted without hesitation. I had come to know and appreciate Dr. Alpenfels. She wanted me to try to explain how a cultural anthropologist could possibly be a missionary. I agreed to be Daniel among the lions, and so prepared a paper which debunked the notion that the normal run of cultural anthropologists, including those of us in that classroom, carried no biases or presuppositions. I suggested that the best way is to be painfully honest and agree that all of us, whether we admit it or not, examine others in light of our own assumptions, no matter how hard we try to have absolutely no opinions about anything. I spoke of my own experiences of living with people of another culture, and how I slowly became aware of my own biases and presuppositions.

Then I made the point that the cultures that I was encountering were undergoing seismic sociological shocks, and that the role of people of other cultures, missionaries, for example, was to sit with them, live among them, and point to options beyond those which were locally available. I reminded my fellow students that ultimately people will decide what they want and what they do not want. The role of the outsider is to broaden the range of options as culture and society change. The idea that an outsider can force cultural change is ridiculous.

Dr. Alpenfels allowed that I had done quite well. I was glad that I did not disappoint her. She never did divulge even a hint of what she believed, except that she believed that believers do not make good cultural anthropologists! I tried to disabuse her of that. I think she dropped a good word for me, because near the beginning of the next semester I was approached by the head of the department, asking if I could possibly help out with a few lectures in the Sociology of Religion course because the teacher had fallen ill. I agreed to and found myself teaching a few classes. Then it became apparent that she could not return, so I finished the year for her as a temporary member of the faculty. They even paid me!

ALAN JOINS THE FAMILY

We loved living in New York. Being near to the United Nations building, we often took the children to the UN's playground. Most of our family activity was limited to our small, sixth-floor apartment. By March, Anna Ruth was huge with child. During a heavy snowfall on March 9, 1960, I hastily called a taxi that took us to the 70th Street New York University Hospital where Anna Ruth had a successful delivery, and we welcomed our dear Alan. He was our only child not born in Africa.

Now and again our wee apartment seemed much too confining to Jane and David who were used to the great wide-open spaces of Tanganyika. Somehow, Anna Ruth managed. She prayed and planned a lot. I could run out in the morning, leaving her with two bundles of pent-up energy. We concluded that one academic year of that was enough. Next school year things must surely change.

MENNONITE CHURCH PLANTING IN NEW YORK CITY

Living in New York, I became acquainted with some young, energetic Mennonite church planters. For example, Glenn and Florence Zeager, who pastored and ran a limousine business all at the same time. We met for fellowship in their spacious house. We learned to know and admire Paul and Miriam Burkholder, John and Dottie Freed, and John and Thelma Kraybill. Since we went to Lancaster almost every weekend, we did not attend services at the congregations they served, but we did try to be in touch with them. I discovered that they, too, were struggling with the issue of denominational discipline as we were in Tanganyika.

They found that it was not all that difficult to lead people to a saving knowledge of Jesus, but it was quite another thing to ask the new believers to submit to the Rules and Discipline of Lancaster Conference before baptism. That hobbled their efforts to plant churches. I sympathized with them.

What impressed me most was the determination of the workers to plant churches, no matter what. I admired their zeal, and the Lord was obviously at work among them. Instead of rebelling against the authorities in Lancaster, they humbly submitted to what was expected of them, even though they might have wished to have more freedom. Some of the workers found new freedom in Christ by deciding to work willingly with the situation that they had little hope of changing at that time.

But What About Culture?

Their dilemma caused me to think again about culture. As I put on those spectacles to examine the New York situation, I saw a troubling fact. The congregations had no significant local cultural rootage. As I probed this, I found that the underlying vision was to plant multicultural fellowships as a witness to the power of Jesus Christ to overcome ethnic and class differences. In light of the civil unrest in urban America at the time, that was a good strategy. If the church was to be part of the healing community, then it had to bring cultures together in Christian love at the congregational level. It seemed so right.

Yet I saw how this vision had its blind spots. No matter if the church was located in a black community, a Spanish community, or a Jewish community, the church planters determined to plant fellowships that included all cultures. They were blessedly blind to what happened, in fact. The congregations reflected the culture of the church planters, not the local cultures.

I recall that every local congregation in Africa that I was acquainted with had its distinct local stamp because it shared the same local culture. These congregations employed their own language as the basic language, and they clothed their beliefs in local forms. Such congregations, all things being equal, had a good chance to grow.

In New York City, the Mennonite fellowships were not rapidly growing fellowships. I began to wonder if each congregation would benefit by having one dominant culture. For example, one local congregation could be black in culture, another Honduran Spanish, and so forth. That did not mean that everyone who belonged to that congregation had to be a child of that culture, but it seemed important to acknowledge that the dominant culture of that particular congregation was what it was.

I was beginning to believe that when planting churches in cultures unlike our own, we must be humbly aware that we can no more expect people from those cultures to deny their inner selves than I could expect it of myself. Each of us brings our culturally-formed inner self to Christ, who cleanses us from sins so that we can each live fully for him in the particular culture in which each of us is at home.

Summer 1960

When the school year ended, Anna Ruth's parents opened the upstairs of their house to us. Our children loved the freedom of the farm. It was a good summer, punctuated with deputation work in the churches. People did not tire of hearing about missions.

As summer drew to a close, we were pleased that the Robert Ranck family offered us their "missionary house." It was a house they owned next to their own. They offered it as low-cost housing to missionaries on furlough, sometimes even free. This was a splendid answer to our prayers. Jane, then five, attended kindergarten. Alan was an infant. So Anna Ruth and David kept each other company. Our house was heated by a self-standing coal stove. One thing, among many,

The missionary home made available by the Ranck family in Lancaster. We lived there for a year.

that Anna Ruth learned that winter was how to maintain a good coal fire. Her mother helped her make the first one.

COMPLETING PH.D. WORK

Unfortunately, I was not around home to help because I returned to New York City for my second year at New York University. Having completed my class work, I concentrated on writing my dissertation. It was a study of social change using a new way of identifying themes in a culture. I applied this scheme to the puberty ritual of the Akamba people of Kenya.

After I submitted my dissertation, I prepared for the oral examination. The day came when I sat there in the presence of six examiners who pelted me with questions. Most of the questions had to do with the material I was working with, which was new material to all of them. They seemed to ask just the right questions. Within a few days I got word that I was approved to receive the Ph.D. All within 20 months! I could hardly believe it. Neither could Orie O. Miller. When I told him, he said, simply but sagely, "Don, you got it. Now forget it!" Good advice. He and I both knew that being a Ph.D. in the little Bible school backed on to the Nyabangi hill in Tanganyika would make little difference. Our daughter, Jane, also pricked the balloon: "My dad is not a real doctor." I chuckled. She was absolutely right.

Parenthetically, the chairperson of the Department of Sociology of Religion, the one who had asked me to fill in as a teacher, approached me as I was wrapping up my Ph. D. with a surprising offer. "I arranged to have you come onto our staff to continue your teaching." Before I could say anything he went into detail about salary, terms, tenure, and the rest. I did not want to appear ungrateful but I had to tell him, "You have been a huge help to me. Thank you very much. I owe you a debt of gratitude. But, sir, I am going to a little African Bible school on Lake Victoria. I did not make that decision, God made it for me." I was quite unconvincing, I am sure, but I was honest.

PREPARING TO RETURN TO AFRICA

The Mission Board had to examine us once again on our beliefs before we could be reappointed. I began to realize how much I had changed since I filled out a similar form seven years earlier. The questions now seemed hopelessly irrelevant to me as a missionary. A few examples, as I recall, were questions that had to do with the seven days of creation and how I would explain the essence of biblical inspiration. The spaces on the form did not allow for long answers. In a way, that was good, for it forced me to say little. I found myself conjuring up an examination that asked the kinds of questions missionaries should be asked. The questions on the present list could not possibly help to determine whether a person would be a successful missionary or not. Maybe it was not designed for that. In any case, I dutifully filled mine out and forgot the whole matter.

REFLECTING ON TWO YEARS IN AMERICA

So what happened to me in 1959 and 1960? First, our little family was subjected to radical changes, from living in Africa without near relatives to getting a bevy of real live relatives—grandparents, uncles, aunts, and cousins that must have been bewildering for our children. My new identity included trying, with Anna Ruth, to shepherd our little family through the maze of relationships and new things. I had some guilt feelings when I returned to New York City, time and again, leaving Anna Ruth with a very heavy burden in Lancaster. I felt constrained to serve my wife and children like never before. My love for Anna Ruth, Jane, David, and Alan deepened. I slowly concluded that my family may not need me, but I needed them, each one.

Another thing that happened to me was that I was able to maintain an active evangelical faith in an environment that made war on faith of any kind. I learned that simple faith could survive in a sea of atheism. In my reading and research, I determined to keep an open mind. I was not prepared to give an inch, however, when it came to what I thought of Jesus Christ. Having so established myself, to my amazement, I could absorb some new concepts and blend them with my integrating self-identity.

I also discovered that I was prepared to be a long-term missionary, probably not for all of my life, but for many years. That served to shift my identity somewhat from being a person who loved to pick and choose to being a person with a distinct and purposeful calling. By embracing the calling of God on my life, I effectively said no to basically everything else. I was no longer an American exploring life in Africa. I was a witness of Jesus Christ in Africa, hopefully open for many more learnings, for better or for worse.

I would be amiss if I did not mention something else. That is, I was perplexed when I realized how the church, and even friends, put me on a pedestal. The label, "missionary," was almost tantamount to sainthood in our circles. I struggled with this for some time. Then I began to realize that in our North American Mennonite culture, I was serving a purpose simply by being a missionary. Our Anabaptist tradition has no tolerance for saints, but our people do revere certain categories, like missionaries, to whom they can attribute the ideals that they believe in. When this began to dawn on me, I finally accepted my culture's need for hero figures, knowing full well that I was the weakest of the weak. In the end I allowed myself to fill a need that my Christian community defined. I realized that I was not what they thought I was, but I was prepared to allow them to live with that illusion. So I found peace in the contradictions.

One thing I was absolutely certain of: I was where God wanted me to be and among the people that he chose for me. And I knew that the work of Jesus in my life opened a storehouse of gifting and grace that was there when I absolutely had to have it. I was learning to open my heart more and more to let God do just what he wanted to do to me and through me.

Chapter 17

SECOND TERM IN AFRICA

1961 – 1966

OPEN-ARMED WELCOME

As our little family of five arrived at Bukiroba in July 1961, our minds went back seven years to the first time Anna Ruth and I stepped on Tanganyikan soil. At that time we tingled with excitement. Everything was new. Not so now. We were welcomed by friends. We felt the warm embrace of missionaries and Tanganyikans alike. This was a hallelujah homecoming! Was the United States our home or Tanganyika? If home is where one's relatives are, then we could not call Tanganyika our home. I recalled the wisdom of our daughter, Jane, when, while traveling as a family, she comforted her brother David who was begging to "go home." "Home," Jane said, "is where we are!" She was referring to family.

As we settled at Bukiroba, we became aware of the chant, "*Uhuru, uhuru*" (freedom, freedom) that filled the air. We could hear and feel it. While we were away in

America for two years, Tanganyika was moving full steam ahead toward political independence. We were away during some of the most exciting times as the movement toward political independence gained momentum. It was spearheaded by Mwalimu Julius Nyerere, whom I knew only slightly. By December of that very year, Tanganyika had become a free and sovereign nation without any violence whatsoever.

THE CHURCH MOVES AHEAD

The euphoria that was in the political air billowed out into the church as well. If the nation becomes independent, should not the churches that were established by the missions also be set free to run their own affairs? I stayed out of those conversations as long as possible, but we all knew that things had to change. The desire of the church was commendable and inevitable. I needed to embrace the new day and prepare leaders to inherit it.

Leadership training took priority. Courses taught in Kiswahili and English featured homemaking skills for women.

My job, to establish the first Mennonite, English-speaking, theological college in Tanganyika, was made easier by the determination of the church to move forward on a course that they would set. I saw my little project as one part of their determination, not only to strengthen the church, but also to enable the church to be a positive influence in their communities. Things clicked for me: "Focus on leadership development." That is what I did. EMM did not need to be convinced of this. Orie O. Miller and Paul Kraybill assured us that funding would be there for the construction of a college on the campus of the existing Bible School.

A Dedicated, Motivated Staff

God provided a superb staff. Dorothy Smoker virtually threw herself into the challenge of honing a curriculum suited to our situation. Working with Dorothy was pure delight. Her quick smile, her brilliance, and her depth of wisdom blessed me. She was deeply involved in the East Africa Revival and, in that context, understood the brothers and sisters in their culture. She was decidedly ready

Dorothy Smoker excelled in many ways.

George Smoker was a perpetual delight.

to do what I also felt led to do, to work on a curriculum that embraced the cultures of the leaders we were to help to develop.

We wanted to do all our "theologizing" in the context of the local world. John Leatherman and George Smoker, while they were not prepared to take leadership in this area, agreed to move with it. We decided to embrace the local culture as we thought Jesus and the Apostle Paul would do. Our primary task was to walk alongside church leaders as they searched the Scriptures for help in pushing back the darkness and furthering ministries of compassion and hope among their people in real-life situations.

Catharine Leatherman and Phebe Yoder, meanwhile, had created a special course for the wives of the students. It was in Swahili and consisted of biblical studies and homemaking.

George and Dorothy Smoker were the kind of people that we would have enjoyed being with, even if we were all unbelievers. They were both as bright as could be, with hilarious and always refreshing senses of humor. Dorothy was a converted comedian! One day I was in their house when George came in after a week or so away building a church. He had not shaved, obviously. Approaching Dorothy for a welcome-home kiss, she took his hand and kissed it, saying, "George, one kiss on the hand is worth two in the bush."

George had a dry sense of humor that made me roll on the floor with laughter. For example, he, like many of us men, got too much sun. He developed a cancer on his ear that Dr. Eshleman removed. In his letter to his friends in America he wrote, "I'll be home in a year and a half with an ear and a half." George was good for me in many ways. And as far as walking with the Lord was concerned,

George and Dorothy were diligent about that, allowing nothing to cloud their vision of Jesus every day. They kept an eye on me, that is for sure, encouraging me to walk in light and liberty, to repent quickly when my attitudes began to sour, and not to get puffed up and stuffy.

It took me a while to get to know John Leatherman, and I suppose he could say the same about me. But we slowly began to understand one another. I think he was a born introvert. It was not easy for him to open up and embrace people. He was a teacher and not a natural leader. He loved to read theology, and he lived in the Scriptures.

In the 1940s, however, God did an amazing work in his heart. As a result, John had a testimony of what the Lord can do to break and remake a person. His introvertedness receded, replaced by a strong personal witness to the grace of God. I heard that when our Tanganyikan friends were witnessing to others about the power of God to change lives, they pointed to John Leatherman. "If God could do that for John Leatherman, he can do it for you."

John based his faith on knowledge. In one of my rare moments of joyous freedom, I made a statement like, "I need Jesus, not theology." Dear John took me aside later and said, rather sternly, "Don, never despise theology!"

I held Catharine Leatherman in high regard. To begin with, she was our expert in Swahili. As to her new life in Christ, as the revival swept through Tanganyika, her testimony was that without any feelings whatsoever she made a determined decision to thrust herself completely on Jesus, trusting him to cleanse her from sin and to give her the Holy Spirit. Her life was completely changed. She said, "Do not wait for a feeling, just do it!"

Recruiting Students

The problem with establishing a college was getting students who could do this level of work, which required some proficiency in English. For most, it would mean studying English and theology at the same time. Some were well along with learning English; others were not. We asked each student for a three-year commitment. Some could come with their wives and families and live in the small houses built for Bible School families. Others would remain at home and come to school daily. We finally had the roster that we felt comfortable with, 16 students who were committed to give their best to developing their leadership potential.

A New Approach

Having brought everything to completion—buildings ready, students in place, staff lined up, and budget assured—we launched into teaching, always keeping in mind that we had to stay connected with the students in their cultures. That was not going to be easy, maybe impossible, because we were all "outsiders." I knew of no theological textbook that dealt authentically with the worldview that our students lived in. We would have to improvise as we went.

Cultural awareness was not terribly important in some courses we taught, like Church History, Anabaptist History, Bookkeeping, English, Current Affairs, and World History. But when it came to practical theology, we simply had to move in our students' world. That was our challenge.

We decided that I would structure an outline of biblical themes and then teach three times a week for an hour, for at least a year, with Dorothy and John present. Other teachers could join in as they wished. I knew that I had to teach the normal theology subjects—God, Jesus Christ, the Holy Spirit, the doctrine of man, the authority of the Scriptures, and so on. The question was, how? How should we approach these biblical themes?

I decided to throw caution to the wind and use the first few months to examine African traditional religion and philosophy. That was a huge risk because I was from Johnstown, Pennsylvania, Germanic in background, and shaped by Western liberal education. Was it not presumptuous of me to try to teach those men something that they did not already know about their own view of the world?

They obviously felt the same way. It was tough going at first. To begin with, they never even thought that it was possible to examine African philosophy in depth. (I doubt that they ever heard those two words together—African and philosophy.) Second, was this not a course in Biblical Theology? Why mess around with traditions they thought they should leave behind? To make it even more ridiculous, how audacious could this teacher be to think that he knew enough to talk to them on that subject?

It was not long, however, before they joined me in the search for the essentials of traditional religion. At this point we were not comparing the traditional way of looking at life with any other way. I kept insisting that our goal was not to judge, but to understand. There would come ample time to judge as we opened the Scriptures and let that light shine on the beliefs that form an African theology.

I might add that I began each session by handing out several paragraphs on the subject for the day, which I had written in English. Sometimes it took a little time to make sure that the students got the full impact of the English text. When we started the college, we had told ourselves that part of our job was to orient the students in English as much as possible.

It soon became quite obvious, however, that English could not serve us well as we moved into deeper, more complex, and emotional levels. I think we all knew when the moment came, and it did, almost inevitably, to abandon English and get on with Swahili. Then things came to life, and we were on our way to some new territory. I tried, at the end of each session, to return to English, but never very successfully.

At some point, unknown to me, we had passed through some kind of pedagogical sound barrier. Now we could talk about these basic things without guilt, illusions, denials, or fears. The class periods became times of freeing, open discussions.

A STUDENT'S EVALUATION

When Bishop Zedekiah Kisare prepared his autobiography, *Kisare wa Kiseru*, this is how he viewed what was going on at the college during those early years:

> Two things happened to me during those three years.
>
> First, I studied English seriously for the first time in my life. Soon I was reading the language fairly well, especially the English Scriptures....
>
> The second thing that happened during those three years was that I discovered my traditional theological roots. Up to this time the missionary approach to our African heritage was to say that it was all savagedom. There was no effort to connect the gospel message to our traditional faith.

It wasn't only the Mennonite missionaries who swept all of that aside. Very few missionaries of any other denomination looked seriously at Africa's traditional faith. This was part of the colonial mind-set about Africa.

Trustingly, we accepted the missionaries' assessment of our traditional beliefs, and we actually thought that as Christians we had to cleanse ourselves of all traditional influences. Don Jacobs changed all this for us, his 16 students. He taught the theology courses.

The first year he taught us African Traditional Theology. At first we were amazed that he knew about these things. This was a subject that had never been discussed with the missionaries except in terms of rejecting it. Now Jacobs taught it as though he himself were an African traditionalist. We found that Jacobs understood us. He helped us to understand ourselves.

We saw that our traditional worldview was there in our subconscious, influencing us in ways we had never seen before. For the first time I became aware of the reality of spiritual power. I saw how satanic power works secretly and in darkness to bring chaos and disruption in a society. I came to understand the traditional answers to the problem of evil. I came to see the traditional role of the family in salvation and life after death.

Often, as Don walked out the door at the close of his teaching period, the whole class would erupt in excited talk as we shared with each other the new discoveries we were making. — *Kisare wa Kiseru*, pages 103–104

Now, we were ready to open our Bibles. We followed the same routine—a set of English notes, a discussion of the English, then a leap off into the subject matter at hand. By this time we had the African worldview much in mind.

We tried to let the light of the gospel shine authentically into local cultures. We agreed that as we opened the Bible, we would employ the mind of Christ that we received by the new birth and deal honestly with the material in both the biblical context and the African context.

May I, again, quote Bishop Kisare:

> The second and third years Jacobs taught us Christian theology through the perspective we had gotten the first year. We saw the answers Christian faith brings to life's issues. We saw these answers in the light of the answers traditional faith brings. We began to see where the Christian faith is in conflict with the traditional faith, and we saw the places where Christian faith is the complement or fulfillment of traditional faith.
>
> The first year I had become especially aware of how the traditional faith manipulates spiritual power. Now I saw how the power of Jesus' sacrifice neutralizes Satan's power, setting us free from its debilitating influence. Again, time after time, the class would erupt in excited talk at the close of the teaching period as we processed together what we were learning.
>
> Through these classes I came to put all ethnic religion on one level, whether it be Nilotic, Bantu, Swiss-German, or Jewish. The lot of them are only guides to life in terms of the insights of people's ancestors. All of them tie people up in ethnic regulations which are a barrier to the discovery of freedom in Jesus.
>
> Salvation is not found in ethnic religion, although ethnic religion may point the way to salvation. Salvation is found only through the blood sacrifice Jesus made on the cross. This same saving blood pushes over the ethnic walls

which separate one people from another. Jesus' sacrifice provides the linkage which makes all peoples one new people.
— *Kisare wa Kiseru*, page 104

A Teacher's Evaluation

It seemed that every day we learned a whole new aspect of something. Our little college got the reputation as a place where leaders were being developed who loved Jesus and the church and who were prepared to go out with the gospel of Jesus Christ in their hearts. It was also a place with an entirely new approach to teaching biblical theology—by coming to grips with local cultures, blessing them, and allowing their questions to emerge to be discussed and wrestled with in the light of the Scriptures.

I think all students and staff grew greatly during those three years. I know I did. We stayed together—one group of learners—for the entire three-year period. We all benefited by the maturity of the group. As I look back over my career, I realize that those three years, when I walked step by step with people who wanted to follow Jesus with all of their hearts, were some of the most fruitful in all of my life.

A Multi-Tribal Community

Most of the students lived in the dormitory or in the small bungalows that we built for families. They developed a very close community, across tribal lines. The college was a multi-tribal island in the land of the Wakiroba, the local tribe, with even some white people living there!

The spirit of revival moved with power among the students, breaking down tribal feelings in a most remarkable way as we learned to walk honestly and repentantly

The first class to graduate from the new Mennonite Theological College

with one another. The Spirit of God was definitely at work, shaping these leaders into useful vessels. Little did we know that almost all the leaders who would lead the church for a generation were in that group.

As an aside, as we began each chapel service, we reverently sang, "Holy, Holy, Holy, Lord God Almighty." Years later I found that when the Mennonite congregations in Tanzania move into a time of sharing the Word of God, after all the preliminaries, almost invariably they reverently sang, "Holy, Holy, Holy, Lord God Almighty," in Swahili, of course. They memorialize, even now, I like to think, our deep times with Jesus at the college in the early 1960s.

Church Music

All of the hymns that we sang in Tanzania in those days were translations of hymns written in the West. Most people who were converted in that era enjoyed those songs. They were their songs. God used them in their lives. They did not seem to give any thought to the fact that they were written in cultures far away. Our little book of *Spiritual Songs,* used for years and found in lots of nooks and crannies in East Africa, contained only translated hymns. Because they were effective among the people, they had embraced them as their own, just like many Americans loved hymns first written in German or Old English.

Before long, however, Africans began to write their own music. It entered the Mennonite churches first by church choirs. Worshipers loved those songs. Soon choirs broke out in every congregation, all singing their newly created hymns, which brought new life into the church. People were coming to Christ just by listening to the hymns. And some young people wanted to hasten the day of their baptism so they could sing in the choir!

At that time, I was the pastor of the Bukiroba congregation. I wanted to use all the African music I could get. In the college the students experimented with a wide range of music. When we had our evening concerts, they sang music that I had never heard. I was amazed, one night, when they enacted the Prodigal Son in song and motion, with an impact far greater than a sermon. I began to see the place drama and music were going to have in the church in the future. The college students moved with this evolution of music in the churches with ease. It fit.

WHAT ABOUT THE DEMONIC?

It was during this time that I finally came to the realization that witchcraft, the appearance of ancestral spirits, and so forth, were Satan's playground and that demonic powers were not simply psychic phenomena. They were empowered by Satan. The only answer to breaking this satanic bondage was to be found in the blood of Jesus Christ. His atoning work alone defeats Satan. I walked with students and the church in releasing the power of Christ to crush the work of the devil. I was way over my head, I know, but that was life and death among the people, and I determined to be on the side of life.

It is difficult to imagine a Gospel ministry among them that did not include casting out evil spirits and praying for the sick. The preaching of the gospel and the worship of God remained the center of everything, but one must be prepared to do battle with Satan in ways that may not feel familiar to someone like me. I was a slow learner in that regard. I recall vividly praying for the mother-in-law of one of our students. I was only beginning to see that the power of Satan was truly at work in spirit worship and elsewhere. The woman was being tormented in ways that startled me. I felt the Spirit of God say, "Go ahead, cast out the evil spirit in the name of Christ." What else could I do? So I did. Nothing happened that I could see. She continued to writhe and cry out. Hours later, I was given the good news that the evil spirit left her, and she was helping to prepare meals. I found that it was necessary to have some level of belief before the prayers had any effect. In that incident, I learned more about the power of the blood of Christ than I could have learned in a semester of seminary, maybe more.

Chapter 18

FULFILLING DENOMINATIONAL EXPECTATIONS

WERE WE AUTHENTIC MENNONITES?

I found myself thinking about this question: As a missionary whose faith has been highly influenced by Anabaptism, how successful have I been in transferring that faith understanding to the minds and hearts of those with whom I've lived and to whom I've ministered? I probably did not ask myself this question enough. I am writing this now in a reflective mode after many years, so I am looking back.

Here is the line of thought that we lived by. Our challenge was to do our best to make sure that the theology we were discussing addressed the urgent life questions of the students and of their cultures. The question seldom, if ever, came up, "How did the early Anabaptists reflect their culture's questions?" Our focus was always on the present. We reminded ourselves that God was at work in the cultures in Tanzania, preparing them for the liberating good news in Jesus long before we got there. We thought it best to highlight the power of Jesus Christ to set people free from the powers of darkness that bind aspects of cultures everywhere on the planet. Powers of darkness come in different shapes and forms, depending on the culture. The point is, Jesus crushed the powers of darkness and invites us to allow him to do the same thing in our lives, no matter what our culture.

As a teacher, I did not believe that an in-depth study of northern European society of the 16th century would be worth the time and effort for the group of men that we were privileged to teach. In addition to that, I found that when I thought of Felix Manz, Conrad Grebel, and even Menno Simons, I thought "tribally." They were Germanic, like me. I found that when I think of historical Anabaptism, I stay within my culture. My students did not have

Bishop Donald Lauver, representing Lancaster Conference bishops, and Paul Kraybill, representing the Mission Board, meeting here with Shemaya Magati and Imori Mtoka. The bishops and Mission Board were determined to work together.

that connection. That does not mean that they could not learn of radical discipleship from them, but they would have to think beyond their own culture to do so.

I began to understand this when I asked my students who their own "saints" were. Not biblical saints, but their own saints. They admitted they hadn't given that much thought. I believe that groups eventually recognize heroes who can be emulated. Who might they be in the Mennonite Church of Tanzania? Bishop Kisare? Pastor Ezekiel Muganda? Maybe some who are not Mennonites. I assumed that after the Tanzanians were comfortable with their own "heroes of the faith," they might be prepared to include a few from northern Europe like Conrad Grebel or Menno Simons. This would be interesting to watch.

The students were eager to be Mennonites. I felt that they did not resist seeing themselves as authentic Mennonites, whatever that meant. Instead of rejecting being Mennonites, they wanted to know and constantly asked how Mennonites were different from their church neighbors—the Anglicans, Lutherans, Salvation Army, Catholics, Africa Inland Church, and Seventh Day Adventists. Why be a separate denomination, they kept insisting, if we do not embrace what is unique in our theology and history? When we got onto that topic, we may as well have just dropped everything else and jumped in. The discussion was predictably spirited but without resolution. However, almost every time it came up, one issue stood out—peace and nonviolence. That went deeper than the most quick and common response, "We are in the Mennonite family because that is who we are."

A CENTRAL MENNONITE CONFESSION — NONVIOLENCE

As we were forming the college in the early 1960s, the nation was moving toward independence from colonial rule. I applauded that, of course. The church, then numbering about 1,500 baptized adults, was also negotiating with the Mission Board to be able to govern itself. As part of the process, the church leaders drafted a document of beliefs along with a constitution. They relied heavily on the faith statements of non-African Mennonite churches which included, among other things, promoting peace and living nonviolently. This was included in the documents that supported their request to be officially registered as The Mennonite Church of Tanzania.

This happened just after Tanzania instituted a program requiring all able-bodied young men to serve the country for a period of national training. Fearing that this was paramount to military training, the church sent Zedekiah Kisare and me to Dar es Salaam, the capital, to explain our church's position on bearing arms. We explained our convictions to top government officials. It was not strange to them, and they assured us that no Mennonite would be sent into combat if doing so violated his or her conscience. They assured us that in the National Service, marching drills were usually done with dummy guns. With the assurance that our position was heard, we returned and reported to the church. That seemed to settle the matter.

THE CHURCH ON ITS OWN

The Mennonite Church in Tanzania today numbers about 75,000 baptized believers. The "missionary influence" ceased about 30 years ago, even though ties remained with EMM and the Lancaster Mennonite Conference. This autonomy has enabled the church to push its roots deeply into its local cultures, while at the same time taking its place in the global Mennonite Church. How much the Tanzania Mennonites will value their place in the global Mennonite world remains to be seen. One thing is sure. They are certainly well established among the churches in Tanzania.

A New Mennonite Thing—Planting Churches in Other Cultures

Our denomination, born in 1525, took root in Europe among German and Dutch cultures and in no other. When persecution and hard times combined to make living in their homelands more and more intolerable, many migrated to places like North America and Russia where their neighbors were not Germanic. In order to survive and prosper, they formed relatively secure Germanic islands in threatening seas of national cultures. That served as the norm for most Mennonites who lived outside northern Europe for the next two centuries. They carried their cultures with them wherever they went. That aided them in their survival but became a hindrance in evangelism, because all who wished

Typical deputation. Paul Kraybill and Orie Miller represent Mission Board; Amos Horst on right represents Lancaster Conference

to join them had to put on their Germanic culture. Therefore, they did not plant churches in their neighboring cultures.

After about 13 generations, during the 1890s, a few
mission-minded Mennonites decided to do what the
church had not done for almost four centuries—try to
plant Mennonite churches in non-Germanic cultures.

So, how are we doing? As I write this, Mennonites who
live in Germanic subcultures are but a small fraction of the
total denomination. Now the question emerges, "Do all of
these churches of many tribes and nations see themselves
as members of one global family? Should they?"

The verdict is still out on whether that vision is coming to fruition. Is it possible that these new churches will
see themselves as Mennonites? Will the older, established
churches recognize them as Mennonites? Will the newer
churches embrace the older churches as authentic brothers and sisters in Jesus Christ, bound together by a spirit
of love rather than by institutions or a common culture?
Time will tell.

*Mennonites gather from across Africa to establish the
African Mennonite and Brethren in Christ Fellowship.*

Birth of an African Anabaptist Fellowship

As for African Mennonites, first they reached out to one another across Africa. Many former colonies emerged as independent nations at a rapid rate in the 1950s and '60s. A feeling of pan-Africanism grew as the colonial powers withdrew. That feeling was experienced by the Mennonite and Brethren in Christ churches as well. The time had come to reach out to sister Mennonite churches in other African nations as part of their family. Until then, the primary relationships were between the churches established by missions and their mission boards. So the Council of Mennonite Ministries in North America agreed to finance initially the Africa Mennonite and Brethren in Christ Fellowship. Elmer Neufeld from Africa Inland Mennonite Mission, who was in Congo, took the lead in this. I had the privilege of working with him to make it happen.

We held our first meeting in 1962 in Limuru, Kenya. That marked a huge step forward. Now for the first time, leaders of African churches got to know one another.

Across Africa, consultations bring the churches together for fellowship.

As I recall, the Fellowship included churches in Nigeria, Ghana, Zimbabwe, Zambia, Congo, Tanzania, Ethiopia, and Somalia. I had the joy of being in the mix as the African Anabaptist churches discovered one another.

At that time, Africa counted roughly 60,000 baptized Mennonites. Roughly one-tenth of them were in Tanzania. I might add that the statistics at present are astounding. Today one of every four Mennonites in the entire world is African, just about 450,000.

THE TEACHERS ABROAD PROGRAM

Soon another responsibility landed on my desk. The Mennonite Central Committee (MCC), sensing a need to expand their service to Africa, was exploring the possibility of placing teachers there. A team headed by Robert

The first group of TAP teachers to East Africa

Kreider visited Africa and returned home with a dream of setting up a Teachers Abroad Program (TAP), a cooperative effort of the Mennonite colleges and MCC. I appealed to my friend and first-rate administrator, Hershey Leaman, to manage this new program.

Soon Hershey and I found ourselves looking for places in Kenya and Tanzania to place North American teachers. We worked with sister missions in the Christian Council of Tanzania and the Christian Council of Kenya. In addition to placing these teachers, we were responsible for their orientation and for directing their annual retreats. At any one time, we had 20 to 30 teachers, each on three-year contracts, which meant that we had a new batch arriving each year. It kept me stepping to keep up with this, along with my other assignments. Hershey Leaman carried the heaviest end of the administrative load.

The TAP program grew rapidly.

Chapter 19

PERSONAL
AND FAMILY
DEVELOPMENTS

PAUL'S ARRIVAL

February 1, 1963, was a red letter day. Anna Ruth had gone to the Shirati Hospital a few days before the due date for our baby. She wrote this about her experiences:

> Mid January, Alan and I went to Shirati to await Paul's birth...After two weeks without any change in my situation, Dr. Dorcas Stoltzfus decided that the baby was big enough to be born, and so she gave me medication to induce labor. I waited in a room at the hospital and still nothing seemed to be happening. I thought that I could walk over to the Leaman house for lunch.
>
> Everything was fine until we were eating dessert, when I realized I needed to get to the hospital. I set out walking, and as I passed the nurses' residence, one of the nurses came out and then alerted Dr. Dorcas. As I walked, I experienced contractions so that I needed to stop and bend over

several times. Hershey could see me from the dining room window, and he went to the car to give me a ride. But the car wouldn't start, so he jumped on his motorcycle and came by and picked me up. So I went the last several hundred yards on the back of the cycle. We thought we should name our son "pikipiki," which is the Swahili name for motorcycle. Dr. Dorcas and a nurse met me at the hospital, and within several minutes Paul made his entrance into the world.

Don and David were at home at Bukiroba. That evening on the inter-station radio contact, Alan, who was almost three, went with Hershey to announce the news to his dad and brother, as well as his sister Jane, who was in school at Mara Hills. During the conversation with Don, Hershey told Alan, "Say to your daddy, 'The baby looks like me.'" So Alan obediently said, "The baby looks like Uncle Hershey."

FAMILY LIFE AT BUKIROBA

When we returned to Bukiroba in 1961, Jane had turned six years old. The mission had gone to great trouble and expense to establish a primary school for missionary children on the great Rift Valley escarpment just south of the Kenya border. It was in a lovely setting, well watered and high in altitude. They called it Mara Hills because it overlooked the famed Mara River valley that teemed with wildlife. It was just assumed that all of us missionaries would take advantage of what they provided, so we made plans to send off our little six-year-old Jane. The school was only 70 miles or so from Bukiroba, but there was no way she could come home for weekends. We could plan, however, to have her home for Christmas and Easter breaks, and then for the summer. It was always a sad day when the Missionary Aviation Fellowship (MAF) flight picked up Jane and headed for Mara Hills. Likewise, it was a day of rejoicing when she returned.

Two years later, David went off as well. We found reasons to drop in at the school now and again, just to stay in touch. The missionary house-parents there became like second parents for the children. And the two teachers did their best to provide a basic education. Jane and David had many good memories of their time at Mara Hills, but they also had times of intense loneliness. Boarding school was bittersweet at best. Many good things happened there, but the loneliness they experienced must have been almost intolerable.

As we look back on our family life, we wish we had considered home-schooling our children until they were older. But the thought never entered our heads at the time. We do not fault the Mission Board. They went to great lengths to make a welcoming and homey atmosphere at the school, but that did not alleviate the feelings that six-year-olds have of being bereft of family just when they need them most. The mission seemed to have assumed that both husband and wife needed to be free to do the task that they were sent to do—strengthen the newly planted churches—so there would be little time left over for home-schooling.

MAXIMIZING TIME AT HOME

Anna Ruth and I determined to guard jealously those weeks when our children were home over the summer and Christmas holiday-time. We tried to give ourselves completely to the children. We could not make up for the many months that they had to spend away, but we did our best to make the most of the days that they were at home. We spent many happy hours exploring the great granite outcroppings in our neighborhood which gave the landscape its distinctive look. One impressive massif we called the ship rock. Our picnics up there, surrounded by

Time for some fun on the motorcycle. Hold on!

rock conies, were always tinged with apprehension as the children got closer and closer to the edge to look down, a precipitous drop of more than a hundred feet.

Our house backed up against a hill that was essentially a granite outcropping covered with lush "bush." On top of the hill lay the concave rock that once served as a grinding stone on which the last great local chief's grain was pounded for his ugali. The hill took his name, Nyabangi. There were remnants of rock embattlements there as well. During tribal wars, cattle and women found sanctuary in that fortified hill. It was a hill with a rich past.

Often in the evening, we scrambled up that steep hill to enjoy the freshness of the air and the marvelous scene before us, stretching all the way to the mighty Lake Victoria about a mile to the west. Way off in the distance, white sails of boats cut through the evening winds, carrying fishermen eager to lay their nets for a night's catch. In the distance, dogs barked, roosters crowed, people called to one another, and then, as the red sun set on the golden lake, we felt the cool of the night. Now and again we took flashlights with us so that we could enjoy the miraculous appearance of a heaven full of stars, clear as crystal. As the Little Dipper appeared, we traced a line through it to the

Southern Cross, low on the horizon. Nature does wonders for people like me, who need to relate to something "out there" that does not change. That settled my spirit as I was undergoing changes.

As we went up and down the hill, we had to be careful because snakes lived there. Now and again, especially during the dry season when food on the hill was scarce, we found them among our houses. We feared two bad ones, the mamba with its deadly poison that killed in a half hour and the spitting cobra that spewed out stuff that could blind.

Some evenings, all six of us piled onto our shiny black motorcycle and sped the mile or so to the shores of the lake where we had a picnic. Frogs croaked their welcome, the fish eagles, high in the great fig tree, stretched their necks and screamed as only fish eagles can. A variety of doves cooed in the distance, singing their twilight songs. A red-breasted gonolek started a tune, in the distance another joined, and together they treated us to a vesper hymn of joy. And then we hear the "bumpf" of a hippo out in the water, eager for the sun to go down so that it could emerge from the water and forage. Off in the distance, in a shoreline village, the drumming had begun. We loved Africa.

We enjoyed picnicking. As often as we could on Thursday evenings we drove to Musoma and climbed to the top of the hill that dominated the town. We tried to be there to spot in the distance the lumbering DC-3 that brought our weekly airmail, and then watch it land in a cloud of dust. It took about three weeks for a letter to reach us from the States, even via airmail.

That airfield held many memories for us, both pleasant and sad. I suppose the saddest ones were when the MAF Cessna landed to pick up Jane and David to take them off

Our family while at Bukiroba

to Mara Hills for school again. It was hard to hold back the tears. We would not see them for several months. It was hard to walk away from the airstrip then, having waved to the little plane as it lifted just high enough to clear the tall sisal poles and the distant jumble of giant granite boulders. We listened as long as we could to the receding engine sound, ever lighter, then, silence. It is hard to describe the throb of that pain.

The scene was reversed, however, when Jane and David arrived home for the holidays or for the summer. Utter delight. Those were very busy days for me because I carried heavy bishop responsibilities, was the principal of the college, and had a heap of other involvements. But I determined to clear my schedule, as much as possible, to be free to give my best to the family. That usually worked. When the children were all home, our family came first. Fortunately, my friends and co-workers understood this and gave us space.

GRAPPLING WITH DEMANDS
OF FELLOWSHIP

Our most meaningful fellowship experiences were at Bukiroba among our friends, both African and American. I received both blessings and jolts in those fellowship gatherings. I recall the day when my newly-purchased motorcycle became the focus of some pointed questions. No one on our hill at that time had a motorcycle, but I had decided to buy one. I rode it home, parked it behind our house, and there it was. My bike. But not for long.

After a spirited and meaningful time of fellowship, the group pressed me on my purchase. "Whose motorcycle is that?" "Mine." "Where did you get it?" "I bought it from the garage in Musoma." "How much did you pay for it?" "250 dollars." "Could you afford it or did you have to go into debt for it?" "No, I paid it all." "Do you have enough money to operate it?" "I think so." "Why did you buy it?" "Often I wish to run the seven miles to town to take or bring mail and that sort of thing, and it is cheaper than a car to run." "Is Anna Ruth happy that you bought it?" The questions went on and on. When they had exhausted all their questions, the leader said, "Now, let us pray. Thank you, Jesus, for giving us a motorcycle." In one prayer I lost control of my motorcycle! They, in effect, owned it. If, after that, I saw one of them on the road walking and I had the rear seat open, I knew that I was duty-bound to stop and say, "Get on your motorcycle with me."

I was slowly learning the freedom of walking in the light. For example, it bothered me that we missionaries had kerosene-operated refrigerators while the local people did not. In a fellowship meeting, I expressed my desire to do whatever the Spirit directed with regard to our refrigerator. I did not want anything to cloud our fellowship in Christ. Their response surprised me. "When we are thirsty we know that we càn get a cold drink from your refrigerator. If you should choose not to share the refreshing water, then get rid of your refrigerator!"

As I reflect on those days, I am surprised that we even dared share openly about our personal finances, which until then, had been a closed subject. Africans talked about financial challenges in life, not us missionaries. We missionaries had more money than the Africans in the fellowship, a fact that we kept out of the light. When the Spirit of God helped us to share in the area of finance, a new day dawned, opening the door to our secret room. Soon we were able to ask one another's advice on what portion to tithe and whom to help. It was as though our money was becoming a common purse.

HOLIDAYS ON THE INDIAN OCEAN

Each month the Mission Board sent us a check. At the beginning of the year we sent in the current cost of our supplies, and the Mission Board then decided how much money we would need. They got it about right. What came was just about what it cost to live. This was mission socialism at its best. The M. D. and the mechanic received exactly the same monthly allowance, adjusted only for the number of children each of us had.

Somewhere along the line, the Mission Board decided to supply us with an additional month's payment each year so that we could take an annual three-week holiday. Our favorite holiday spot was Mombasa where the Africa Inland Mission had a cluster of thatched cottages that missionaries used at a small cost. Those annual holidays punctuated our years. The warm Indian Ocean became our favorite spot for rest and relaxation. There is nothing like an hour of snorkeling among the coral reefs to transport one into another reality. We never tired of swimming among the flashing, dashing fish, as varied as the colors of a rainbow, with a ray or small shark thrown in for good measure. We could never get our fill of the sea. And where else does one find local fishermen coming by peddling huge lobsters? Oh, the delight of boiled red lobster on the beach as the sky darkened to highlight the glow of our fire. Those days of wonder and family bonding on the warm Indian Ocean can only be described as exhilarating and wonderfully satisfying. They had an eternal quality, we thought. People who are working cross-culturally need such times to clear their heads and get ready for the next challenges and delights.

The moon rises over the Indian Ocean.

DEATH OF A CO-WORKER

It was on one of these beach vacations, in 1969, that we got the news that the MAF plane had crashed on the Ngong Hills outside of Nairobi, killing our dear friend and co-worker, Alta Shenk, Clyde's wife. We were shocked. We packed quickly and drove to Shirati for the funeral. It was a sad day as the entire Shirati community, and many from a distance, stood by Clyde and his family as they said their farewells to one of the most wonderful women we had ever known. Anna Ruth and I knew Clyde and Alta very well. They were our first mentors when we were new, green missionaries, stationed at Bumangi. We were heartbroken by the tragedy. Yet that funeral service was marked with hope and with thanksgiving to the Lord for sharing Alta with us for all those years. She was a solid sister, beloved and cherished by Africans and people like us who knew her as a co-worker and as a woman who knew what it meant to walk with Jesus.

I recall the tragic day when we learned that the two children of David and Erma Clemmen's inadvertently ate sugar-coated malaria pills and died within a couple of hours. That was one of the most difficult burials I ever officiated at in my entire life. I was shaken as we lowered the two wooden boxes into small graves, dug in that sacred spot at Shirati in which we buried those of our missionary family who died.

Chapter 20

ADDITIONAL RESPONSIBILITIES AS BISHOP

1964 – 1966

PLANS DISRUPTED

The year of 1964 was tumultuous for me. In addition to administering the college, I was directing the Teachers Abroad Program for Mennonite Central Committee. On top of all this, our Mission Board decided to open a satellite office in Nairobi, headed by me. They had big plans in mind. That was Paul Kraybill, again, always pushing and overrating me! The Tanzanian Church did not want to hear that at all. But little regard was given to the feelings of the local church at that point. It was a Mission Board matter. We were set to move to Nairobi as soon as it could be arranged. I wanted to protest—"Not so fast." Little did we know what the following weeks would hold for us.

That was the year when Bishop Elam and Grace Stauffer announced that they had reached retirement age and were going to return to the States. This was not a surprise. Simeon Hurst who had served as bishop in the northern area of the church had already left Tanzania. I had great admiration for Simeon. He and his wife, Edna, both walked with the revival fellowship and had a clear, marvelous testimony. Simeon's smile stole the day, and his meticulous grooming put no one off.

The Stauffer family prior to their leaving Tanzania for retirement

In any case, the church leaders did their best to select a Tanzanian bishop. A big sticking point proved to be the matter of ethnicity in the church. Each of the 12 or so ethnic groups in the church was hoping that the bishop would be from its particular tribe. They failed to find the person who would just fit.

The Church Makes a Quick Decision

Under some pressure to do something about the impasse quickly, the ordained persons—pastors and deacons—met to choose the bishop to succeed Stauffer. Their discussions were lengthy and urgent. They knew that the church was not yet of one voice about the choice of its first Tanzanian bishop. After lengthy deliberations, the church decided unanimously to nominate an interim bishop. That was the first decision. The second was just as unanimous. "It will be Don Jacobs." The haste with which

Elam Stauffer officiates at my installation as bishop.

this happened was quite un-African. What could I say? I could not in all good conscience say, "No," because I knew the straits they were in.

This threw me into a dither. I thought that being a bishop was a diversion from my major calling of developing leaders. Furthermore, I knew enough about African culture to know that white hair is honored and wisdom is golden. I was 35 years old, comparatively young in that culture, and I knew that my reservoir of wisdom leaked badly.

Before I could digest what was happening, I was, in a flash, made bishop a day or so later on February 15, 1964.

That week Anna Ruth wrote to her parents:

> This is really an amazing thing in this day for an independent African church to choose a white man for such a position when "Africanization" has been the key word which they lived by for the past few years. It does show that the Spirit of the Lord is here, because I am sure this could not have happened otherwise. Also, Don is younger than any of the African ordained men. This also is contrary to their culture, to put a young man in the authority over his elders. All in all, it is quite a challenging commission, and we feel the need of the grace of the Lord in it. We know you will include this in your prayers for us.
>
> On Saturday morning there was a little service here in the church, sort of an installation service. It was not large, it was called just the day before, but it was quite impressive.

I might add that Anna Ruth, who has a lively sense of humor, consoled me with a line I will not forget. "You always wanted to be either an actor or a politician. Now, Don, you can be both!"

Working with Church Leaders

Because I had been serving on the major committees of the church, I was well aware of the challenges. I set to work to develop a five-year plan in consultation with the church leaders. There were about a dozen ordained persons at the time. The church urged me to lead out. Our long-term plan was to triple our membership and our income in 10 years. There were plenty of checks and balances to stop me and my little committee if we went down the wrong track.

We set out to follow the first part of the agreed-upon five-year plan. I had no idea how long I would be in office. That did not bother me in the least. I was going to give leadership to the church, in close fellowship with the church leaders that God had chosen to be around me. While doing all that, I was still the principal of the college. It is a wonder that I did not go berserk. I was quite excited by the opportunity to shape the newly independent church for a big advance into the future.

In Tanzania, being a bishop carries weight, like being a tribal chief, I guess. I hadn't felt that until I was ordained bishop. No matter what, the people elevated me to a height that made me distinctly uncomfortable. This was not the real me. I fought against it. I am just me! Believe me. Try as I might, the image of being a bishop that they had in their minds was much stronger than my adamant refusal to be so identified. The way they thought about bishops somehow contradicted my belief that leaders should be servants. I still believe that.

But I soon discovered that I needed to just bow my head, try to fit into what the people thought, and get on with it. I realized that it was going to be impossible to change their concept of "bishop" at once, and it was futile for me to fuss and fume. I just had to accept what I could not change and push on to do the job they expected me to do. I decided to put off thinking about who I was until some time in the future. For now I was their bishop, a title that I had to live with.

While I was dealing with this bishop issue, I got news that my father had died. It was not completely unexpected, but it still shook me. One of the joys of my life was being the son of Paul Jacobs. Now he was gone.

DEATH OF MY FATHER, PAUL JACOBS

For some reason, the telegram informing me that my father died on July 27, 1964, did not arrive until after he was buried. Because of that delay I could not even consider going home. I received the news, digested it, praised God for the joy of knowing that Dad was now on to glory, and prayed that Mom would have the wisdom and strength to deal with the mountain of decisions that had to be made. My grieving would have to wait.

Eventually I gave myself time to digest how my father influenced me. During our most recent extended home leave, I spent time with Dad. He was suffering with the ravages of arthritis, I guess. It was especially painful across his shoulders where I massaged him. He seemed so small, and his bones were just under the skin. I could feel each one as I rubbed him. I pressed love into that shrinking body. All the while he was getting cortisone shots. He had little zest for life which was so unlike him. When I gave him my good-bye, I knew the next time I would see him would be in glory.

Dad was a deeply pious person. He loved Jesus, that was for sure. And he held the Mennonite community in high regard. He did his best to belong. He bent over backwards to show that he was one of them. I suppose Dad became as integrated into the Mennonite community as a Jacobs could. I often felt a bit like Dad, not sure who my real community was.

I knew that Dad was pleased about what I was doing, and that I had his favor and support. He was not a letter-writer; Mom was. Now and again she passed on to me something that Dad said. I did not expect more from him. I knew that he cared for me. With those sentiments, I embraced the reality of his passing and got on with the pressing work ahead of me as a servant of Jesus in Tanzania. After all, I was now the bishop and the principal of the Theological College. The people expected more of me than I could possibly deliver. Thank you, Dad. I love you dearly.

Trips to Germany for Funding

As bishop, I helped the church to think about how we were going to fund things. The Mission Board was stretched just paying the immediate, mission-operating expenses, so I began to look elsewhere for funds to expand our medical and educational services. I learned that in Germany a portion of tax money was set aside for overseas charity. They established a committee to administer these funds.

In order to obtain these funds, we needed to have the Mennonite Church in Germany endorse our requests. At that time I did not know anyone in the German Mennonite Church, but I did know that Mennonite Central Committee had an office in Germany, under the direction of a person who was to play quite a significant role in my life, Peter Dyck. Peter offered to help. He was a Mennonite phenomenon.

As we sat in his house in Germany, he introduced me to a whole chapter of Mennonite life that I knew dreadfully little about. He was born and raised in the Ukraine, in a German colony that was first established during the reign of Catherine the Great of Russia. He spoke of the Mennonite colonies there, their religious life, the revivals, and how the colonies came under pressure as Russia tried to assimilate them into Russian life. Many fled. Peter, as a young MCC representative, had assisted hundreds of them to settle in Canada and Latin America. Here I was, learning from one of the key players in the Russian Mennonite scene. And he had time for me and my projects. I was also pleased that we had a similar faith, based on God's saving grace and with the mandate to make Christ known to all nations.

Peter, on my behalf, asked the leaders of the Mennonite Church in Germany to authorize our projects so that the government committee could consider them. I think our first proposal was for funding to upgrade our leprosy facilities, a large project, indeed. That request was approved, followed by others. Germany provided tens of thousands of dollars while I was involved in Tanzania, all done with the blessing of the German Mennonite churches and our own Mission Board.

Another benefit of going to Germany for funding was that it put me in touch with some of the Mennonite church leaders there. I think particularly of Franz and Erma Esau, who opened their hearts to me and made me feel right at home among the German Mennonites.

LEARNING PITFALLS OF LEADERSHIP

As a bishop, my style of leadership was in need of some major adjustments if I was going to learn the skill of bringing leaders to a consensus on any issue. I was used to the parliamentary method that heard all arguments before the question was voted on. In my mind, the vote was the important thing, not the arguments. I discovered that my Tanzanian colleagues did not think like that. They elevated the discussion of an issue to an art form. In their discussions, I found that often they were way off somewhere, not speaking to the issue at all, and enjoying it immensely—a proverb, a little pithy story, a humorous event. They lost me. Then, to complicate matters even further, we seldom voted on anything, unless it was something trivial. I wanted to cut through the fog and vote! Get it into the Minutes.

I slowly learned that when it came to anything important, we simply had to run the course with great patience, allowing the normal verbal circumlocutions to go on and on. Only then could we possibly come to an agreement that all could own completely. I discovered that if this process was short-circuited, we paid for it later with harmful disunity.

I recall that one time I thought we were getting nowhere as the verbiage expanded, so I asked, "What is the consensus?" Their answer surprised me, "Weren't you listening to us?" They had been artfully couching their answers in idioms and stories. They expected me to be smart enough to catch on. "Oh, my," I thought, "will I never learn?"

On another occasion I got frustrated because I wanted a straight answer and made that known, with vigor. I got my way, but afterward one of the pastors took me aside and gently reprimanded me, "Today, Bishop, you were a male goat with sharp horns." That was not a compliment.

I also discovered that I had to bend a little in my own self-understanding so that I could hear what was going on and could feel the hurts and the hopes. At times I simply closed my ears to what I did not want to hear. That worked when I was just a member of a group, but not as chairperson. In order to be one bit effective, I had to deliberately wipe clean my slate with its prejudices and my likes and dislikes and try to really hear what each had to say. And I had to pay heed to what was not being spoken as much as what was being spoken.

This was different than preaching or teaching. I could do either of those without listening. I found that listening was key to leading the group to consensus. When leading a meeting, I had to remind myself to listen, not only with my ears but with my heart.

Enjoying the Absurd

I was fortunate to be able to walk hand-in-hand with a soul mate of mine, Zedekiah Kisare, then a pastor and fellow teacher in the Bible School. As our houses were close together, we sauntered into one another's place now and again. On a Saturday afternoon, he found me mowing my grass. Sitting comfortably on my stone wall, he asked, with a twinkle in his eye as he prepared to tease

me, "What are you doing?" Here is the story. We built our
fine new house on campus on a severe slope. It is custom-
ary in that community to clear and keep swept an area of
about 20 feet around the house. This was considered to
be part of the living space. Were we to follow that custom,
the rains would quickly cut huge erosion channels, so I
decided to plant grass, a novel but expensive concept for
that time and place. I had a wall built to retain the soil in
front of the house.

At the highest point the wall was three or more feet
high. I then had the area filled with soil, at no little expense.
Grass seed was not available locally, but I learned that
Kikuyu grass was available in Nairobi. I got some. The
day came to plant it. It was like planting rice, a stalk here,
and another there, in rows. Then I hooked up the sprinkler
and watered the newly planted grass. By that time the
mission had installed a water system which brought water
from the lake to a tank on the Nyabangi Hill. Sure enough,
the grass grew. That Kikuyu grass was tough, not the kind
that yielded to the normal tin "grass slashers" that we
used. The only answer was to buy a mower.

Let me get back to that Saturday afternoon when I
was out there mowing my precious grass, when Zedekiah
Kisare came along and sat on the wall. I understood that
he expected me to stop and chat with him. So I did. We
passed the time of day, and then he asked me, chuckling,
"What are you doing?" I was absolutely stumped. He had
seen me go to great expense to prepare a plot for planting, and then, when my plants began to grow, I cut them
off before they could bear anything at all. Good question,
"What are you doing?"

I thought for a moment and then decided to be honest.
"Brother, this is an American tribal ritual. Every Saturday

afternoon we men get out our little machines and push them back and forth as we wave to other men who are doing the same. Then we put our little machines away, sit on our porches, and we feel good." We both had a good laugh at that. It was something of a tonic, just to call a spade a spade. What I was doing, mowing grass, was obviously absurd.

A few weeks later, when I saw his children dancing naked in the first refreshing rain, I asked him, "What are they doing?" "It is a tribal ritual," he replied with a knowing wink.

MEETING REVIVAL LEADERS

During this time I also got to know better the leaders of the revival movement, especially the Anglican ones, including Dr. Joe Church and William Nagenda of Uganda, Bishop Yohanna Omari of Tanzania, and Festo Kivengere, a Ugandan then living in Tanzania. We ministered together often

Festo Kivengere, my mentor and friend

at revival conventions. One of my favorites was Bishop Omari, the first Tanzanian Anglican Bishop. He told me that when he attended his first international Bishops' Conference in Lambeth, England, the archbishop took him aside, wanting to know more of the East Africa Revival that was causing some buzz in the UK at the time. He asked Omari, "Tell me how this revival got started." Omari, flashing a smile for me, said he was very polite and answered, "You will recall that Jesus died on the cross. I think it was about two thousand years ago. That is when it started." I am sure the archbishop had a good laugh at that. And I am sure it blessed our dear Bishop Omari as well. Incidentally, he was right!

Choosing the First Tanzanian Bishop, 1966

In February 1966, after I had served two years as bishop, the time had come to once again try to choose a Tanzanian bishop. Tribal feelings ran high those days, even in the church. The Tanzania Mennonite Church contained many tribes and languages, clustered into two groups: those whose ancestors migrated into the area from the south, the Bantu, and those who migrated from the north, from the lands of the Nile, the Nilots. Both pressed hard for their choice. I suppose it would have been easier to select two bishops, one a Bantu and the other a Nilot, but the consensus was to choose only one. It came down to a choice between Ezekiel Muganda, a Bantu, and Zedekiah Marwa Kisare, whose father was a Nilot but whose mother was Bantu.

Fortunately, Muganda and Kisare consistently rose above tribal loyalty even though they were surrounded by people, even some Christians, who employed tribal

Zedekiah Kisare and Ezekiel Muganda, equally qualified to be bishop

identity for gain. Those men knew the renewing power of the Holy Spirit. I was privileged to walk with them, in fellowship with others, as they found true freedom in Christ, which diminished the power of tribalism in their relationship. Time after time when issues came up in our councils that had a tendency to divide along tribal lines, Muganda and Kisare were absolutely clear in their renunciation of self-serving tribalism. I knew some of the pressure they were under from their fellow tribesmen and admired them immensely.

Their close fellowship in the gospel was to be tested when the ordained persons in the Tanzania Mennonite Church convened to select their first Tanzanian bishop. Both men were qualified to be bishop, and both were duly nominated. The next step was to boil it down to one. As they deliberated and prayed, it slowly became evident that God's choice was Zedekiah Kisare. Unity of the Spirit had overcome the power of tribalism. It was one of those special "hallelujah moments."

Zedekiah Kisare, chosen to lead

Those who participated in the momentous selection process were satisfied that God had led. However, the Bantu tribal elders, some Mennonites, others not, found the decision to select a Nilot a bitter pill to swallow. Some of them were even prepared to break and form a new church for the Bantu people. Muganda listened. But he would not budge and yield to the pressure. Now we come to the issue of the refrigerator!

BROTHERLY LOVE TRIUMPHS
OVER TRIBAL LOYALTY

Two years prior to that, when Bishop Elam and Grace Stauffer retired from the field, they had a mission-owned refrigerator, a rather scarce item at the time, that the mission did not need just then. It found a home in the Muganda house. They were neighbors on the same compound. I do not know what the agreement was, but it became common knowledge among Muganda's tribesmen that the refrigerator was the bishop's refrigerator. They contended that Bishop Stauffer moved the refrigerator to the Muganda home before he left Tanzania, indicating that he would be the next bishop.

In light of all that, Muganda's tribal friends said, "Keep the refrigerator; it is the refrigerator of a bishop, passed from Stauffer to you." This put Muganda on the spot. He and Zedekiah Kisare were extremely close friends and, above all, brothers in Christ in the revival fellowship. They loved one another deeply. I was beginning to grasp the power of tribalism, so I knew he must have agonized about the decision that he had to make. Finally, he said, "The refrigerator goes to the house of Bishop Kisare at Bukiroba!" I think I am safe in saying that the following 20 or more years of unity in the church resulted from Muganda's selfless, praiseworthy determination not to split the church for his own advantage. He stood valiantly against the demands of tribal loyalty.

As for myself, my hope that tribalism would not gum up the works was realized. I knew in my heart that the outcome was the direct work of the Holy Spirit. That gave me all the assurance that I may have needed to close that chapter, my tenure as bishop of the Tanzania Mennonite Church, and move on.

REFLECTIONS ON AN AMAZING FIVE-YEAR JOURNEY

For almost two years, I had been bishop of the church and principal of the Theological College, while looking after many, many people and projects. In hindsight, it was good for me to spring out of there, lest I be given more to do or simply implode. I was young and committed and had good people around me who were well able to run with their assignments. Orie O. Miller once confided to me, "You can always do more if you can hire good secretaries!" Poor Naomi Smoker, my dedicated and supremely able personal secretary, took the brunt of the load, often working late into the night. Bless her memory!

Now the time had come to bid good-bye to Tanzania. Years before, when I first lived in Tanzania, I had no true African friends. They were "Tanzanians." My stance was, "Stand outside the culture, look in with interest, but do not step inside." But that all changed when Eliezer Mugimba opened his heart and led me to intimate fellowship with Christ and, little did I expect, to an intimate fellowship with him, a Ugandan. That one genuine friendship was the sharp edge of a wedge that broke my prejudices and presumptions. Following that, I got more local friends, and more. A notable example was Zedekiah Kisare. We became friends in Christ first, and then that friendship grew into an all-of-life friendship.

I was understandably humbled by what he wrote years later about our friendship:

> With the arrival of Don Jacobs, our situation began to improve. He knew his own aspirations in life, and he was not upset to see us wishing to wear leather shoes and have cement floors in our houses. He was well educated and it

didn't offend him that we loved learning, too. He did everything he could to help us to rise above our low economic and intellectual state. His greatest gift to us was that he saw us as brothers and sisters on equal standing with him. He saw us as fellow human beings on the same level.

Don Jacobs wasn't just an intelligent person. Solving people's problems only with intelligence gets us nowhere. For change to happen, change that is good, Jesus must be at the center of that change. Soon after Jacobs came to Tanganyika he met Jesus in the same way we had met him, along with Bishop Stauffer, back in 1942.

So from near the beginning of Don's experience as a missionary, his work and his estimation of us were based not only on his good education and his bright intelligence but on the blood of Jesus which breaks down the walls which separate people from each other. In this way, Don Jacobs, like Bishop Stauffer before him, was our brother at the foot of the cross.   — *Kisare wa Kiseru*, page 100

Seeing the End of My Work in Tanzania

Bishop Kisare and I never talked about whether I should stay in Tanzania or not after he was designated the bishop. It was just understood between us that it would be best all around if I would move into something else. By that time, Paul Kraybill at the Mission Board was reviving his earlier dream of establishing a regional office for East Africa, located in Nairobi, and he had his eye on me to do that. I knew that my work in Tanzania was coming to an end.

It was a bittersweet leaving. Our family will never be able to repay the Tanzania Church for their openhearted love and sympathy. If ever a missionary could say, "The Lord has done what he promised," I could say it with hearty emphasis.

That original group of 16 men had now completed the three-year course and graduated. The college was off to a good start. Bishop Kisare was now bishop. It was time for the Jacobs family to move on. We enjoyed several weeks of heartfelt farewells, and, as school closed in June 1966, we said our good-byes and were on our way into the unknown future. We were ready for a break.

FIVE YEARS OF LEARNING

At this point in my story, I should try to explain what happened to me in those five years. I cannot even begin to do that. Let me employ similitude. That may help. It was as though I had a complete internal rearranging of furniture, maybe even a new room or two added to the house, new large windows, doors out of their jambs, some that said, "Come in," replacing those that said, "Stay out." I saw striking new décor with cardinals, chickadees, and downy woodpeckers, as well as flamingos, hornbills, and fire finches. There were Guernsey cows, along with zebras, wildebeest, and hippos. There was a German room. A British room. A Bantu room and a Nilotic room. A room with the pictures of ancestors and martyrs and saints, and a room where our little family lived, off to the side a bit, but open to all.

It was not just *my* house, but *our* house. In the center was the great room where we gathered to worship, learn, and pray. In the hub of that room that was lit by the light of heaven stood a cross, a reminder of the shed blood of Jesus Christ. That spot was precious beyond measure, for it was there that all in the house found forgiveness and newness of life. As we moved toward Jesus, nudged by the Holy Spirit, we found we were not alone. Our unity was the unity of the Spirit. We ate the same loaf and drank the same drink, the broken, resurrected Jesus Christ.

All these rooms were covered by a strong roof that caught the precious rains and sent them to the fresh water tank for drinking when it got hot. Under it all was a foundation stronger than the granite and igneous boulders of Bukiroba—Jesus Christ, God in the flesh, crucified for sinners, raised to herald the new day of love and brotherhood. It was his house. He lived there. It was a house of meeting for all people. In the refrigerator water cooled, the water of divine love, for thirsty ones. Come in, have a glass of cold water.

I was humbled as Anna Ruth and I took hands and strolled through the wonders of this house. We rejoiced with what we saw, the additions and the subtractions. And we were aware that we could not stop building and arranging and rearranging and bringing in new furnishings and saying good-bye to what we no longer needed. No, it was a good house, made by God with our permission and assistance, but it was a house in the making, his house. We would welcome changes until the ultimate change, when we will stand as happy, contented, saved sinners in the very halls of mercy, a mansion of rooms.

Second Furlough, 1966

As usual, the Mission Board had a rather full summer laid out for us. The centerpiece was a family trip to Colorado where I was scheduled to speak at the Mennonite Youth Convention. That youth convention put us in touch with what was happening in the younger generation of Mennonites in North America, and we were quite excited by what we experienced. I recall praying earnestly that, having been away for more than 12 years, without any experience with the tumultuous happenings in their culture in the 1960s, I could communicate with these young people. The Lord answered that prayer, and I felt a genuine and deep response to my simple message of walking with Jesus.

Time sped quickly as we visited brothers, sisters, and cousins; attended family reunions; and, of course spoke in churches again and again. For our children, it was a blur of activities. For us, it was a time to ponder who we had become or were becoming. We could not brood long over that, however, as we were soon packing for another term in Africa, this time for three years, not five or six, and not to Tanzania, but Kenya.

Paul Kraybill's plan was on again, to establish a Mission Board office in Nairobi to serve all of East Africa, including Ethiopia, Somalia, Kenya, and Tanzania, and to make Nairobi into a center of missionary services, in an effort to liaison with the churches. Paul envisioned it as the first overseas branch of the Mission Board. The guest house, which the Board had purchased about five years previously, and the Rosslyn Academy which replaced Mara Hills School, would provide some of the services. So we began to plan in that direction.

Chapter 21

NEW LOCATION — NAIROBI

1967

MENNONITE WORLD CONFERENCE IN HOLLAND

The first leg of our trip to Africa took us to Holland where I was scheduled to speak at the Mennonite World Conference. I enjoyed the interaction with Mennonites from around the world. As I understood it, this was the first Mennonite World Conference with a heavy contingent from the non-Western world. I felt right at home.

I had the joy of being with Bishop Kisare in this, his first Mennonite World Conference. He was sharp. His English was not all that great then, but he got the gist of what was going on. However, he did not hesitate to ask me to confirm anything that puzzled him. That was the case when we sat together as various Mennonite mission boards reported on what they were doing. During the Dutch mission reporting, I saw him squirm a bit.

After the meeting he told me that he needed help with his English because he was sure he misheard something. The Dutch mission board reported that their special project for the year was to help build a mosque for a Turkish community in Holland. That way they could show that they had no prejudice against Muslims. I must admit that it took me quite a while to explain to Kisare how it could be that in the birthplace of Menno Simons, Holland, the church there now saw evangelism as building an Islamic mosque. I am not sure that what I said made sense to Kisare, because it barely made sense to me. This was an eye-opener for Kisare who had no exposure whatsoever to the theologically liberal wing of Anabaptism before.

OUR NEW HOME, NAIROBI

Having lived in rural Tanzania for many years, we did our best to adjust to life in a burgeoning, world-class African city, Nairobi. With the able help of Hershey Leaman, the Mission Board administrator in the Nairobi office, we located and purchased a suitable house only a half-block from the guest house on St. Michael's Road in the Westland section of Nairobi. It was a concrete-block bungalow with a corrugated iron roof, iron windows, and a polished red concrete floor, originally built for a British railway overseer. It was located on about three acres of well laid-out Kenya lawn, large enough for a go-cart track for our boys.

The house was not laid out all that well for us, but we were pleased with what was there and inhabited it with joy. A favorite spot was the living room with a fireplace topped with a crafted mantel. That was our cozy area during the cold months of July and August.

Our home in Nairobi for six years

DOWNTOWN OFFICE IN NAIROBI

We located office space in what was called Church House in Nairobi, owned by the Anglican Church, not far from the headquarters of the East African Railways. Hershey, Helen Rufenacht, and I gave ourselves to serving the needs of missionaries and to relating to the growing Mennonite churches in East Africa. From our sixth-floor windows we could see, on a clear day, Mt. Kilimanjaro to the south and Mt. Kenya to the north. We were not far from the equator.

MENNONITE FELLOWSHIP IN NAIROBI

It was not our intention to plant churches in Nairobi. However, when we moved there, we found that Hershey Leaman had taken the initiative to provide a time and place for Kenyan Mennonites to meet on Sunday afternoons. Quite a few Mennonites from western Kenya lived in Nairobi. A group of 20 or so met on a regular basis. All of us expatriates attended churches of other denominations. Our family enjoyed the growing Nairobi Baptist Church which was under the dynamic leadership of Tom Houston of England, a man who loomed large in my life as time went on.

We got to work developing and administering services like the Mennonite Guest House, Rosslyn Academy, Mennonite Central Committee programs, and other services to meet the needs of the dozens of missionaries that were in northeastern Africa at the time. Hershey also took over the Teachers Abroad Program and had it functioning marvelously. I admired Hershey for his administrative skills and his strength in human relations. Helen Rufenacht ran the office with her extraordinary efficiency and friendliness. Elizabeth Hostetter, who graduated with me from High School in 1945, ran the Guest House with her usual attention to detail.

I also served as the Mission Board representative in East Africa, so when a mission problem popped up in Tanzania, Somalia, Ethiopia, or Kenya, I was expected to help. Since I knew where the Mission Board stood on most matters, I could usually speak for Paul Kraybill. I thoroughly enjoyed interacting with my missionary friends in Ethiopia and Somalia and visited them often, even if there were no problems.

BEGINNING A FACULTY OF RELIGIOUS STUDIES

David Barrett was an Anglican missionary who served as a chaplain at the new University of Nairobi, the first university in Kenya. He asked me to join him and a few others to establish a Department of Religious Studies in the new university. I agreed to teach African Religion and Philosophy, gratis as my contribution. That was not enough for David, he wanted me to help raise funds and find staff. What could I do? I agreed. Fortunately the renowned Anglican Bishop Stephen Neill, author of the epochal mission book, *The Unfinished Task*, was closing out his tenure in India. He agreed to head the department. We had no money to hire faculty, so we asked qualified lecturers to help, like myself, but also Islamic and Hindu scholars in addition to Christian ones. As promised, I taught the course on African Religion and Philosophy. The university doubted whether such a department could survive. It not only survived but prospered sufficiently so that, after a few years, they funded it.

This put me on the map, so to speak, as someone around town who could explain what made African cultures tick. I could have spent all my time answering invitations from Bible schools, churches, and many other institutions who wanted help to understand cultural issues. I recall that, after I taught the course at the large Nairobi Baptist Church, Tom Houston, the pastor said, "Don taught us how to think black without seeing red!" I preferred that to when an African introduced me to audiences, saying that I had a white skin but a black heart.

Euphoria in Tanzania

One of my assignments was to be a link between the local churches and the Mission Board, a tricky spot, if I may say so. With regard to Tanzania, the church was in a post-independence, euphoric mode, eager to establish itself as a self-governing church in a new nation. Sympathetic to their desire, I determined to listen carefully and then try to share their concerns with the Mission Board.

I took a great deal of comfort in knowing I could lean heavily upon the counsel and advice of Bishop Kisare, a sage if there ever was one. Our relationship was one of the factors that added purpose to our being in Nairobi. He could pretty well predict how I would respond and seemed happy with that.

Imperceptibly, things began to change in my relationship with the Tanzania Mennonite Church. I was seen by some, but not by Kisare, as a spokesman for the Mission Board and not for the church. Dark clouds appeared on the horizon.

Go with me, back a few years, to where I think this problem started. When I was the bishop in Tanzania, I knew that the church would need spiritually mature, well educated leaders to meet the challenges that lay ahead. That led me to obtain scholarships at Eastern Mennonite College for two capable, promising, young leaders whom the church felt led of God to send, Thomas Migire and Shemaya Magati. They did well in their degree programs and returned to Tanzania where, within a very short time, the church gave both of them very influential positions. That was when I felt the cold shoulder.

Migire and Magati had paid several visits to our Mission Board in Salunga, Pennsylvania, when they were students. These visits and their own personal interests convinced them that, if and when they held offices in the Tanzania Mennonite Church, the Mission Board would be favorable to their requests.

Bishop Kisare had doubts about their motives but acceded to their desires to deal directly with the Mission Board, bypassing me, of course. They managed to push Kisare aside and effectively squeezed me out of the picture. A consequence of this was that one of the major reasons for my being in Nairobi fell away, ironically because of the "success" of the men for whom I arranged scholarships.

I hasten to say that this situation of being elbowed out of the way by the Tanzania Mennonite Church after having served them for 12 years became another opportunity for me to break and to forgive. Not only did I feel that Migirc and Magati were rejecting me, but I dreaded the thought that this might drive a wedge between Kisare and me. I deliberately refused to let my mind dwell on what was happening in Tanzania. I was deeply hurt and profoundly disturbed. I concluded that the best thing was to bury myself in my present jobs in Kenya and forget about Tanzania. I felt that I was a dismal failure.

That feeling was not new. I always felt that way when I believed that I was being rejected. Oh, how I dreaded rejection! That pushed me up against Jesus in a most remarkable, redemptive way. I slid into a relationship with Christ that shared the suffering of rejection so that I did not need to bear the loss alone. I found consolation in knowing that the suffering Savior was suffering in me all over again. Or was I suffering in him?

RELATIONSHIP RESTORED

Months passed. I feared that Kisare had pushed me right out of his mind. I didn't dare to reach out to see what was left of our friendship, because it may have been nothing. When I got up the courage to do so, I was overjoyed to find that Bishop Kisare valued our friendship deeply and, in spite of what was going on, asked me for forgiveness if his actions had hurt my feelings. I forgave with joy, and he forgave me for my coldness and my tendency to withdraw and just hide in my own cave of hurt. To my utter delight, our relationship was restored. Then we moved forward in true brotherhood.

To bring this saga to an end, I need to leap forward a year or two. In time, the Tanzania Mennonite Church discovered that Migire and Magati could not deliver on what they had led the church to believe they could do. The two probably overrated their ability to obtain from the Mission Board just about anything they desired. Disillusioned, they simply abandoned the church and turned to their personal matters. I grieved for the church that saw hope diminished and for Bishop Kisare who had to pick up the pieces.

I have been asked time and again if it was a good idea to send African students to Western schools. I still do not have a very good answer. I helped more than 40 from both Tanzania and Kenya, members of a variety of churches. Magati and Migire were but two of them. Some returned to their country of origin and made lifetime contributions. Some failed in their studies. Some returned with degrees but could not find the niche that fit them. Some of them stayed on in the U.S. I saw some return, who, eager to serve in the church in Tanzania or Kenya, but not finding employment there, went into Civil Service or business. There was no pattern that I could discern.

GETTING ACQUAINTED WITH AFRICAN ENTERPRISE

When our family returned to Nairobi after a furlough in 1969, Tom Houston, pastor of the Nairobi Baptist Church and by then a close friend, startled me with the report that the Nairobi churches were asking African Enterprise of South Africa to lead out in a major evangelistic campaign, the first of its kind on such a large scale for Nairobi.

"Hold on, there," I said, "not South Africa, the land of apartheid!" I lodged my protest loud and clear. However, I soon learned that Michael Cassidy, a white South African leader of African Enterprise, insisted that it would be a truly multicultural ministry of evangelism to all people.

I then recalled that when George and Dorothy Smoker, our missionary colleagues, were on home leave in California, they met regularly with this young South African student, Michael Cassidy, and his little prayer group, at Fuller Theological Seminary. They said, "Don, you just must meet Michael Cassidy!" With this background, I knew that when I met Michael, I would know that he was a man under God's anointing for Africa.

I dropped my defenses and did what I could to make the campaign successful. We invited Festo Kivengere, the gifted Ugandan evangelist, to join Michael as one of the speakers. He agreed. I looked forward to seeing how he and Michael might get on. They clicked.

It was great to see a white South African and a black Ugandan standing side by side, proclaiming the gospel of peace that breaks every barrier and makes, of two very different people, a new thing on the earth—fellowship in Christ. I was designated to translate their afternoon evangelistic messages in Nairobi's great Central Park — Michael's messages into Swahili and Festo Kivengere's Swahili into English.

The relationship between Festo and Michael deepened. In a very short time after that, Michael invited Festo to begin in East Africa a group similar to the one in South Africa, both responsible to a single International Board. They did so and called theirs "African Evangelistic Enterprise." I was much involved in that step forward, not only as a member of the Kenya Board but as a friend of Michael and Festo.

PRESSURE FROM KENYA MENNONITE CHURCH

"Now that Bishop Kisare is bishop in Tanzania, will you be our bishop in Kenya?" I heard this loud and clear as I was sitting in my office in Nairobi, before a delegation from the scattered Mennonite churches of western Kenya. They were there because they desperately wanted their own bishop, even though their membership was only a few hundred people.

The Kenyan Mennonite churches were the result of Mennonite migrations out of Tanzania. Many of those who left Tanzania for Kenya, all Nilotic, were really going home to where their ancestors had lived. They moved to Kenya for economic reasons. The Kenya economy was thriving. Wherever they settled, they planted churches, Mennonite ones. They looked to the Tanzanian bishop as their spiritual leader. Shortly after Kisare was made bishop, bad blood developed between the nations of Tanzania and Kenya as Tanzania embraced socialism. It was becoming increasingly difficult for Bishop Kisare to move freely into Kenya.

These circumstances moved the Kenyan Mennonites to take things into their own hands and organize themselves as a Kenyan Mennonite denomination. They concluded that the way to go about this was to approach me to become their bishop. I knew in my bones that, if I agreed, it would drive a wedge between me and Bishop Kisare, the officially designated bishop of Tanzania and Kenya. He did not think that the Kenyan churches were far enough along to require a bishop of their own. He served them the best he was able to from Tanzania.

I felt for them and did hope that they could some day stand on their own feet. But I had no option; I had to decline their kind invitation. That was not their last visit. As relations between the nations deteriorated, they approached me again. I had to decline.

As I saw the Kenyan Mennonite Church struggle in those days, I wondered all over again if I had made the right decision to refuse to be their bishop. I always came to the same conclusion: my relationship with Bishop Kisare must take priority. Furthermore, I had no stomach for schism and determined to keep peace between the Tanzanian and Kenyan Mennonite churches no matter how their nations quarreled with one another.

Gladys

Meet Gladys, a strong, hard-working, Kikuyu woman who lived about five miles outside of Nairobi on a little farm with chickens, goats, and at least one cow, and a dissolute, alcoholic husband. It was not easy for her to raise her family—she was for all intents and purposes, a widow, even though she was legally married. Gladys, cradled in revival, was a dedicated Presbyterian and absolutely committed to following Jesus Christ no matter what. We were fortunate in that Gladys agreed to help Anna Ruth a few mornings a week. She was very good for us. When we faced any hardship, we reminded ourselves of the way Gladys was facing life in spite of all that loomed up before her.

A Martyr's Funeral

It was the fall of 1969 when Gladys asked us to pray for her and for those in her fellowship group who were being harassed by the Kikuyu tribal oathers. It was election season. Jomo Kenyatta was President, and his tribe wanted him to have another term. For that, they needed every Kikuyu to vote for him.

To assure that, the tribal elders revitalized an ancient ritual that had been used for political purposes during the Mau Mau days of the 1940s and early '50s. While drinking a potion of animal blood and intestinal material prepared by the tribal oathers, persons swore to obey the commands of the tribal ancestors. Most of the Kikuyu people, a quarter of the nation's population and the largest of the dozens of tribes in Kenya, drank the oath without protest, if not gladly. But not the "saved ones," who simply refused to drink the oath. They could not possibly swear allegiance to anyone other than their Jesus.

Gladys came to work one morning with the distressing news that the oathers took several people from her fellowship group during the night to force them to take the oath. We soon learned through Gladys that it was Evangelist Samuel, his wife, and daughters, leaders of their group. We were acquainted with Samuel. They were taken to the oathing place in the forest where, Gladys told us, they refused again to take the oath. For that they were severely beaten and left alone in the cold, stripped naked.

When morning dawned, the oathers were back. Again Samuel and his family were beaten. We learned later that Samuel protested, "We have already drunk the blood of Jesus, and this blood that you have in the gourd will not mix with that blood that we already drank!"

The brothers and sisters, realizing what had happened, hired a pickup truck to look for the family. They found them at the oathing place, beaten. Loading them all on the truck, they proceeded to the nearest hospital, a government one, which disdained treating anyone who refused to take the oath. They had to drive a long distance to the mission hospital where Samuel died from loss of blood. His wife and daughters recovered.

Gladys invited us to attend Samuel's funeral on a little hill near her place, where the congregation worshiped in their rather small, corrugated-iron church. We arrived to find the place swarming with people. As the singing, testifying, and preaching proceeded, I sensed that the place was being transformed. It was full of light.

Then a little white Ford sedan came up the hill. Inside was Samuel's wife, wrapped with bandages. With a warm smile on her face, she said that before he died, Samuel, realizing that he would not survive, told her that he forgave his killers and asked that God would forgive them, too. She then said, "In the name of Jesus, you are forgiven." Presumably, some of the oathers were in attendance. At once the signature song of the Revival filled the air, "Glory, glory, hallelujah. Glory, glory to the Lamb, for the cleansing blood has reached me. Glory, glory to the Lamb."

Another oathing death followed in about a week in another part of Kikuyuland. There was such uproar that the government prohibited any more tribal oathing. The elections which followed were entirely peaceful. Those martyrdoms produced a harvest of peace more or less immediately, unlike many martyrdoms in church history.

The martyr's funeral touched me deeply. As a student of Anabaptist history, I had read the *Martyr's Mirror*, which was first published in 1660 in Dutch by Thieleman J. van Braght. After retelling the stories of early Christian martyrs, Van Braght described the martyrdom of many Anabaptist martyrs. This book often lay beside the Bible in Mennonite homes. We did not have one in our home, but I grew up knowing that there was such a book. When I finally saw one, I studied the woodcuts of martyrs being burned at the stake or sawn through. It all began to make sense that day when I attended Samuel's funeral.

Following Christ is serious business. Standing among those hopeful mourners, I recommitted myself to Jesus anew. I knew in my heart that no matter what, his grace would enable me to stand by him. Another conviction hit me: "I will live like Samuel died." I mark that event as one of the crisis events of my life.

For me as an Anabaptist participating in a martyr's funeral, denominational lines became very blurred. I was standing beside Evangelist Samuel, a Presbyterian, on that Kikuyu hillside in Africa in a simple corrugated-iron structure. But as I reflected, I was, in spirit, standing with Felix Manz's mother and sister and the little praying band of Anabaptist believers on the banks of the Limmat River in Zurich, near the famed Grossmünster church on a cold winter's day, January 5, 1527. They stood there as Felix was being bound for drowning and pleaded with him to cling to his faith in Jesus and to suffer as Jesus suffered. Manz was the first Anabaptist to suffer martyrdom at the hands of the Protestants.

Evangelist Samuel was another martyr for the exact same reason—to suffer for and with Christ rather than disown him. I felt unworthy and shaken as the 400-plus years between these two events collapsed into a moment of holy unity. I praised God for Felix Manz, and with the same lyrics I praised God for Evangelist Samuel. I had one foot in 1527, another in 1969, and I realized that the ground on which I stood was holy beyond telling. I wept.

LOOKING THROUGH NEW EYES

Something was changing in me. I was open to looking at things from a new perspective. I was discovering that when I changed my perspective while viewing something, I saw it slightly differently. I was beginning to question why I looked at life the way I did, and I wondered if that was keeping me from seeing things as they actually were. How did I know if something was true, when it seemed to change, depending on where I stood as I looked.

I illustrate this by what happened to me on one of my many trips to Somalia. It was morning, just before the sun appeared. I was walking alone on a high bluff near the sea, looking east. Few morning skies are as crystal-clear as daybreak skies in Somalia. I could see for miles out to sea. As I stood there, I saw something that astounded me. As the first sliver of sun appeared I had the distinct sensation that the sea before me was going down and down, allowing more of the sun to appear. I was riding the earth downward! When I got my bearings I heard myself saying, "The sun does not come up. The earth goes down!" It is true; the sun was there all the time!

I was nurtured all my life on the fantasy that the sun comes up. It is even enshrined in the English language. What do I do now? The earth goes down; it just looks like the sun is coming up. Now and again, as I tried to see things from new perspectives, I recalled that morning in Somalia. It was there in my mind as a metaphor. Question your presuppositions. Some are right; some are not. Bring them out and look at them honestly.

Chapter 22

OTHER RESPONSIBILITIES IN NAIROBI

Working with MCC

As I worked more and more with Mennonite Central Committee I was eager to learn more about it. I had long conversations with Bill Snyder, then General Secretary of MCC, who visited us now and again. Since we were administering the MCC Teachers Abroad Program from our office, we developed a relationship with MCC, work-

Jim Bertsche, a man of wisdom and warmth

ing with Robert Miller and Vern Preheim of their staff. Hershey and I felt good about this relationship. Somewhere along the line I began to wonder if MCC might work with the emerging Mennonite churches in the area of community development. Bill retold the story of MCC, noting that it was formed to help Germanic ethnic Mennonites who were struggling in Russia. Later, they assisted those ethnic Mennonites who wished to relocate in North and South Americas. Then, in the WWII era, MCC broadened out as a relief and service agency wherever there was need.

I sincerely wished that in East Africa, Eastern Board and MCC could work together, one concentrating primarily on evangelism and church planting and the other pursuing economic development. I thought the concept was sound. I thought that our office might be the place to coordinate the two. As with many of my ideas, this one flopped. MCC eventually set up its own office and served where they thought it could do the most good.

SOUTHERN AFRICA SURVEY

Mennonite interest in South Africa grew in the late 1960s. One reason for this was the entrenchment of apartheid politics there that flew in the face of almost everything Mennonites were supposed to believe. Was there a niche that the Mennonite church could enter and try to do a little good? A second reason had to do with the growing interest in the African Independent Church movement in much of South Africa. In any case, Jim Bertsche, a highly regarded veteran Congo Inland missionary in Zaire, and I were asked to spend a few weeks in southern Africa, sniffing out what we might possibly recommend regarding a way forward.

Those weeks with Jim Bertsche, a real soul mate, set my mind to thinking in several new directions. We undertook this survey with the general understanding that any ministry that the Mennonites might possibly have in southern Africa would not include church planting. As I write this years later, I am astounded that we did not even consider planting churches in southern Africa. I suppose it reflects the mood of the time. Was there fear that fellowships would not engage the issues that we were most deeply concerned about? Or had church planting become synonymous with denominational imperialism? A bad thing. The report that we submitted with our conclusions was simply silent on the issue of church planting.

Jim Bertsche and I were both intrigued by the expansion of the many indigenous Christian movements. He had studied the Kimbanguists, an independent church movement in Congo, and I was doing research in Kenya with a similar indigenous church. That may have been one reason why we tried to discover if there would be a way of partnering with such movements. Major missions and denominations were not inclined to help those churches, nor were the indigenous churches particularly looking for help. We believed, however, that it would be good to develop relationships with these churches where possible. We were also interested in the nonviolent movement among many Christians in South Africa. We felt a kinship with them and recommended that we might be able to help a little there.

What is a Missionary Family?

Where did our family fit into our lives as missionaries? Next to our relationship with God and with one another, Anna Ruth and I happily elevated family as our most important calling. I valued highly every minute of home life. Serving the family was in no way a chore but a delightful privilege for which we shall be eternally thankful. I personally have experienced the grace of God in family life more than in any other relationship. It is in those special love-bondings that we see ourselves for who we are. Every flaw I have is exposed in the close family bond. And every virtue is extolled. It is in the family that I test my faith in God, and it is in family life that I forgive and am forgiven. I have discovered that if things are not right at home, there is no use going out to help someone else. The whole gospel is lived, in its entirety, in the home. Anna Ruth and I loved Jane, David, Alan, and Paul dearly. That love never wavered.

Life in Nairobi was a happy time for our family.

Chapter 23

ACCOMMODATING TO CHANGES IN THE U.S.

1973

Decision to Leave East Africa

When our family returned to Nairobi in 1969, we had the general feeling that this was to be our last term as missionaries in East Africa. Realizing that Jane would graduate from high school in 1973, we focused on that date.

As far as our work, we could see that others were there to carry it on. Hershey Leaman was a far better administrator than I was, and he had a vision for what he was doing. I felt good about his leadership in the Eastern Mennonite Mission Regional Office in Nairobi.

One of my jobs as area representative for EMM was to relate to the churches as a mouthpiece for EMM. That was brought into question by the mixed response of the church in Tanzania, as I already described.

Furthermore, one of the reasons we went to Nairobi in the first place was to provide services for missionaries in Somalia and East Africa, such as the Guest House and Rosslyn Academy. Little did we know that Somalia would eventually deport all missionaries, so no more children came from there. We also saw a reduction in the number of missionaries sent by EMM, since the local churches were managing pretty much on their own. In summary, I felt that I had more or less completed or passed on the assignment that had been given to me.

We had family considerations as well. In the forefront was Jane, then 18, a graduate of Good Shepherd High School in Ethiopia. Some missionary parents who had college-age children arranged for their children to live in American college dormitories so that the parents could continue their work in the field. We felt that we should be with our children as they progressed through high school and on to college. David, at age 16, completed his sophomore year at Good Shepherd as well. Alan and Paul were day students at Rosslyn Academy. I was 45 at the time, and Anna Ruth was a year older. It was clear to us that we could go one of two directions: retool and seek a new role in East Africa, or move to the United States to begin a new career. We felt moved to do the latter.

Life does not always permit much time for contemplation between major transitions, and I was in for a major one—from being a missionary to becoming a returned missionary, whatever that was. I was soon to find out. I do recall that I was once teaching at Eastern Mennonite College when I wrote on the board, "Old missionaries never die, they just..." One student blurted it out—"They just go on showing their slides." Dear me!

SEEKING DIRECTION

"But what will I do?" I kept asking myself. I had three live options. Fuller Theological Seminary was looking for a replacement for Allen Tippet of Australia. As the anthropologist in the School of World Missions, Tippet did an amazing job of opening the eyes of his students to the cultural implications involved in missions. Since it was time for him to retire, he arranged for me to visit Fuller to test the waters. I had lectured in the School of World Missions several times before that, and I knew Allen and the rest of the staff and felt right at home there. In my mind it was the best missionary training staff that I had ever known. So when Allen asked me to consider coming on as his replacement, I could have wept. I was truly overwhelmed with gratitude. But should I?

I also had an invitation from President Myron Augsburger to join the Eastern Mennonite College staff. He thought I might be interested in making the Shenandoah Valley my new home in America. I could not believe that Myron was honoring me that way.

All the while, Paul Kraybill, who engineered the creation of the Mennonite Christian Leadership Foundation (MCLF), hoped that I would give half time to developing a vision for that program. It was then four years old. He and Raymond Charles, President of the Mission Board, went ahead and worked out an arrangement where I could serve half-time with MCLF and half-time as a consultant to EMM. What should we do?

I realized how fortunate I was. At my age my peers were well into building careers. For them to make a huge career change was nearly impossible. Being a returned missionary definitely does have some advantages!

Times of transition, like that, are divine opportunities to ask the questions once again, who am I and what
have I become? I realized that I could not fully answer
those questions, but just thinking about them gave me the
courage to take some risks. All of the options before me
demanded drastic changes. I was ready.

We prayed earnestly. It slowly dawned on us that,
above all, we needed to reconnect with our cultural roots.
That meant plunking down in a Mennonite community
and serving the whole world from there. As we thought
of it, our compelling desire for community could not be
fully met for us in an academic institutional setting, either
in Virginia or California.

In reality, that community existed at the Chestnut Hill
Mennonite Church. They helped to support us when we
were in Africa, and we knew almost everyone there. That
settled it; we would attend that small church. The question about community was taken care of. So, having made
that decision, I agreed to serve MCLF and Eastern Board,
half-time each.

Anna Ruth and I were well aware that the Mennonite
community that we desired to belong to was flawed like
every other community. The people were like us in that
regard. We knew that if we were to grow in grace, in
humility, and in vision, we needed to be surrounded by
fellow believers whom we could love and who could love
us. We had no exalted delusions about Lancaster Conference. The Mennonite community there was going through
huge transitions. To expect it to be perfect was foolhardy.
And it was just as stupid to think that we could be much
help as the community reinvented itself.

BACK TO LANCASTER

We were welcomed home to Lancaster by Anna Ruth's mother, her brother, Raymond, and his wife, Anna Lois, and Dwayne, Twila, and Linda, then living together in the old farmhouse. Her father had died while we were in Nairobi.

Raymond Charles was a prize. He and Anna Ruth were the only children of Jacob and Cora. Everyone in this world should have a brother-in-law like Raymond. In addition to running a productive farm on 22 acres of land, the family homestead, he served as bishop for the Landisville District of churches and president of the rapidly growing and energetic Eastern Mennonite Board of Missions. He was in great demand as a speaker and counselor. He also helped to start the popular Voluntary Service department at EMM, Friendship Community, Partners in Evangelism, and Gateway Evangelistic Ministries. Probably others, too.

As president of the Mission Board, Raymond had visited us in Africa. The way he handled himself there, and the way he could relate to the challenges that I was facing, impressed me. He and Orie O. Miller cooperated beautifully in bringing the mission interest to the fore in Lancaster Conference. I cannot say enough about this man.

We purchased a house on Southview Drive in Landisville. As we settled in, Anna Ruth's mother, Cora, asked if she could live with us. She had been living, since becoming a widow, with Raymond and Anna Lois. We agreed to that, even though we were ourselves going through a transition. At that time she could help Anna Ruth around the house to some extent, but she slowly lost her mental abilities. For about two years, she was dimly aware of her circumstances, but then disorientation set in, and during the next six years, she required more or less constant supervision. Our children were open to having her live with us, and they did marvelously well as she deteriorated. In 1981 she died peacefully in her bedroom in our home, at age 89.

The Charles family and ours. Front row, left to right, Anna Lois, Alan, Cora, Jacob, Paul, Anna Ruth. Back row, left to right, Raymond, Twila, David, Dwayne, Jane, Linda, me.

Chapter 24

FAMILY
LIFE

Seeing Anna Ruth's Needs

"I cannot go on like this," Anna Ruth confided. Those early years on Southview Drive were not easy for her. She was stretched to the limit. In Nairobi she knew who she was: a missionary, a teacher, a wife, a mother, a hostess for our many guests, and a spiritual counselor. She flourished in those roles. But change had come for her. She now had her mother to look after, she had to relate to each of our four children as they tried to find their ways in this strange land, and she had to make do with a husband who seemed to be running about everywhere with only limited time at home. Furthermore, in order to make ends meet, she took a part-time job teaching remedial reading. All the while she was expected to do what returned missionaries do, speaking here and there. She was stretched to the limit. I was but little help, unfortunately.

Because I had two official jobs, plus a lot of irons in the fire, my date book included one assignment after another, many promised even before we left Africa. At times I arrived at our house in Landisville, spent a day or two, and then was off somewhere else. And often, on the spur of the moment, I invited someone to come to our place for a meal. Anna Ruth, bless her heart, endured this without complaint; at least I didn't detect any. I was oblivious to her needs and, worse yet, to her yearnings.

We had learned to walk in light with one another, the secret of our rich life together, but those days it seemed as if we just did not have the time or energy, maybe even the desire, for that. Finally, when the pressure became too great, Anna Ruth poured out her hurt and frustration and confessed that her attitude had become judgmental and hard. Broken, she asked for forgiveness for her rotten attitude. I was devastated. Of course I forgave her, but I still had no idea how much my self-centered attitude and lack of concern for her needs hurt her.

At night the Lord met me and pulverized my pride. I was responding to calls for ministry here and there, but was absolutely deaf to calls from my dear wife for love and human companionship. How could it be that, after all these years, I could take her for granted? The next morning after pouring out my heart in repentance, I produced my date book and laid it on the table between us. "From today, nothing goes into that date book that we do not agree on. I give my date book to the Lord and to you." That series of events put our relationship on a new footing.

As a result of our new commitment to one another, I had the courage to say no to invitations that I would not have even questioned before. Our commitment to pray about and to seek God's will on incoming invitations for ministry brought us closer together as well.

I also learned not to speak for Anna Ruth again. When I got invitations to speak on missions, I was often told,

"And we look to Anna Ruth to give the children's meeting," or something like that. The Lord gave me the grace to say, "Fine, please ask her." I assured Anna Ruth that I would back her to the hilt if she declined and would pray for her heartily if she accepted. That helped immensely.

Knowing Myself in a New Setting

Part of the problem, maybe the biggest one, was that I was still trying to figure out who I was in this new setting. Upon leaving Kenya in 1973, I had some sense of who I was. Unfortunately, that identity could not be transferred to Lancaster. I found myself wishing that I could just be Don on Southview Drive, just Don Jacobs without any labels, just a happy believer, filled with a deep appreciation for the grace of a loving God. I soon discovered that my new community saw me through a different set of spectacles. I was a missionary, an educated person with a testimony, an author, an achiever in missions, an "International Christian Statesman." I cringed time and again when I was introduced by well-meaning people in such lofty terms. I knew who I was, and it was not as advertised.

I suppose one reason I liked home so much was that I was just Daddy there. Our children knew me, and they had no illusions about who I was. When I entered our home and closed the door behind me, I determined to be nothing but a grateful, contented, and fun-loving father. Then I was the real me. Being with Anna Ruth, Jane, David, Alan, and Paul just felt right. When we were around our table, eating hot dogs or ugali, all my other identities faded. I was Daddy and Anna Ruth's husband. It was what I could imagine heaven to be.

Furthermore, I liked to sit, unnoticed, in the Chestnut Hill Mennonite Church congregation because there I was Anna Ruth's husband and a regular attender, nothing special. I preferred to have no identity at all in the public mind. In fact, I wanted to slip into anonymity. I realized, of course, that was hogwash. I was in a group, a culture, a community. But, mercy days, who was I to me?

CHESTNUT HILL CHURCH

We had decided to make Chestnut Hill our church home. It was not an easy decision. We could shop around and find a congregation that represented the kind of world we were accustomed to—a multicultural, mission-minded, rapidly growing Mennonite congregation with a compelling vision. We actually had a few invitations from congregations like that. But we were drawn to Anna Ruth's ancestral congregation, the small

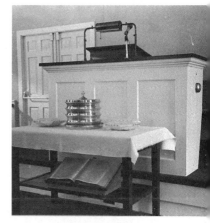

Chestnut Hill Mennonite Church, Columbia, PA

but friendly, often struggling, Chestnut Hill Mennonite.

We felt loved there, although it took effort to try to understand how they looked at things. It finally dawned on me that this was like going into a new tribe or culture. The idea was not to have them understand me, but for me to understand them. Just like in Africa. This approach helped me to relax and learn from this group of disciples. I found that they represented a cross-section of Lancaster culture, and I needed to understand them if I was going to live happily in Lancaster.

I am not sure that our children found life at Chestnut Hill to be as positive as we did. Life there did not resemble life in Nairobi for them by any means. In hindsight, perhaps Anna Ruth and I should have considered the needs of our children more. This was one of the cases where my commitment too often trumped the needs of our family, a tendency that I repented of often but never fully resolved. The fact that we could talk about it helped to some degree.

Having said that, I am a strong proponent of learning to walk with the Lord by deliberately joining a group that is not entirely like you, such as a local congregation, and then hanging in there no matter what. Chestnut Hill Mennonite Church passed through rough waters. We saw much—untimely deaths, unemployment, bankruptcy, marriage problems, leadership struggles, changes in worship styles, the lot. We also enjoyed innumerable precious things. In all this we admired the pillars of faith and love in the congregation who bore the heat of the day. Pathos mingled with hope.

We had no impulse to leave. We had made our commitment and that was that. A Christian congregation is all of life compacted into a worshiping community. All of the needs of all humanity are often contained in one congregation. We began to understand that.

OUR CHILDREN

Each of our children brought a distinct personality to our family. Jane had a heart as tender as any devoted friend. David loved to be independent, to do it himself. Alan was Mr. Inquisitive. If his head was not in a book, it was out inspecting every bug. Paul could pick and choose to be like any of his older siblings, but he chose to be himself, a contented, happy Paul.

As we got established in Landisville, we were already thinking of how we could best walk with our children as they eased into life in America. To be honest, Anna Ruth and I were also facing some real challenges in this regard. We were as anxious as our children were about fitting into this strange, new world, probably more so. It was tough going for all of us. We found that it was one thing to visit the US as missionaries on furlough, and an entirely different thing to get it into our heads that this was not a furlough, but a life shift. It was permanent.

If Anna Ruth and I would have known our new place in the community, which we admittedly did not, we may have been more helpful to our children as they were making huge adjustments. I suppose we all just floundered together, hoping for the best. Our children are not all the same, not by any means, so each one had to rediscover who she or he was all over again. Each had a known place in the family but not in the community. As I look back, it is small wonder that we did not all just collapse. God helped us to survive, not without scrapes and bruises, but we kept going. Let me explain.

Jane decided to find work for a year and think of college later. I think it was a lonely year for her, coming from Kenya, where she had friends, to a place where her old friends were not replaced by new ones. How she came through that first year is a surprising work of God's grace. Her walk with the Lord gave her the stability that helped her through some grueling times.

Following college at Goshen where she qualified as a teacher, Jane joined the Voluntary Service program of EMM, which landed her in Norris Square, Philadelphia, as head of a Voluntary Service unit. There we saw her leadership gifts and her counseling skills mature. While there she met Glenn, the son of a Mennonite bishop in the Delaware Valley and his wife, Luke and Miriam Stoltzfus. Glenn was a medical student interning at a hospital in Philadelphia at the time, the city in which he grew up. Jane and Glen married and moved to New Mexico where he had obtained his medical doctorate. Jane and Glenn had their first child, Zel, in 1982, and Sara in 1984. Marie was born 11 years later. Sara, now married to Joel Waltermyer, has given us a great-grandson, Isaac.

And we embraced Heather, Glenn's daughter to a prior marriage, and her husband, Jeff, two jewels. They were both born and raised in New Mexico but moved to Boston where Jeff obtained his Ph. D. at the Massachusetts Institute of Technology. They continue to live there, raising their fine family of three—Emily, Eric, and Jonathan.

When Sara was but a girl, the family served a three-year term under EMM at Mugumu Hospital in Tanzania where they enjoyed African living. For Jane, it was like going back home. Mugumu will always have a big place in the hearts of their family.

Jane looks back at her experience as an MK (Missionary Kid) as generally positive. Her toughest times were in her first grades when she lived in a boarding school. As the years pass, the negatives seem to be eclipsed by the positives. Being raised abroad in a missionary setting is problematic in many ways. We thank God that she came through it all with peace and a thankful heart.

David was 16 and about six feet tall when we settled into our Landisville home. He attended Lancaster Mennonite School for his final two years of high school. The fact that he lived in Africa gave him a positive identity, but among his peers at school in America that fact was not always appreciated. David struggled with that. I think he just wanted to be an American. His desire to belong followed him into Goshen College. While trying to place the African phase of his life behind him and live a wholesome life in the American culture, he was in a world that he did not fully understand. He found an anchor when he gave his heart to the Lord in college, but he still had personal and cultural issues to deal with.

David eventually joined the staff of a new program being developed by Lancaster Mennonite Conference, a ministry to the disabled called Friendship Community. That seemed to be the place for David to give a life of service. He found fulfillment in looking after people who needed love and assistance. He built his life around that ministry. He enjoyed four years of marriage with Melody Milburn and her two daughters, Nicole and Ashley.

In his maturing years, David embraced his African roots, so to speak, and found a good deal of peace in feeling comfortable about his past. David never rejected his roots; he just saw his "African-ness" as something of an impediment in the way he was seen by others. He just wanted to be "David."

Alan had the capacity to create his own world from the time he was a child. He loved reading and just going off doing his thing. It was not that he was antisocial. He had a winsome personality and a great sense of humor. But when he saw an ant or an animal, for instance, he was off examining that while others were interacting. He kept his sanity and self-worth by shaping his own world. He was 14 when we moved to America. At Lancaster Mennonite School he developed some lifelong relationships, including a fondness for Sharon Lopez whom he eventually married.

Like Jane and David, Alan had the opportunity to learn to know his Uncle Merle and Aunt Liz when he attended Goshen College, where Merle taught and did research. After his freshman year, he returned home to finish his degree at Millersville University. He enjoyed many areas of study, but the one that dominated all others at the time was cultural anthropology. He spent one of his most delightful summers on a Native American excavation site in the American Southwest. At another time he, along with Phil Ruth, his cousin, spent several weeks as backpacking students in East Africa, just enjoying the excitement of once again exploring that land.

His fondness for Sharon Lopez was not to be stifled, even though she went off and graduated at Eastern Mennonite University while Alan graduated from Millersville University. They married, settled in Lancaster city, and had four children: Von, who is a graduate of Drexel University in engineering; Jody, a law student at Temple University; Sasha, who is employed in a pharmacy; and Annisa in veterinary school.

Alan found his place on the management team of Isaac's Restaurants, a cluster of 20 restaurants around Lancaster, and Sharon established a law firm, Triquetra Law, located in downtown Lancaster.

This brings us to Paul, our youngest. His adjustment to America was comparatively trouble-free. He was only 10 years old, a very malleable age, when we moved to America. Having an African background was, on balance, a positive thing for him. But Paul never dwelt on that. He was an American young man. His older siblings attended Mennonite high schools and, at least for a while, Mennonite colleges, but he did not. He received a degree in Fine Arts at Millersville University. All the while he worked at

Charles' Studio as a professional photographer. Paul was happy to be a Mennonite and enjoyed participating on the worship team at Chestnut Hill Mennonite.

When Paul got to know Tammy Smith of Lancaster, a flame was lit that burned brighter and brighter. As they approached their wedding day, Tammy discovered that she had Stage II Hodgkin's Lymphoma. She and Paul were both hovering around 40 years old. They agreed to proceed with their plans for marriage. After their honeymoon, Tammy submitted herself to 16 weeks of powerful chemotherapy. With prayer and excellent medical help, she got through the treatment. In less than two and a half years, Evan was born and, three years after that, Elizabeth. For that reason, we still think of Evan and Elizabeth as special miracle children.

Paul has a soft spot in his heart for Africa. When as an adult he revisited Kenya and Tanzania, he reconnected with his past and had not the least hesitancy in re-owning it. For Paul, growing up in Africa borders on the ideal.

THE VAGARIES OF FATHERHOOD

Predictably, the question arose within me, "How am I doing as a father in this culture?" I must admit, it was a roller-coaster ride. My love for my family never wavered. But I found that when things were going well, I praised God. When things did not please me, I blamed myself for being a poor father. Anna Ruth saw this happening and made a suggestion: "You give credit to God when he does good things, don't you? Then, why not just leave the bad things in his hand as well?" I had never thought of that. I had been pushing myself to find out where I was derelict as a parent. Was it right to go flitting all over the world, telling people that Jesus satisfies, while my children needed me at home? Maybe. Maybe not. In any case, a completely satisfying answer eluded me.

Nothing made me feel better than when my children succeeded (which they usually did), and nothing made me feel worse than when they faltered (which was seldom). I must admit that the self-image that I had as a good father when the children were younger underwent some pummeling when they entered the American culture and went on to live as maturing adults here. One thing is for sure: even though I could not figure it out, it gave me compassion for all fathers like me who find it difficult to depend on the grace of God to hover over and guide their children.

Chapter 25

RETHINKING THE MISSION OF EASTERN MENNONITE MISSIONS

1973 – 1980

New Positions

Let me change gears now, moving from personal decisions and family life to the task that was before me, finding my role in the workplace. After all, I was 45 years old, full of energy and a desire to get on with living. As already noted, MCLF and Eastern Mennonite Missions (EMM) agreed to employ me to serve half-time as Director of MCLF while I worked half-time as a consultant to EMM. Since neither of these jobs existed before, I had to find my way.

HOME MISSIONS CONSULTANT

In my half-time role as consultant to EMM from 1973 to 1975, I had regular chats with departments that were dealing with ministry. I was especially interested in the Home Missions work, then headed by Chester Wenger, a former missionary to Ethiopia whom I admired greatly. He was a man with vision and a determination to get things done. He, too, was relatively new in his job. When he left Ethiopia, EMM corralled him to work as Secretary of Home Missions, a department which was becoming more and more multicultural in outreach along the Atlantic seaboard, all the way to Florida. He loved the work.

Chester wanted to know why some of the churches that were planted as new cross-cultural church plants within the past 30 years were growing, and others were not. I was as interested as he was, so we got to work, incorporating Paul Landis, a bishop who had worked among Spanish-speaking persons in Florida. We found a common narrative as we pursued our study. Early efforts to evangelize produced results, and quite a few people came to believe in Jesus Christ. Some of them were baptized into the newly-formed Mennonite fellowships. Others found church homes elsewhere.

At first, this puzzled me. As I thought about it, I realized that what was happening in the church plants here was what we experienced in Africa. If the church planters carried a heavy cultural agenda they were headed for trouble. More likely than not, the churches that they planted would reflect their culture and not the culture in which the churches were planted. That stunted growth.

Our study led me to conclude that the issue was not theology but culture. When the local believers discovered that they could not shape the congregational life to reflect their cultural ways of doing things, they simply walked away. I recalled that it took 20 years in Tanzania before the church had become part of the local cultural scene. I also noted that the stabilization of the Tanzanian church was hastened, in large part, by the revival movement that made cultural issues peripheral.

I have found that churches thrive and grow where believers are bound together by a common love for Jesus and a determination to follow him, and not by commonly held church forms or traditional ways of doing things. Many church plants suffered by not having that clear.

As a consultant to the Home Missions Department, I believed in church planting and tried to help fashion a way forward that would help the newly-planted churches to push their roots deeply into the local soil.

OVERSEAS MISSIONS CONSULTANT

I was a consultant to the Overseas Missions department as well, but I felt uneasy there. That was strange because that was my world! I soon learned that, at that time, they were in a tight spot. They were trying to walk alongside maturing churches who were now asking for ongoing help from EMM. Much of that help was needed to keep the institutions going, like schools and hospitals and church organizations, all of which EMM had helped to begin.

I was interested in seeing how our sister mission board managed this issue, the General Mennonite Mission Board, located in Elkhart, Indiana. They were in overseas missions 30 years longer than we were. The churches they planted in India and Argentina at the beginning of the century matured into self-governing national churches, but they still needed help to maintain the educational, medical, and even some administrative institutions. It was quite normal, as missions got established, for the Board to provide such services. It was one hand of the "dual mandate" that carried both church planting and social services, while the other hand carried evangelism and church planting. The newly independent, rather small churches could not bear the weight of many of those institutions. It is no wonder that the General Mission Board felt compelled to help, and they did.

At about that time, critical voices were being raised in mainline denominations that equated denominational church planting with "colonialism," a bad word. That attitude seeped into some Mennonite thinking as well. I recall being scolded by a Mennonite mission administrator, "Don, why do you think you need to go all over the world planting the Mennonite flag everywhere?" I got the point, but should we have stopped planting churches because it smacked of Mennonite colonialism?

Because of this confluence of events, I think the General Mission Board turned from frontier church planting, their original purpose, to providing inter-church aid and to becoming salt and light in existing non-Mennonite churches. That meant helping other denominations to think again about Anabaptist theology. In my opinion, they found a way to continue to be a mission board but without the determination to multiply congregations of believers around the world.

I may have misread or misinterpreted what happened, but I was convinced that Eastern Mennonite Missions must not evolve into another inter-church aid society or take its eye off the task of making disciples in all nations.

This was about the time that The School of World Mission at Fuller Seminary was emphasizing evangelization and deliberate church planting, especially for what they called the "Unreached People Groups." The stance of The National Council of Churches and that of the Church Growth Movement of Fuller Seminary polarized the debate.

Things began to coalesce for me around three goals. First, promote church planting as the priority in missions. Second, release the new churches to proceed with church planting unencumbered by institutions that they should not need to carry. Third, stand with the growing churches as they establish institutions that they truly own. Little did I know that I would be called upon shortly to put these lofty ideals to the test.

DIRECTOR OF OVERSEAS MINISTRIES

After I served two years as a consultant, EMM approached me about serving as Director of Overseas Ministries on a half-time basis. MCLF reluctantly agreed to the new arrangement, realizing that I would need to give priority to administering the overseas ministries programs. So, from 1975 to 1980, my major energies were expended in reshaping or updating EMM's vision for overseas ministries.

Behind me, urging me forward, were marvelous people on the board and staff of EMM. Prominent among them were President Raymond Charles, my sterling brother-in-law, and the treasurer, Ira Buckwalter, a man of remarkable faith, a faith that challenged me again and again. He was something of a father to me. When I faltered, he lovingly pushed me forward. Norman Shenk, Ira's right-hand man at the time, was a gifted administrator with granite wisdom in financial matters. Jay Garber was the remarkably able chairperson of the board. With that kind of backing, I moved forward with the vision that God had given me.

I agreed to assume responsibility on the condition that Hershey Leaman, my friend and former colleague in Kenya, would leave there to help out. I was relieved when Hershey agreed. So, within a very short time, I was back in administration. It was not something that I desired, but I knew that I had to do it. Fortunately, Helen Rufenacht, whose administrative skills became evident in our Kenya office, also joined us in Salunga. She did her usual stellar work.

First, we examined each area in which our mission was involved. Our experience led us to believe that all of those churches wanted to grow and expand. We determined to sit with them to see how we could best work together to do that. If they were having problems with any of the institutions left over from the mission era, we offered to walk with them to restructure or shed that burden. One of the givens was that EMM would channel most of its assistance into the growth and development of the churches, especially into Christian nurture and leadership development.

I reviewed the programs in Europe, Central America, and the Pacific, while Hershey did the same for Africa. This represented a shift in EMM's overseas ministries strategy. EMM would carry some of the burden for the institutions created during this era, but on a reducing basis. At the same time, we tried to assure the churches that we were completely behind their efforts to strengthen their local congregations, church administration, leadership development, and ongoing church planting.

We believed that our central focus as a mission board was to plant, strengthen, and walk alongside churches as they spread the good news wherever they could. The concept behind it all was to shift more resources into church planting. I was convinced that, given time, the maturing churches would inevitably establish institutions that would meet their needs—institutions that were theirs to love and to pay for.

That is not to say that church planting and nurture would be our only involvement. We were also convinced that we should give a substantial portion of our budget to other ministries that were not intended to plant and grow churches. I thought that 20 percent was a proper portion for those activities. This strategy guided us through the reordering of priorities at the mission board.

I carried the conviction that the Scriptures taught that the church must multiply fellowships. My own experience underlined that. Projects and good works supplement the growth of the Christian community, but they are only signs of the grace of God at work in the fellowships, in the churches. Institutions come and go, but the church, as flawed and as weak as it often looks, has an amazing capacity to survive and prosper. For me, missions became a matter of introducing more and more people to Jesus and walking with them as they fulfilled their own callings. This was the rubric that Jesus announced, to go on making disciples of the nations.

I would like to think that by refocusing our attention on our primary task—church planting—the base was laid for new advances by all parties to extend the Kingdom of God around the world. It is the task of both older churches and younger churches to call out communities of faith in all cultures, who will then follow the leading of God to bless the world, beginning from where they are.

Chapter 26

SETTING THE COURSE FOR MCLF

1980 – 2002

From EMM to MCLF

During those five years of working half-time for EMM, I gave some attention to developing the Mennonite Christian Leadership Foundation. Paul Landis, who was employed half-time by MCLF, as was I, gave stellar leadership to developing MCLF ministries, focusing mainly on North America. We held many seminars and encouraged churches to create programs aimed at developing leaders. Paul Landis was especially gifted for that and enjoyed it.

It was then, in 1980, that Raymond Charles resigned as president of EMM in order to give more time to his bishop work. It seemed as though either Paul Landis or I would be called upon to fill the opening, even though it was not up to us to make that decision. Paul and I had a heart-to-heart talk about it. I had no vision at all for that role, primarily because I did not feel a call to continue to administer missions. I was called to help in the development of leaders internationally, and I wanted to minister interdenominationally. My calling was clearly to walk alongside the worldwide church as it developed its leaders.

Paul saw the presidency of EMM to be a challenge that he was prepared to take up, which left me free to jump into the development of MCLF. We agreed that, when possible, Paul would assist in MCLF ministries, something that he was open to doing. When we made our views known, both agencies decided that Paul should be president of EMM, full-time, and that I should be director of MCLF, full-time.

When it was decided that I should leave the Overseas Secretary post at EMM, the board asked Hershey Leaman to replace me. I was enthusiastic about their choice. He gave himself entirely to heading up the department and administered the program wisely. Through overseas travel he developed friendships with many church leaders and walked with them in such a way that their dreams could be fulfilled.

I enjoyed my five years as Overseas Secretary, but the time had come for me to trim down and commit myself to international leadership formation. EMM kindly provided office space for MCLF. Helen Rufenacht assumed the role of Administrative Assistant, for which she was well suited. It was a small staff, indeed, just she and I. We were made to feel a part of the EMM family and enjoyed interacting in many staff activities there. I took comfort in knowing that EMM was eager to see our ministry go forward.

MCLF BEGINNINGS

In 1945, several Mennonite businessmen, mostly in the Midwest, established the Mennonite Foundation to assist those who had been in Civilian Public Service to become established in business ventures. It worked. The Foundation grew by leaps and bounds, eventually concentrating on mutual insurance programs and on retirement policies. It was a superb concept.

Somewhere along the line, some Mennonites, primarily along the eastern coast of the United States, felt that the time had come to establish a similar foundation. Orie O. Miller and Paul Kraybill pursued the idea. In January 1969, they pulled together a group of businesspersons and church leaders at the Willow Valley Conference Center in Lancaster, and there they established the Mennonite Christian Leadership Foundation (MCLF). The name itself indicates that the eastern foundation was not to be a duplicate of the Indiana-based Mennonite Foundation, but would concentrate on developing Christian leaders. The group

MCLF Board and Staff in retreat at Camp Hebron, an annual feature

had no clear strategy about how to do that, but they set their sails in that direction.

When Miller and Kraybill shared their vision with Lewis Strite, President of Shenandoah Equipment of Harrisonburg, Virginia, he needed no convincing. He threw his weight behind the vision and was elected President of MCLF. Later on, Lewis figured prominently in my life because he was not only president, but a worker in MCLF until he retired. What a man! I might add that Richard Detweiler, my lifelong friend, became Vice-Chairman; Elvin Byler, the Secretary; and Dale High, Treasurer.

GAINING A VISION

Orie O. Miller believed that MCLF should establish a missionary training institute in New York City in conjunction with the New York Theological Seminary, on whose board he served. So Dale Stoltzfus, a church planter in the city, was employed part-time to bring it to fruition. He tried his best, but it never got off the ground. MCLF then financed some small projects for five years, until 1973 when I took up residency in the US. I knew that my future lay, in some way, in the hands of MCLF.

MCLF, A NEW CONCEPT — WILL IT FIT?

As MCLF gained momentum, two questions had to be answered. First, by what church authority did MCLF operate, and second, would MCLF compete with EMM for funding?

When it came to accountability, MCLF was set up so that it reported to no one except itself. Furthermore, MCLF had full control over the appointment of its own board of directors. Some of my friends who worked in official Mennonite agencies chided us for not submitting to the authority structures of the Mennonite Church in North America. This remained a bone in the throats of some who felt that we were setting a bad example. All we could promise was that all members of the board would be active members of their congregations, and that their beliefs would be in line with the vision of MCLF. Since we knew that our ministry would serve many denominations, we decided to be autonomous yet cooperative.

FINANCING MCLF

The second issue had to do with funding. EMM had ample reason to question MCLF on this point. There was some fear that MCLF would become a quasi-mission board which might siphon off funds that would have gone to EMM. The MCLF and EMM executive committees met on occasion to discuss this issue openly. MCLF assured EMM that it would not become a missionary sending agency and that it would not solicit funding from those sources of funding that had made EMM a success.

As far as I know, MCLF remained true to that commitment. That enabled it to grow up alongside EMM as a supporting agency, not as a competing one. MCLF deliberately kept its budget quite low, thus not alarming its sister agencies.

THE MCLF VISION

The vision and mission of MCLF got sharpened as the ministry went forward. Its purpose was clear: to conduct training seminars for leaders, to get behind laudable leadership development programs and visions in churches, and to promote their growth and welfare. One example, among many, of the latter was our involvement in helping to shape a seminary without walls in Central America. James Sauder, an EMM missionary, and then Amsey Yoder, also an EMM missionary, together with local Central American staffpersons, proposed a prototype that they called *Semilla* (Spanish for "seed"). MCLF walked alongside the planners and provided some start-up funds to shape it. The program flourished and continues today.

MODE OF OPERATION

We also decided to focus our attention on newer churches overseas, rather than in North America where leadership development programs abounded. We would deal with leadership issues facing indigenous churches that were moving from the status of mission churches to full churches in their own right, doing things that vital churches need to do. Since these new churches were growing at an amazing rate, the Western pattern of Bible schools, seminaries, and the like could not possibly produce the hundreds of leaders that the churches needed right away. I recall describing the problem as moving from the Western way of preparing leaders like you fry fish— slowly on one side, then the other, then back again, and so forth until the fish is indeed fried. I suggested that we think of leadership training for the many like cooking in a microwave—maybe not cooking thoroughly through and through, but getting it hot!

But, how? We decided against promoting a single program to fit all situations. Instead, with some generally agreed upon theological beliefs, we decided that we would sit with the local churches to try to help them envision their own training efforts. MCLF was unique in the Mennonite church in its twofold mission: to develop effective leaders with a vision, on the one hand, and to offer some tools to meet the challenges of planting local churches that grow and prosper, on the other.

We also decided to keep overhead low and to maintain a nearly invisible presence. Instead of maintaining a large staff, we brought in board members and others to help as needed. For example, Paul Landis, with whom we had a good working relationship, participated in many training events with the blessing of EMM. I think also of John Martin, a teacher at Eastern Mennonite Seminary, who taught widely in Africa. Richard and Mary Jane Detweiler and Myron and Esther Augsburger ministered across Africa. Vivid in my memory was the trip businessman Dale High and I took around the world in three weeks, teaching in many cultures. We both came down with a retching intestinal flu in Bangladesh. We missed not a session of teaching, between intestinal volcanic eruptions!

Our ministries with Lewis and Ethel Strite took us to South Africa, Nigeria, Australia, New Zealand, and beyond. Ike Risser and I ministered in Haiti many times. Ivan Martin had a soft spot in his heart for Australia. Board Members Leon and Karen Moyer, along with Melvin and Elfrieda Loewen, found themselves teaching in East Africa and Congo. Ervin and Bonnie Stutzman, also on the board, taught in Indonesia and beyond. I could go on and on. By incorporating such magnificent resource persons, along with those unnamed, we managed to touch the lives of church leaders in a host of places.

Now and again we asked people to do specific assignments on a no-pay basis. Since we had no French-speaking people in our leadership circles, we asked Samuel Gerber, principal of the European Mennonite Bible School in Bienenberg, Switzerland, to help out. The fit was perfect. He and his wife, Irma, agreed to travel to the Congo several times to do extended leadership training, a ministry that was greatly appreciated.

It is impossible to compress what happened in 20 years into a few paragraphs. Suffice it to say that I believe we taught roughly one-fourth of the Mennonite church leaders in what we then called the Third World, plus many others. How many nations? God kept track—but at least 50. How many miles did I travel? Maybe eight times the distance to the moon.

It was a kaleidoscope of cultures, each requiring special sensitivity. For instance, in India the group we taught put on a street drama portraying the Prodigal Son, all reflecting life in India. Crowds cheered as the son returned. I was puzzled as the father wanted a sheep killed for the feast. I elbowed the man beside me. "A sheep? It should have been a calf!" He replied, "Hindus do not slaughter cows of any age." I was sheepishly hushed. The drama continued with telling results.

I was taken aback in Bali, Indonesia, when I heard, "The Lord is my duckherdsman." Really? They actually herded ducks there, huge flocks of them, a big business. Time after time, I was reminded of the power and usefulness of culture.

A ministry of leadership encouragement and training like that does marvels for the spirit. Many times I went away from training experiences deeply humbled by the zeal and the selflessness of this generation of leaders. Truly, the future looks bright, because this generation of leaders is determined to make Christ known throughout the world. As a rule, local leaders teamed with those sent by MCLF to keep the ministry rooted in the local context and to provide wholeness to the training experience.

Our intention was to train the trainers. In no way could we hope to do much more than that. Since calls came in from all over the world, we were kept nicely busy.

MCLF Board of Directors

I might add that the board consisted of 16 members, usually about 12 business-owner couples, plus four couples employed in church ministries. This combination of business-acumen and gifted-ministry people produced some interesting moments! At times we visionaries needed

Lewis Strite and Marlin Thomas served marvelously in MCLF and Global Disciples ministries.

to be pulled down a bit by our coattails by the sound financial wisdom that one gets in business. The blend worked. It produced a ministry that impacted hundreds of leaders around the world. This board directed the activities of MCLF and made sure that the money was there to pay the bills.

Our full board met twice a year, one of which was a weekend fellowship. Strong bonding occurred in those settings. Spouses participated fully in both the business meetings and the fellowship and fun times. I praise God for that group of extraordinary people. I could not have done what I did without them.

MCLF maintained a budget of about $100,000 per annum throughout the years. This covered all expenses. As noted, we were able to do what we did because of the generosity of friends and board members who gave freely of their time and gifting. No year ended in the red for MCLF. Not only that, but, as we ministered, our corpus grew to almost a million dollars, due largely to the grants of stock in Herr Foods, contributed by Jim and Mim Herr. Jim served for many years as the Treasurer of MCLF. He could make things happen!

I was parsimonious when it came to spending money, too tight for some people. Maybe I was a missionary too long! An example: I could see the end of my tenure with MCLF and wanted to make sure that the team that followed me would have enough money to carry on the work. So I sat tight on the egg as it grew, not allowing it to hatch. I assumed, of course, that MCLF would continue after I was gone, with a paid staff, and that they would be happy for some butter to fry the pancakes. As I look back, I think I should have been a bit more intentional about expanding the program in my last decade with MCLF. The Lord knows. In any case, the board was over-generous on every account. Finances were never a big problem for the board.

ME, AN AMERICAN BISHOP?

While I was fully engaged in international leadership development, Raymond Charles was diagnosed with cancer. The doctors encouraged him to move quickly to seek a successor as bishop of the Landisville Mennonite District. Raymond asked if I would be a candidate. I dreaded the thought, but how could I ever say no to Raymond? So votes were taken and, after discernment by the ordained

persons in the District, it came down to either Ervin
Stutzman, then the pastor of the Mount Joy church, or
me. A meeting was called to move the process forward.
The question was raised as to "calling." Ervin admitted
that he had felt a call to that kind of church leadership.
My joy was unbounded. I had no call for that whatsoever,
but was there because of my respect for Raymond. That
was one of the happier days of my life.

Chapter 27

GLOBAL DISCIPLES

1996 – 2011

WORKING WITH GALEN BURKHOLDER

"God is calling me to pursue a vision he has laid on my heart for an international training cooperative." When Galen Burkholder shared that with me, I knew that he was captured by a vision, nebulous but profound. For 12 years he and his wife, Marie, developed the Youth Evangelism Service program, YES, within EMM, patterned after Youth with a Mission (YWAM). Philadelphia was their base, but the world was their stage. Galen made sure that YES teams included young people from around the world, and he planned outreach ministries in many countries. His international vision grew.

He was directly responsible to EMM but pulled together an advisory board to walk with him. I was pleased to be in that group. Interacting with him, I saw the fire that burned in his soul to follow Christ and to impact the world. I was not startled, therefore, when he told me of his new vision. So, the vision he had; the means to pursue it he had not.

As a member of his advisory group, I suggested that he apply to MCLF, my employer, for start-up funds. He had

Galen Burkholder, founder of Global Disciples

nothing, not even a salary for himself. Galen jumped at that and soon presented me with a request for $50,000 to launch his new vision. That was Galen! I squirmed. "When?" I asked. "Half this year and half next," he replied. I said I could not promise anything, of course, but that I would suggest MCLF give $5,000. Never had MCLF given more than that for a project of any kind beyond itself.

When I presented this request a few days later, I expected a protracted discussion with the usual penetrating questions. That was not to be. Chairman Lewis Strite listened politely, then asked, "How much does he need?" I relayed Galen's request for a jaw-dropping $50,000. I timidly urged that they give five.

I was not prepared for what followed because it was completely out of character for our board to give to something like this. Treasurer Jim Herr said, "If he needs $50,000, let's give it to him. I believe God wants us to do that." Heads nodded. Done! "Twenty this year, 30 the next." That day a vision met a sponsor, and what was to be known as Global Disciples Network was on the way. Galen had a new partner, MCLF.

EARLY VISIONS FOR YOUTH SERVICE PROGRAM

As Director of Overseas Ministries at EMM, I saw the potential for developing a program for young adults that included a solid training emphasis, coupled with team ministries on location all over the world. I felt so deeply about this that I worked it into my schedule to spend a few days at the sprawling YWAM base on Kona, Hawaii, when Loren Cunningham, the director, would be there. It was not a new idea to him to have a denomination adopt a facsimile of YWAM as its own program; he had hoped that might happen. So he blessed the idea and prayed for me.

When I presented the concept to EMM, it did not get a warm reception. The Voluntary Service (VS) program was still in place, and this new concept seemed to threaten the future of VS. Next, I spoke of the dream at a meeting of the Mennonite Council of Overseas Ministries. It received a mixed reception at best. I was convinced that the idea was sound so concluded, sadly, that I was a weak presenter! One response startled me, "Don, that's just another glamorous travel experience for affluent American kids. We have enough of that already." So I drew in my horns, convinced myself that it was not for me to pursue it further, and just left it there.

After three or so years, others such as Nathan Showalter, Galen Burkholder, and Jeryl Hollinger caught the vision, and then things began to happen. I learned through that whole experience that a vision remains a vision no matter what, but its implementation must wait until the Lord's appointed moment.

As for Galen and Marie, they served as the youth pastoral team at Hesston Mennonite Church on the Hesston College campus, and then went on to study at Eastern Mennonite Seminary. Following that, they moved to Lancaster where Galen served as Director of Youth and Young Adult programs under Lancaster Mennonite Conference. It was then that EMM invited him to develop YES (Youth Evangelism Service), which was patterned similarly to YWAM. Hurrah for Galen, I thought. Dreams do come true, in God's time and in his way.

The Burkholders felt the call to move from Lancaster to develop the Philadelphia YES Center. As already noted, Galen invited me to serve on his unofficial advisory committee. So I walked with him for 12 years as he sent teams to many parts of the world. That took him into many international settings where he spoke with church leaders. Through that, a vision for an international ministry began to form in his heart, ever so slowly.

It did not surprise me terribly much that God was leading him into such a ministry. What did surprise me was his determination to get moving! That is when he approached MCLF for funds to inaugurate his ministry vision. Assured of initial finances, he gathered a staff around him. They formulated a plan in which his new ministry, Global Disciples, would pursue realistic ways to train the next generation of young adults, similar to YES, through self-sustaining programs, supported by local churches around the world.

This pleased his friends at MCLF, and so a relationship developed in which Galen reported regularly to MCLF about what was happening. Galen made valuable contributions to MCLF as well.

MCLF AND GLOBAL DISCIPLES
FORM ONE MINISTRY

In time we began to consider merging MCLF with Global Disciples. The two boards concluded that there should be a single board, and that the ministry would be called Global Disciples. Remarkably, it happened, and Marlin Thomas agreed to serve as president of the new entity. All the board members agreed to stay on for at least a year to assure full support for Global Disciples.

I agreed to become a board member in the new structure. I was pleased that the MCLF Board had the humility and courage to, in a sense, lose its identity, hoping that the leadership training ministry that was the backbone of MCLF ministries would find a place in the Global Disciples programs. MCLF believed that, as a grain of corn, it must fall into the ground and die, for then it would have a chance to come back to life in a new form to produce even more fruit. I was consoled by this thought as I prayed and worked for the development of Global Disciples.

I served on that board, then, for 15 years. When I retired, finally, from the board at age 82, there was not a happier man on the face of the earth. I could not have possibly planned a better way to move the ministry forward that had consumed me for over 30 years. This was obviously God's plan.

A PATTERN BECOMES OBVIOUS

I began to see a pattern in my life. It was shaped, I suppose, by being a missionary. As I look back, I see that as soon as I picked up a new responsibility I knew that, in time, I must relinquish it. Effective missionaries do not cling to a role as theirs, but seek to pass the baton to others when it is possible to do so. I was not only a missionary but a teacher. A teacher's greatest delight is to see a student surpassing even the teacher. I think I can honestly say that one of the great delights of my life has been seeing others pick up something from me, or from someone else, and then run with it. Therefore, I tried to hold lightly what I had in my hands, knowing full well that I must pass it on. To do so with joy and grace is a marvelous gift of God.

Chapter 28

MENNONITE CHURCH — AT HOME AND ABROAD

RESTRUCTURING THE NORTH AMERICAN MENNONITE CHURCH

Paul Kraybill was my close friend for many years. He watched me from afar as I found my place in East Africa. He must have seen things that I did not, so he kept pushing me beyond where I felt I should go. He had much more faith in me than I had in myself. I tried, mostly unsuccessfully, to live up to his expectations. That contributed to my growth and my humility.

Paul and I could not have been much more different. For example, I do not think he ever misplaced anything. I lost stuff. While traveling in Europe one time with him, I misplaced my passport twice. He said, "I am going to put your passport on a chain and hang it around your neck." I needed that! Even though organized to the hilt, he made allowance for slovens like me. Paul paced himself. I was erratic. How we ever worked together with such sizzle and charm is a miracle. In so doing, he did give me the courage to be me. Few people in my life shaped me like Paul Kraybill.

I dreaded to think that, just when I was getting involved in EMM at Salunga, he was leaving. The Mennonite Church of North America asked him to move to Chicago. There he would work on developing a consensus about how to restructure the Mennonite Church that had grown up as a patchwork of conferences and regions.

He, together with the boards that surrounded him, decided to disband the historical conferences that had grown naturally through the years, and to bring all congregations into a new configuration of five geographical regions. For the first time in my life I wondered why he was doing something. I could not speak to him officially, but as friend to friend. "Paul, the conferences are built on relationships that have developed through the years. They work! I wonder if the five-region, cookie-cutter approach will do the trick." I discovered at that point that I thought relationally; Paul thought strategically. I concluded, that is no problem, we can complement one another.

We genuinely enjoyed each other. Paul surprised me when he urged me to sit on the newly formed denominational Commission of Faith and Life. I jumped into that with both feet. This brought me into contact with Lawrence Burkholder, President of Goshen College. I found in him a kindred spirit. I enjoyed exchanging views with all the commission members, but Lawrence stood out.

In our commission, we felt obliged to speak to several overarching issues. Among them was how to allocate funding, assuming that the denomination would adopt a unified budget. The bone of contention was that the institutional staff, like those at the publishing house, colleges, and seminaries, felt that too much money was going into missions. They believed some of that money should go to education and literature, which should also be understood as mission. (Even Lawrence was slightly tainted by that heresy!) It all sounded very sensible, but I could see in that approach a demise of mission. Interest in overseas missions and church planting was already under attack by many as Mennonite colonialism. I was distressed as I saw mission interest waning.

As I served on that Commission I became aware of how parochial I had become. I had given my life to missions, so everything revolved around that. Serving on that body forced me to view the denomination as a whole. I tried my best to do so, but always came back to what I considered the bottom line, extending the Kingdom of God by going into the entire world with the gospel of Jesus Christ.

Parenthetically, as to the overall reorganization of the denomination into five regions, only the eastern region did well, and it eventually collapsed, too. And there was no unified budget. Good try, Paul.

KRAYBILL SHOULDERS MENNONITE WORLD CONFERENCE

Having done his best to reorganize the Mennonite Church of North America, with mixed results, Paul accepted the invitation to resuscitate and restructure Mennonite World Conference (MWC) which had first met in Basel, Switzerland, in 1925. It began as a meeting of white Mennonites, representing Europe and North America.

Mennonite demography had changed dramatically since then. It was time to reformulate Mennonite World Conference to reflect the fact that the Mennonite Church is a truly multiethnic body, stretching around the world.

Because of his prior work as the executive secretary of EMM, Paul was a good choice for moving MWC into this new mode. He had a feel for the needs of the international church, even though he and his wife, Jean, never served as overseas missionaries. I was one of his sounding boards as he suggested some new, risky ideas. I enjoyed dreaming with him about a true round table around which all Anabaptist-oriented churches could sit, each with a special place. This uniting vision was to me, a large part of my "Anabaptist Vision." I felt the time had come to emphasize the expansion of the body of Christ in the world as the chief joy and duty of the church. I suppose I felt that way because it did, after all, represent my life's calling.

Paul and Jean Kraybill. Paul had a huge influence on me for some years.

MWC GATHERINGS

I participated in the MWC assemblies in Amsterdam in 1967; in Wichita, Kansas, in 1978; in Strasbourg, France, in 1984; in Calcutta, India, in 1997; and in Bulawayo, Zimbabwe, in 2003. I tried to comprehend what happened to the worldwide Mennonite family between 1967 and 2003, a period of 36 years. I recalled that the Amsterdam

Conference of 1967 was marked by racial problems in America. It seemed to me that the internationals were observers only. Good things happened there, no doubt, but it failed to embrace the entire Anabaptist family. When I contrast that Amsterdam Conference in 1967 to Zimbabwe in 2003, I am utterly amazed. During those three decades the number of Mennonites in Africa, Asia, and Latin America shot ahead of the number of those in Europe and North America.

Before I describe my feelings about Zimbabwe in 2003, my mind goes back to 1978 when Mennonite World Conference convened in Wichita, Kansas. Paul Kraybill asked me to prepare to preach on the closing Sunday night service, wrapping up the major concerns, issues, hopes, and commitments of the week, with a challenge to move courageously into the future. So all week I had my ear to the rail, making notes and processing what was happening. I was working on my presentation late Saturday night when I learned that the guest speaker for Sunday morning,

Mennonite World Conference in Calcutta, India, 1997

Bishop Festo Kivengere of Uganda, was delayed in Jamaica where he had been ministering. I got a call from Paul Kraybill, "Don, you are on for Sunday morning. Forget about that summary. Just preach!" I sent one of those arrow prayers to Jesus. Help! My mind had been set on summarizing the week, not preaching!

Jesus is supremely dependable. He opened my mind to the story of the cave of Adullam, when all kinds of needy people left where they were and joined God's anointed King David to form a new fellowship of grace because everyone needed it. Hopeless, they needed to be with their new captain, the anointed son of Jesse who was full of hope. They had no vision for their lives. They needed a leader with a godly vision. They had no purpose in life. They needed a king who exemplified purpose. We need to make Jesus our captain, just as they rallied behind young David.

Such thoughts ran through my head and heart. I wanted to underline that we had come together at Wichita, not strong but weak, not satisfied with the way things are, but hopeful in what we would be as Jesus forged us into a company of disciples.

When I stood before 14,000 Mennonites from around the world in that stadium in Wichita, Kansas, I sensed that I was privileged to live in a Kairos moment when the dream was coming true. The Mennonite Church, though halting, had been faithful in following Jesus' great commission to make disciples from every nation. It was one of the most exhilarating moments in my life, the peak of a mountain that allowed me to look backwards and forwards, but mostly up!

I knew that I was exactly where the Lord, my creator, redeemer, and friend, wanted me to be, shaped by the past, envisioning the future, enveloped by the Spirit of God, and bursting with joy among a community of people who desperately desired to follow the Lamb wherever he led. I knew in my soul that was the real me.

That may have been the peak of my experience in Mennonite circles up to that time, because I saw myself there as a link between the past and the future, between evangelism and doing good deeds, between "old" Mennonites and the burgeoning "new" Mennonites of all tribes and cultures around the world, sharing a burning compassion to bring Christ to the nations. I felt that, had I been swooped off to glory that morning, I would have lived an entire life and a complete vision.

When the Zimbabwe Assembly met in 2003, I was 75 years old. That gathering was breathtakingly multicultural. Could these Mennonites become something of a family within the great Christian family around the world? I became hopeful.

Something happened there that stirred my deepest emotions. A song rose from the people that was not on the prepared song sheets at all. I do not know how it happened, but a simple song, arising from the heart of the African churches, found its way onto the platform and into our consciousness. Its echoes rose above all differences. The lyrics went something like this, "There is no one like Jesus." It was as simple as an African breeze but as profound as life itself. For some reason it touched me deeply. I could barely sing, I was so humbled and inspired. That song said it all. "We looked everywhere but found no one like Jesus. Everywhere! We concluded, there is no one like Jesus!" (A loose translation.) "Jesus binds us together. Jesus is our Brother. He is our Savior and Lord. We found him! Let's celebrate." My eyes misted over. This is what I lived for. Now I was seeing it with my own eyes.

Bulawayo was, to me, a fitting climax to my own 50-year involvement in the planting, growth, and nurture of newer churches around the world and as a trainer of leaders. All this happened in my lifetime. How could I keep from singing? Truly, "There is no one like Jesus."

DIVISION AMONG NORTH
AMERICAN MENNONITES

I was not surprised when I heard that the Mennonites in Canada intended to form themselves into a national denomination. That seemed like the next step in redrawing the Mennonite map in North America. For some it was a happy moment; for others it was tinged with sadness and some legitimate fear. Some Mennonite groups in Canada simply did not go along, but the great majority did, blending many traditions into one denomination, the Mennonite Church of Canada, in 2000. Somehow we got through that one. But that was not the end of the story.

Next came the desire to do something similar in the United States where there were many, many more diverse Mennonite groups than in Canada. At the turn of the 21st century, many Mennonite groups faced the issue of joining the new Mennonite Church USA, or standing outside.

This presented a huge challenge in some areas, such as in eastern Pennsylvania. I saw four distinct streams flowing in Lancaster Conference. There was the traditional one that wished to maintain behavior boundaries in the areas of dress, lifestyle, church structure, and piety. This group leaned toward limiting communion only to those who were in agreement with their particular rules and regulations.

A second was represented by the majority who felt comfortable with a denomination that was becoming more accommodating to American society but who honored and even revered the historical and cultural life of Mennonites through the years. They invited other believers to their communion table.

A third stream included those who were renewed and revived through the Holy Spirit (charismatic) movement. Some congregations leaned heavily in that direction and fashioned their leadership styles around the apostolic mode common in those circles.

A fourth group, feeling that the Mennonite denomination was losing its evangelical underpinning and playing loose with biblical texts, insisted on a more literal interpretation of the Scriptures.

It is not my intention here to express my own preferences but to note that these four streams had been running through Lancaster Conference for almost 20 years without serious schism. By the grace of God, they remained together. All that was threatened, however, when the time came for Lancaster Conference, the largest of all the Mennonite conferences in North America, to decide whether to join the new Mennonite Church USA, or not. By a slim majority the Conference decided to join.

Those days jarred me. I saw old friendships strained, families torn apart, old partnerships fail. I knew in my heart that the pressure that would be put on the conferences and congregations would simply widen gaps that were already there and would actually lead to greater division. I did not hold any office in Lancaster Conference, but when the schism clouds gathered, the Conference Moderator, Keith Weaver, asked me to address the assembly, appealing for unity. I was only one of the voices that urged all to go slowly and to try to move forward without spinning off yet more Anabaptist splinter groups. There were enough already!

That appeal was too little too late. Many of the charismatic churches in the Conference split off, others who called themselves Evangelicals split, and yet others abandoned the Conference because they thought it was too weak to stand up against most anything. In the first few years of the 21st century, Lancaster Conference lost up to

20% of its churches. In the process, the pressure produced a few more mini-denominations. I might add that in the years that followed, some of that loss was made up by including 20 or so "minority" churches—Spanish, Ethiopian, Tai, African Americans, and so on. The color of Lancaster Conference is changing in the process.

As a Mennonite—So Far, So Good

I believe that when my two oldest brothers decided to be baptized as Mennonites, even though for them Lutheranism was an attractive option, they did the right thing. For at least that brought our family into the Mennonite church. That set the stage for my own involvement in the denomination. And that put me into things at the right time at the right place, as I see it, so good things could happen in my life.

Had Willard and Gerald, my oldest brothers, become Lutherans, the Lord would have had an equally good but alternate plan for my life! However, I am grateful to be a Mennonite because of the enduring witness of the denomination through its emphases on community and missions. I am a Mennonite still. I suppose others will need to tell me what kind of Mennonite I am. It seems there are many kinds these days. That is probably good.

Being Mennonite is not a peripheral factor in my self-awareness. If not at the very core of my self-understanding, it is very near it. Through the years I have blown hot and cold on the issue, but I never had the desire to hide my Mennonite identity. The church gave me a sense of belonging and purpose through the years. God used denominational affiliations in my life to bolster my view of the church and the world. For me, that was grace. I viewed the Mennonite church as a member of the great body of believers, bringing its learnings and its hopes to build up the entire body. It is one among many.

Reckoning with a Multicultural Mennonite Church

When I found myself in the forefront of the postwar expansion of the Mennonites in the 1950s, global North Mennonites outnumbered global South ones by a ratio of about 95:5. The ratio is now about 40:60, with the global South membership gaining ground convincingly every decade. Roughly one-fourth of those in the Mennonite World Conference are African.

Some are asking, quite legitimately, "What binds us together as a multicultural family?" As we think about that we need to factor in that up until 1900, that is 375 years after we began, we had a cultural identity. We were a German subculture. That shaped our identity.

Now what? Our denomination, because of mission, embraces people of dozens of cultures and languages so we cannot be identified by a common culture. If that is the case, then what does hold us together as a denomination?

My mind goes back to when I was involved in helping to plant Mennonite churches in Tanzania. We, that is the missionaries and local believers, gave little thought to the state of the broader Mennonite church in the world. We concentrated our attention on establishing fellowships of believers within Africa. In the back of my mind, I had no doubt that Tanzanian believers would some day, in some way, want to relate to the worldwide Mennonite family, but not because these newcomers to the table saw themselves as products of 16th-century radical reformation.

Instead, just like everyone is part of a family, so every church that comes into being through the efforts of Mennonites belongs to the Mennonite family. The larger question of denominational identity must surely follow. That is now happening.

An African Vision

In his autobiography, *Kisare wa Kiseru*, Bishop Kisare envisioned the church as a cluster of villages made up of many different kinds of people, but all within one encompassing large village. The head of the village is Jesus. Kisare carried this vision throughout his life. He knew it could happen, because he saw Jesus breaking down walls between repentant missionaries and repentant local believers and between Africans of different tribes. The winds of revival brought the idea of a large village to reality as the Holy Spirit did remarkable things in reconciling that which seemed irreconcilable.

For some, like Kisare, we are a village. For some we are a body, with each member contributing to the whole. For some we are a family enjoying life together as we love one another and experience give-and-take while sharing the same table. For some it is a tree with 16th-century Anabaptism as the trunk, with all sorts of branches reaching out. For others the heavenly scene says it all, each nation, each culture, kneeling before the Lamb of God, humbly removing their crowns and placing them before the feet of him who is the King of Kings and Lord of Lords, forever and ever.

Most will be content with imagery such as this. Others will press for a cluster of common beliefs. This is an exciting moment because from fluidity, energies are released for the building of the Kingdom of our Lord.

Chapter 29

PAIN FOR THE CHURCH IN TANZANIA

1980

Bishop Sarya's Ordination and Its Aftermath

Few things have caused me as much personal pain as seeing schisms occur within the body of Christ. How could it be that brothers and sisters who once lived in harmony and love, turn their backs on one another and go their different ways as though it was the right and proper thing to do? I am not now referring to Mennonites in America, but, horrors, to the Mennonite Church in Tanzania, where I poured out my life. The schism bomb exploded there in the 1980s.

Let me explain. After we left Kenya, the Tanzania Mennonite Church determined to ordain a second bishop. I knew that this was not a pleasant prospect for Bishop

Kisare, but he told me that he felt pressure from within the church and from the Lancaster Mennonite Conference to do so. He guided the process as best he could. He was acutely aware of the sectional struggles that were going on inside the church all the time and felt that a one-bishop structure was best to keep the many groups in the church together.

By the grace of God, Bishop Kisare and the team around him managed to maintain peace and unity in the church for a dozen or more fruitful years. The ordination of a second bishop carried with it a disquieting risk. Nevertheless, the process went forward, and Hezekiah Sarya was chosen to be bishop. I knew Hezekiah very well as a student, and also as an aggressive church planter with boundless energy. He stood out among his peers. He was of Bantu origin. As noted earlier, Kisare had a Luo father and a Bantu mother.

Not long after Sarya was ordained bishop, his own people put heavy demands on him to make sure their voices were heard. He no doubt did so because his relationship with Bishop Kisare soured. When Sarya saw the Mission Board backing Kisare, he turned against them also.

Happier days! Bishops Kisare and Sarya and me.

Let me return to a tumultuous day in 1979 when preparations were made for Sarya's official ordination in Musoma, Tanzania. I saw in what happened then the early signs of schism. It was to be a day of celebration and hope for the future. The church invited me and a representative of Lancaster Conference, Bishop David Thomas, Moderator of Lancaster Conference, to attend. We flew to Tanzania, hoping to participate in a major advance in the Mennonite Church. Sarya was to fly in from Dar es Salaam for the occasion, well ahead of the time set for the ordination service.

The church was in a festive mood on that bright sunny Tanzanian morning. The church building was festooned with flowers and ribbons of all colors. Choirs sang like angels, one after the other. Still no plane. Time passed. It was decided to proceed with the formal service, assuming that Sarya would turn up any time. We were not far into the service when a whisper, then a louder voice, rustled through the congregation, "Sarya will not come." They were right. He did not appear.

So instead of ordaining a bishop, they asked me to preach a sermon! Somehow the Lord gave me a word for the occasion, Revelation 5, and then it was all over. Bishop Thomas, Bishop Kisare, and I made the best of it and left without knowing what was happening.

Word came through later in the day that Sarya apologized for not showing up for the installation because of sickness in his family, and he was not sure that the flight was going to be safe. I may be wrong, but I believe that was the way Sarya rebuffed Bishop Kisare and Lancaster Mennonite Conference, the two obstacles that stood in his way of leading the Bantu charge in the church. In due course he was ordained, surrounded by his people. There ensued many dreadful years of disunity in the Tanzania

Mennonite Church. Even the Tanzania police had to step in at times.

Painful Days of Schism

How did this affect me? I was devastated. First, my pride was wounded. I loved that church. I held it in high regard. In the past, when people asked about how things were going in the church that "I had a part in," I could scarcely hide my pride just thinking about it. All that came crashing down around my head. I wanted to disown Bishop Sarya and all that he was up to. I wanted to wash my hands of the whole sad affair.

I was an easy target for Satan to send his barbs: "How much of what happened was your fault?" I should have reminded old Screwtape that I left that church almost 15 years ago. He kept taunting, "You loved it when it was doing well and disowned it when it was in trouble." I could scarcely believe that people like me could have such thoughts.

I have always hated rejection. I developed the art of detecting the slightest sign that I might be a target for rejection. With regard to Sarya, I needed no subtle sign. While I dread feelings of rejection, they invariably take me to the cross of Christ where he was rejected. There I find cleansing and healing. So it was in the Sarya matter. Having been set free, I wrote him a letter expressing my desire to see him in Dar es Salaam. His reply was cold as an igloo: "You are not welcome in my Diocese." Once again, I was crushed. So I had to get back into my prayer closet and forgive again and again.

Candidly, this was one of the most difficult periods in my career. The fact that my heart was still in the church made the pain of these wounds plague my spirit. I suppose I could have said like Peter, "I never knew him!" and walked away. But I could not do that. Never.

The bright spot, however, was that Bishop Kisare and I were still bound together by cords of love. I hasten to say that even that love got strained somewhat when I challenged him to take the initiative in reaching out to Sarya, although it was crystal clear that Sarya was not interested in anything that Kisare might say or do. As I walked in Kisare's shoes for a while on this, I could see that he was suffering 10 times more than I was, so I backed off and just prayed and did some spiritual groaning.

This affair brought me to a place of helplessness. I had fixed many things in my life. I prided myself on being a good fixer. But this! This I could not fix! I was so weak that I wanted to forget all about it and dwell on other things. But the Lord would not allow me to do that either. So for months, years, in fact, having repented of personal pride, I carried in my person the suffering of disappointment, buoyed only by the realization that Jesus bears the cross with me.

Eventually Bishop Sarya died. Most of his followers found reconciliation and returned to the original church. A small group who called themselves the Tanzania Evangelical Mennonite Church gathered a few of the congregations and registered themselves as a separate denomination. I was greatly distressed by the schisms in the church.

Another Blow, a Second Schism

Since I am dealing with the pain of schism, I will add here that another hurtful split occurred several years later, in about 2002. The Tanzania Mennonite Church ordained two additional bishops, Christopher Ndege and Joseph Nyakyema. Fine, until Bishop Ndege led yet another schism out of the church. I thought, "What is going on here?" Like the former split, this one had tribal overtones as well. I was dismayed, of course, but not as crushed as I was when Bishop Sarya led the first revolt 20 years earlier.

The Bishop Christopher Ndege split lasted about five years. He then repented, and, in a blessed season of reconciliation, the rift was healed. As I write this, I am pleased to note that the church is enjoying a period of peace, aided by its bishops, John Nyagwegwe, Joseph Nyakyema, Christopher Ndege, Stephen Mang'ana, Jackson Magangira, Amos Muhangira, and Joseph Osiero.

I am convinced that the Holy Spirit has not abandoned that church, or any church that holds on to the practice of living and teaching the gospel. It occurred to me that as long as the Holy Spirit is there, I should not give up on it. I can no more disown a church than the Holy Spirit can.

When I despaired, the Spirit of the Lord never gave up; he continued to pull people toward peace. As my dear friend Lewis Strite said often, "Do not forget, Don. Jesus said, 'I will build my church. It is his.'" I needed to be reminded of this fact a thousand times as I watched the Tanzania Mennonite Church grow and prosper, split and heal, preach and pray. The miracle is that in the midst of ethnic demands and hosts of internal tensions, the church survived. It is still there and growing rapidly! As I write, I am told that there are now 72,000 baptized members in that church! This is a miracle. In 1934, that number was zero. Today about five percent of the entire Mennonite family are Tanzanians. Humbling, indeed.

Chapter 30

PROMOTING REVIVAL

NEED FOR RENEWAL

I asked myself again and again, "How is an old movement, such as the Anabaptist movement, now almost 500 years old, to experience ongoing renewal? Can spiritual renewal be generated from within itself, or must it come as a wind from outside?" I am not sure that my observation is correct, but I am coming to believe that restoration movements, such as the Recovery of the Anabaptist Vision movement, have a basic problem to overcome. I believe we tend to look through our own cultural lenses as we examine our spiritual roots, our Golden Age. We see only what we want to see. It seems inevitable that recovery movements pick and choose in light of their own immediate set of questions. Therefore, we recover only in part and often miss the very life-spring that shaped the movement in the first place.

For example, while living with African Mennonite churches I reread early Anabaptist writings often. From that perspective I found how their central message of conversion, baptism, and newness of life in Christ reflected precisely what happened to us there in Tanzania. We cherished that commonality. So far, so good. Then I turned to the highly regarded Anabaptist Vision, written by Harold Bender in 1942, when Europe was being torn apart by a dreadful war. Bender's essay addressed the issues of the day, particularly, why were Christians rushing, en mass, into war? Bender did not set out to present an Anabaptist theology, otherwise he would have gone to the heart of the issue by emphasizing the Anabaptist insistence on conversion and renewal of life. I understood that, but I became more aware of the fact that theologies speak to questions that society is asking now.

I began to ask, "What benefits are there in a spiritual heritage?" No doubt many. However in my experience, heritage is a bit like a wax nose, it can be turned this way or that depending on our own whims. We usually find what we are looking for and simply ignore what we do not want to own. This is the peril in recovery movements.

As I surveyed the phenomenon of Christian renewal movements in older churches such as ours, I concluded that the most powerful movements originate somewhere else, not within the group itself.

I have also seen another quite startling phenomenon. If the new stirring of the Holy Spirit connects with some spiritual memory in a group or tradition, then the renewal has a definite chance of making a significant impact.

That was true of my own experience in the East Africa Revival. It emphasized the need to be radically changed by surrendering oneself to Christ and then living as Christ lived, as faithful disciples in communities of light, doing the works that Jesus did. That connected with my own Anabaptist roots, which held to the conviction that it is not only important to be forgiven by Christ, to be converted, but that discipleship also means following Christ day by day in self-giving service and witness, again in community. That theme of following Christ in community is a silver thread running through the life and ministry of the East Africa Revival as well. I have found these connections to be almost electric.

OUR HUNGER FOR FELLOWSHIP

One issue that became urgent for Anna Ruth and me when we moved to the United States was our ongoing need for spiritual fellowship. We had come to expect, because of the Holy Spirit's work in our lives in the past years, that we would have access to deep fellowship in Christ in America as we had in Africa. We remembered that in the '60s and '70s there had been live revival fellowship groups in eastern Pennsylvania, central Canada, and California, all inspired by and related to what was happening in East Africa and the revival fellowships in Europe and the UK. I recall vividly the life-changing fellowship meetings in the homes of Herbert and Erma Maust and Mary and Mervin Miller that we attended on furloughs past.

In the mid-70s, when we were getting settled in Lancaster, we found no such fellowships. Anna Ruth and I knew that we would not prosper spiritually without the input of fellowship. This does not discount our experience at Chestnut Hill. We always felt at home there, but we needed some heart to heart, constant, rugged fellowship with a few "on the way." In due course we asked Paul and Ann Landis, together with our missionary friends, Nathan and Arlene Hege, to join us in weekly meetings where we could be accountable to God and to one another. We enjoyed that group, with a few changes now and then, for almost 30 years, through thick and thin, as we say.

In the larger picture, we kept running across people who had been deeply touched, many in a life-changing way, by the testimony and message of a long string of speakers who lived in that revival, including Roy and Revel Hession, authors of *The Calvary Road* which summarized the heart of the revival; Methuselah Nyagwaswa of Tanzania, a student in the US for several years; Festo Kivengere of Uganda, among the most gifted communicators that I know; William Nagenda, also of Uganda, whose ministry penetrated deeply; Stanley Voke and David Wilson of the UK; and many others from abroad. Then there were many awakened voices in North America like Chuck Higgins, Bill Liner, Erma and Herbert Maust, Les Simons, Jim Perry, Bill Scott, Ron Lofthouse, plus many more. (Forgive me for not naming all the spouses.) The message was freeing and life-giving. Since the revival in East Africa thrived in fellowships of light, it was assumed that such fellowships would form everywhere. At first they did, but they subsequently sputtered out.

While this was happening, strong fellowship clusters developed in Switzerland, Germany, the UK, and France. The revival was taking on a decidedly international character, sometimes unaware of its roots in East Africa. Anna Ruth and I attended scores of such conferences through the years, often where I was asked to speak. I think particularly of the Les Diablerets setting in the Swiss Alps, the Southwold Conference on England's southern coast, the Rehe Conference in rural Germany, and the Scarborough Conference in England. Now and again we were invited back to East Africa for large, regional, revival fellowship meetings, such as the huge international conventions held every 10 years in Kabale, Uganda. I found that I needed to keep in touch with those people with whom I walked in the fellowship of Calvary through the years.

STAYING ALIVE SPIRITUALLY

A casual friend, a pastor, asked me one day as we played a round of golf together, "How do you stay alive spiritually?" He assumed that I was alive! After I teed off, sending my ball slicing to the right, as usual, and fussing about it, I addressed the question. I knew he wanted a serious answer. I strung my thoughts together as we covered the 18 holes. It went something like this: "I drank my first spiritual milk in my home, and then drank some good, nourishing Anabaptist milk as I grew. Then, in God's providence, I found myself drinking deeply with brothers and sisters in the East Africa Revival, meaningful draughts, because we saw Jesus in a fellowship of light. Walking with them brought me into a deeper understanding of the glory of Jesus in all his aspects, a freeing way to walk, in which I discovered who I truly am—Don Jacobs, saved mightily by the grace of Jesus Christ. Now and again, Brother, I am drawn back to East Africa for refreshment, and I also touch that level of spiritual unity when I am with any brothers and sisters everywhere in the whole world who are sustained by simple faith in the efficacy of Jesus Christ to do all that he said he would do." I heard myself verbalizing what I probably had never said before. And, of all places, on a golf course!

The Charismatic Renewal and East Africa Revival

When we reentered American church life, I was a bit confused. While we were on the other side of the planet, many nominal believers here found release and purpose through what was then called charismatic renewal. I knew the Holy Spirit. He was real to me; he enabled me to walk with Jesus. He was right there showing me Jesus day by day.

I distinctly recall being picked up at an airport in Florida to minister in some churches. That was soon after we returned from Africa. On the way the brother driving asked me, "Don, when did you receive the baptism of the Holy Spirit?" I did not know what he meant by that, but I gave my wee testimony of how the Holy Spirit brought me to Jesus and how I know him as my guide and as the one who reveals my sin to me so that I can run to Jesus for cleansing. I said that I have never felt bereft of the Holy Spirit since I was reborn from above. Sometimes I take my own way instead of his, that is for sure, probably more often than I am comfortable admitting. But the Holy Spirit has always been there. As long as Jesus is there, the Holy Spirit is as well.

Was I deficient when I could not testify to a specific "baptism of the Holy Spirit" in my life subsequent to conversion? I had often experienced, in prayer, the presence of the Holy Spirit praying with me, and I was not particularly surprised when I prayed beyond my knowing, because of the Holy Spirit. I knew that and was blessed by it. But I did not make that the center of my understanding of what it means to be remade by the work of Jesus on the cross. In fact, the revival brothers and sisters were so keen on keeping the cross of Christ central that anything that threatened to obscure the cross was seen as a potential rival for the centrality of Jesus himself, even good things like miraculous healing, which they were experiencing regularly in their fellowships, and other such signs.

The revival message that we came to know and embrace in Africa focused on Jesus, particularly the benefits of his death for us. The center of attention was always Jesus. When we saw yet another facet of the beauty of Jesus, we rejoiced. It all had to do with Jesus. No gift or experience or novel interpretation should diminish Jesus. I remember a brother in Uganda saying, "The role of the Holy Spirit is to take you by the collar and push you up against Jesus!" I think there is wisdom in that.

SPIRITUAL IDENTITY

I am trying to look at myself to figure out what my spiritual identity was through the years. I am discovering that every time I find myself bumping shoulders with people whose experiences are substantially different from mine, I am forced to reexamine my own spiritual identity; not my spiritual experiences, but my spiritual identity. This is especially true when it includes friends and people whom I deeply respect. I have been enriched and challenged by many movements within the body of Christ, and I thank God for that. But I also find that I always return to the foundation that was there when I first believed. When I move away from Jesus, the foundation rock, I invite peril. Instead of growing wider, I find myself desiring to grow deeper, deeper into the things I already know, or think I know. In a mysterious way, that enables me to grow wider.

Chapter 31

WORKING
WITH AFRICAN
ENTERPRISE

❖⋮⋮⋮

When Michael Cassidy of South Africa was studying
at Fuller Seminary in California, Charles Fuller took a
personal interest in Michael and encouraged him to do in
Africa what he, Billy Graham, and others were doing in
North America. That lit a fire in Michael. When he shared
this vision with me in Nairobi in 1967, I believed it was
right, and I have connected with it since that time.

As a friend of Michael
Cassidy, Bishop Festo Kivengere, and many dear friends
of African Enterprise, I not
only served as a board member for many years, but I had
the rare privilege of ministering with them in many
of Africa's major cities, as
well as in Israel, Egypt,

Michael Cassidy of South Africa,
founder of African Enterprise

Festo Kivengere and translator in China

Jordan, Bahrain, India, China, and beyond. I found I was right at home among a multiracial ministry that presented the good news that Christ is Savior of all and the one who brings real, eternal peace among humankind.

Indelible in my mind is China. I went three times to China, the first when the government was fighting against Christianity, so to speak, and the last after reforms were taking place, ever so slowly but surely. One reason I was so affected by China is that when Anna Ruth and I prepared for our assignment in 1953, one big issue was, "Why did missions fail in China?" The existence of the church in China then seemed to hang in the balance. In 1949, the Chinese Communist government had directed that all Chinese churches should sever relationships with overseas missions and churches. The government allowed only those congregations to continue which agreed to be registered by the government, and, of course, constantly monitored.

At that time it is estimated that there were about three million believers in the country. Seldom has the church suffered persecution as it did in China for the next 30 or

I was amazed at the vitality of the huge number of Christians in China

more years. Numbers dwindled at first, but as the church dug in and grew in the Chinese culture, many times in secret, the numbers in both registered and unregistered churches grew. In spite of everything, believers multiplied at a rapid rate, spreading good news and fellowships all over the land. I cannot begin to explain how my three extended visits to China convinced me, once again, that Jesus Christ is building his church. I read again the Book of Revelation. I began to understand the miracle of the survival and growth of the church in China.

I had been invited to that great land by Bishop Ding, the official head of the Protestants in China, who wanted the Chinese church to hear how churches in Africa survived after the Colonial Era. Ding befriended Bishop Kivengere, whom he met at ecumenical conferences. Out of this friendship came Ding's invitation to Kivengere to share with the churches in China about how African churches managed to survive in the Colonial Era and since. Festo said yes, if the trip could be sponsored by African Enterprise. Ding agreed and made all the arrangements. So AE formed a team, that included me, as a testimony to the ability of the Holy Spirit to build fellowship across races and cultures. I shared along with the others on the team that the cross of Christ binds us together in love, regardless of race or culture.

Now, as I write, I understand that there may be as many as 75 million believers in China, and that they have a missionary vision to evangelize both within and beyond their borders. These trips to China, that came in the latter years of my ministry, strengthened my faith in the power of the Spirit of God to enable believers to pass through unspeakable suffering and emerge as a purified, enlivened body, ready to do God's will.

I have a little story to tell about the Bible in China. The euphoria of the Communist Revolution installed by Chairman Mao ran high for 20 or more years. He even produced the famous Red Book that everyone had to read. I recall that on one of my visits to China our little team was traveling by train alongside the Yangtze River. On that particular team we had a Norwegian missionary who knew Chinese, Dr. Sig Aske. He was reading his Bible. A middle-aged Chinese man cocked his head and asked, "What are you reading?" Sig replied, "The Bible." The man asked, "Is this the book that Jesus wrote?" Sig did not want to get into details so just said, "Yes." The man asked, "When did he write it?" The questions were getting harder. Sig just said, "About 2,000 years ago." The chap straightened up and said, "Ten years ago we all read Mao's Red Book. No one reads that any more! You are still reading a book that old?"

Another picture comes to mind as I recall ministry with the African Enterprise teams, this time in Durban, South Africa, during the days when the apartheid white government was doing its best to preserve the status quo. African Enterprise was determined to have evangelistic meetings in a setting where all races could gather. The only place that could happen in Durban was at the International Trade Center building where people from all over the world could show their goods. So that became the venue. Everyone used the same latrines, the same restaurants, everything, whether white, brown, or black.

During one of the sessions when some issues were being discussed, discord broke out. Michael tried his best to quell the unrest. It came down to a black-versus-white issue. It was bedlam as all wanted to speak, or yell! Poor Michael. Here was something that he could not control.

So bowing his head, he left the podium empty and moved back. In a few moments all went silent. It was as though the arresting power of the Holy Spirit fell. I heard soft weeping invading the silence, then more and more. A spirit of weeping and repentance fell with power. I, who seldom weep, found myself pouring out my heart with tears like everyone else. Later I thought, "That is true evangelism." Hearts were changed that night. I know mine was.

INTERNATIONAL CHAIRMAN OF AFRICAN ENTERPRISE

It should not have startled me, but in 1992, the International Chairman of African Enterprise, Warwick Olson of Australia, a gem of a man, fulfilled his six-year term. Bishop Festo asked if I would consider stepping in. I knew something of the challenge of trying to shepherd the work of the 10 African teams with their local boards and the five international support boards, so I did what I often did. I asked to speak to Anna Ruth first. That usually gave me

*Some African Enterprise leaders with
Michael Cassidy in the center*

time to say "No." When I spoke to Anna Ruth about it, she said, "I think you should." Ouch.

It stretched my every fiber to fill my six-year term. I came into office when tensions were escalating between the Southern African region and East Africa. The politics wanted to tear us in two. People with passports from East African nations could not travel to South Africa. I even carried two US passports, one for South Africa only and another for everywhere else. This put a huge strain on the relationship between Michael and Festo, leaders of the two groups.

We arranged to meet at a retreat setting in Glion, in the Alps. Try our best, we could not see our way forward. We were dreadfully deadlocked. The only solution, it seemed, was to split in two. As we gathered for morning prayers, Festo stood, telling us that as he prayed before the meeting, he was pouring out his heart to Jesus. He said, "Jesus, I love you." He heard Jesus say, "I know that you love me, but do you love Michael?" That broke Festo's heart. He left his place, crossed the room, and embraced Michael with the words, "I love you Michael." That opened the door for all to repent, to reach out in love for one another. I believe that saved African Enterprise. The problems were still there, but with unity and love we knew that we would get through.

As International Chairman I experienced times of wonder, like I just described. I also went through dark times when it seemed issues were simply irreconcilable. In almost every situation I found myself between—between East and South Africa, between the piety of the revival movement and the new charismatic movement, between some very strong voices in the international support boards and equally strong voices on the ministering teams in Africa, between those who had money and those who did not, which usually meant, between the support boards and the ministering teams. (I often wished that money would never be part of the discussion. Unfortunately, it always was!)

My term as Chairman taxed my ability to reconcile sincere differences. I became painfully aware, again, that I am a slow learner. I found that I was internalizing the pain of all parties instead of charting a way forward, hoping the relationships would heal eventually. In a situation like that, survival is success, I guess.

One of our challenges was to protect the dignity and integrity of every person involved in AE and every board and team, scattered around the world. Since we all had the same vision and call, and since we were all committed Christians, we were able to push through some of the cultural barriers. But not all. It is a huge challenge to understand each other. Working cross-culturally requires a huge commitment to listen, listen again, and then be willing to change. For me, it was an exercise in dropping my strong opinions regularly so that I could hear the real message behind each person's overt message. I suppose that I was slowly being changed, even though I could not put my finger on exactly what was happening to me. I always had to fight for internal integrity. I did not want to lose that.

On the brighter side, African Enterprise attracted some absolutely marvelous people all across the world. I will mention a few who became not only colleagues but also friends. Foremost were Michael and Carol Cassidy. I was totally committed to standing with Michael and his team as they took huge risks to bring about spiritual and civic renewal in South Africa. When called upon, they played a significant role in the process of softening and finally in seeing the apartheid system vanish. Michael embodied his undying determination to make every person in South Africa stand tall. And he always did it with a Christ-honoring message.

And then there were Malcolm and Bertha Graham, remarkable servants of the Lord. While Michael dreamed the dreams, Malcolm and Bertha and their staff translated those dreams into reality. They were marvelously gifted administrators and the most gracious human beings.

The oldest of the international partner boards was the US board. It was populated with high-level people like Ted Engstrom, President of World Vision, who answered every letter I ever sent to him no matter how busy he was. And it included my hero, Bruce Bare, who was with the Enterprise from the very beginning and a stalwart supporter all his life. The board in England was just as impressive. Its chairperson, Richard Bewes, Rector of All Souls in London, was born and raised in Kenya of Anglican missionary parents, so we clicked immediately. And who would not be impressed by Jean Wilson, a British business owner, a rare blend of power and grace. She managed the UK AE board and served as treasurer of the AE International Partnership board for many years. I leaned on her heavily when I became chairperson.

In Australia, I finally met a person whom I had heard about for years, the author of the popular *Jungle Doctor* series, Dr. Paul White, with his wife, Ruth. He was a member of the Australian Board. Paul had served as a missionary doctor in Tanzania where he gathered innumerable African stories and parables. He had the extraordinary gift of telling those stories for Australian audiences. The fact that he was a compulsive birder like me did no harm!

Today African Enterprise is a partnership of approximately 300 staff and countless volunteers and friends representing national teams, including a pan-African mission team, a reconciliation department, a training department, and support teams in seven countries across the globe. These teams, departments, boards, and individuals have covenanted among themselves to continue the mission given to African Enterprise at its start: "To evangelize the cities of Africa through word and deed, in partnership with the church."

Trying to build cross-cultural and international ministries is fraught with challenges, but these are the challenges of the decades ahead. African Enterprise continues as a viable ministry, doing marvelous work all over Africa today. Such international team-building to extend the Kingdom of Christ is worth the hard work. Even the hurts and disappointments that go along with this sort of work can become opportunities for repentance and spiritual growth. I used to console myself, when there was a blowup, that what we went through was the setting for new heartfelt repentance. That was how we could truly work together with joy and tremendous hope.

RECONCILIATION MINISTRIES

I was pleased that during my term as International Chairman, although African Enterprise was primarily involved in evangelism, it worked effectively at vitally important reconciliation ministries. The South African team, for example, served an extraordinary role in bringing leaders with opposing views together and, in a safe and Christian setting, worked at developing friendships which helped the nation move out of the apartheid era and into the democratic one.

I saw that, without planning for it, African Enterprise had been serving as a reconciling force everywhere it ministered. Seeing this, I suggested that African Enterprise set up a program to focus on ministries of reconciliation. They agreed, and today that ministry is sought after where there is conflict.

It was put into practice first in Rwanda after the genocide of 1994 in which AE experienced a tragedy. The head of the Rwanda AE team, Israel Havigumana, a Hutu, reached out to leaders of both tribes, Hutu and Tutsi, pleading for them to be reconciled. Because of that he became a marked man. When the killing orgy began in 1994, he was one of the first to be martyred, by his own people, the Hutu. I was unable to attend his funeral but determined in my heart that AE must assist in reconciliation and peacemaking.

The first ministry was in Rwanda under the leadership of Antoine Rutayisire, the Rwanda team leader. It proved to be one of the most effective of all AE ministries. Later on, Emmanuel Kopwe of Tanzania assumed leadership. Through the years, AE has been able to help hundreds of people to find forgiveness, reconciliation, and peace.

Chapter 32

SIBLING
BONDING

Gerald's Funeral

Can a family like the one I grew up in grow closer as life goes on? This question haunted me for years. We were a mixed bunch. Seven of us retained membership in the Mennonite church; four did not. I cannot speak for each one, but life and heaps of grace and forgiveness served to bring the tracks of our lives together as time went on. Family bonding got stronger for me as the years progressed. I think we all swallowed a bit in order to accept one another.

For example, on a chilly day in December 2003, I was given the awesome responsibility of officiating at the funeral of my older brother, Gerald, age 91. I was 75 at the time. Gerald made the Army his career. He retired as a full Corporal, an "Eagle," as they say. In our visits, which became more frequent as we grew older, he spoke incidentally about his funeral.

When I got word of his passing, I had assumed that he would have a full military funeral, maybe even in Arlington National Cemetery where he had a right, as a Colonel, to be buried. But he decided to have a service at a funeral home and then be buried beside his wife in a Williamsburg, Virginia, cemetery. I noticed that he wore civilian clothes. On a prior visit, he told me that his uniform was ready for his burial. I had no problem with that. The military issue was always there in our family but not openly discussed. I am convinced that Gerald was saying something by choosing a nonmilitary funeral, in civilian clothes; at least I want to think that. That was so like Gerald, I thought.

I conducted the funeral at the funeral home, and then a hearse carried his body to the cemetery where the military guard took over. Assuming my involvement was over, I grabbed my video camera to record something entirely new for me, a military funeral. Then someone approached me urgently, telling me to come immediately to conduct the interment ceremony at the graveside. I had left my Bible in the car when I got my camera. Fortunately, my

Jacobs family. Seated are Erma, Trella, Paul, Twila. Others left to right, Dorothea, Willard, Gerald, Merle, Dwight, Arnold, Duane, me.

brother Duane was at my side. He whipped out his pocket New Testament, and I rushed to the burial tent, found appropriate verses, and said my final good-byes to Gerald. I no sooner said the final "Amen" when the silence was shattered by the deafening, startling, 21-gun salute. I wondered, is this me standing here?

I recall presiding at my brother Merle's funeral as well. He and his wife, Liz, were true friends. Merle was so unlike Gerald that it was hard to believe that they were brothers. I remember my mother saying "They do not come much different," when referring to her children. Yet God gave me grace to learn from each of my brothers, and from my sisters, for that matter. Merle and I agreed on almost everything. He was head and shoulders taller than I in almost everything but height. If I laid aside his massive achievements and his off-the-chart IQ, I found him feeling just the way I feel about the core virtues of life. I carry with me the closing moments of his funeral. As we turned from the grave site to return to the church, a snow-white pigeon fluttered down from the sky and landed, cooing, on the eave of the church for all to see. A nice, Merle-like finish.

Thinking of common values, I do believe that we were shaped by the same environment, speaking generally. I began to discover that the best way for siblings to relate is to melt down together, into the deeper level of being where achievements and public opinion mean nothing. Realizing that has blessed me tremendously. I value that unity of core virtues with all my siblings. In many ways, our separate lifetime paths converged so that we are now more than pleased to call each other brother or sister and mean it. I draw immense consolation from that fact. It is a miracle of God's grace. My longing to see harmony in the family has been satisfied beyond my fondest hopes.

As I mused on the course of my own family relationships, I could see, dimly, the entire scope of my life. It is
as though all in the family leave the station on the same
track. Then our tracks take different routes, over hills and
valleys, until, at some point, the tracks begin to merge
imperceptibly into something that, when examined, point
to a common origin and hopefully to a common destination.

Chapter 33

RETIREMENT—
TIME TO REFLECT

❖

MORE THINKING ABOUT FAMILY

I am still trying to figure out why, at age 70, I was overcome with a compulsion to try to find out everything that I could about my ancestors. Maybe it was because my life's calling has required me to squeeze through the needle's eye of one culture after another. As I grew up, I discovered that my own home culture bore little resemblance to the dominant culture of our area. As I became an adult, I went from embracing a Mennonite culture to living for a few years in Appalachia, then England, and then to the wrenching adjustments of living in African cultures on the shores of Lake Victoria, then in urban Nairobi, the new Africa, and back again. On and on I went, finally globe-trotting as a lecturer and teacher in the art of Christian leadership.

I was like a butterfly flitting from flower to flower in a bewildering kaleidoscope of cultural colors and shapes. Or like malleable iron on an anvil, I was hammered this way and that, probably more than most of my generation. How could I possibly retain an inner integrity? To be honest, I didn't give it a thought. I just got up, brushed off the dust, and got on with life as a child of God. I lived under the constraints of a call to reach out in love to all.

The cultural whirlwinds that I went through in my life are now mercifully stilled, or, should I say, not as violent. I'm thinking more about me. As I do so, I find that there is one part of me that I need to know more about. That might help me to understand how I survived a lifetime of bending and then blending, time after time, recovering rather than fracturing. Granted, the grace of God was at work, but I do believe that I have a core that holds. Where did that come from? I know it is there. It is also there among my siblings. Is it possible that we owe that to our ancestors?

My time had come to ponder my origins. I began by asking, again, what kind of parents were Mom and Dad? What shaped them? What gave content to our family ethos? How was I influenced by my brothers and sisters? How did we get through tough patches as a family? How did we deal with success and painful setbacks? What influenced the way I react to things? Have I changed in that regard?

Grandma Jacobs, a praying woman

When it came to the Jacobs' side of the story, I fell in love with Grossmom, my father's mother, the only grandparent I knew. I use the word, "knew" lightly because I never did know her really. She was German!

Years later, her grandson, Curt Cover, Jr., with whom she lived, told me that after supper she withdrew to her room where her Bible and prayer book were. There she sang and rocked and no doubt prayed for herself and her family. Curt remembers that rock, rock, rock sound. I can hear it now. Did she pray for me, in German?

When I studied the Jacobs family history, I met things that startled me. For instance, my cousin shot and killed his wife in a fit of rage, then killed himself, leaving their only child, a three-year-old daughter, to be raised by her mother's family, the Kapps, who were nominal Catholics at best. The daughter, Phyllis, dropped right out of the Jacobs family life. When I decided to write the Jacobs family history, I got an address through the alumni association of her high school and wrote to her — in Idaho, of all places. She had been out of touch with our family for more than 40 years. She responded by not only being ready to include her own family in the Jacobs family tree, but she also wanted to link with us because she, her husband, daughter, and son were all keen Christians and rejoiced that there were some believers in our line!

Phyllis is a bit older than I am. I visited her three times in Idaho. When I heard her story of her hunger for God in her grandparents' home, and how that was not satisfied then, but was later in life when a friend led her to faith in Jesus, I had my answer. Grossmom's prayers! As I collected stories like this, I found a golden thread, laid there, perhaps, by a praying grandmother.

Now, some thoughts about my mother's side.

MUSING ON MEMORIES

I had my mid-morning coffee under the red maple tree in our backyard today here in Lancaster. A tufted titmouse snatched a sunflower seed from the feeder, flew to a perch above me, and proceeded to break open the seed with deft strokes of its wee bill. Presto, I was sitting beside the grape arbor as a boy, watching the exact thing in Johnstown. Then I recalled the strikingly colored, large oropendula of Costa Rica feeding on palm nuts. I was with my brother Merle as he made a video for his book on animal behavior. I was seeing the marvels of nature through his eyes. So there on my porch, warmed by the spring sun, an entire slide show flashed across my mind. It was a moment of joy. A time of no time. Johnstown, Costa Rica, Lancaster, and untold places between, kissed one another. Life is a whole.

I mused further—Felix Manz, a 16th-century martyr, Christian and Magdalena Blough who settled in Somerset County in 1767, Samuel and Susanna Blough, my ancestral Mennonite bishop who lived near where I grew up, Paul and Trella, and now me. I looked the other direction and saw our children, spouses, grandchildren, and their children, off into the future. I believe that life has more continuities than shake-ups. I see that the effects of changes in my life tend to get ironed out over time, and I find myself more like I was than I ever would have expected.

I find it hugely satisfying to know that I live life in a stretched picture, a picture that includes not only what I experienced, but what my ancestors did as well. Why should I gain so much satisfaction from looking backwards? I think it has to do with the mechanisms that constantly strive to compact diversities in my life. I will never weave everything that I experienced in my fourscore years into a single, unified braid. But I never stop trying, and maybe even succeeding to some degree. Now I must feed into that braid what I received from my ancestors. That golden cord may be the most important part of me.

I inherited physical traits from them. I also inherited a place in culture. I did not fashion that culture; I found it fully blown when I became aware of it. I was American and heavily stamped by that fact. I was born into a home that was shaped by history and experience, decidedly Christian and decidedly multicultural. Furthermore, we as a family had to forge an identity within our particular mixed cultural context. The way we did that rubbed off on me. The fact that I was child number nine out of a string of eleven certainly had a profound effect on me.

I was shaped by values that my family embraced, all of which were passed down to them. Hard work. Do your bit. Do not complain. Help one another but look out for yourself. Mom kept repeating, "Remember who you are." That did not mean, who "I" was, but who "we" as a family are. I felt strange and disobedient when I disregarded any of the virtues. I did not think of those virtues as inherited because they were so much a part of us. They were there as family furniture. It was our very own furniture.

In summary, a huge part of me was given to me. How do I handle that as a free moral person? The only sane thing to do is to acknowledge it and start from there.

Here is where being "born from above" comes in. Our new birth, that is made possible by the reconciling work of Father, Son, and Holy Spirit, speaks to what we have inherited through no effort of our own. My new birth in Jesus embraces what I have inherited. I recall reading the Apostle Paul's defense before the Jewish elders. He

recounted what he received—born a Jew of Jewish parents, raised a Jew, subjected to Jewish rituals, and shaped
by Jewish values. If there ever was a born-again believer, it
was Paul, yet he could not disown his Jewish inheritance.
He never did, even though it cost him years of impris-
onment in Rome. Ultimately, every person must embrace
what is inherited and start from there.

My active imagination and internal memory are always
receiving, always sorting, always deleting. The narrative
extends back, way back, to the heartbreak of my grandmother when the flood of violent waters swept away her
husband and left her abandoned, without family except
for her own six children, in a strange land that she could
barely call home. My memory extends to the ends of the
earth, from the sensation of walking on the Great Wall in
China to enjoying ballet in the Sydney Opera Hall in Australia. It drinks water from the imagined springhouse on
the Blough farm where my grandmother, Almira Blough,
learned how to live productively, nursed by family and
herd. It knows the exhilaration of standing on the summit
of Kilimanjaro and on the massif Jungfrau. It also knows
the blast of oppressive heat coming off the Dead Sea and
of heart-shaking tragedy.

Why is it that everything that happens finds an echo in
my soul? Is that the God-consciousness that God breathed
into every human being? I do not know. But I do know
that there is something deep down in me that simply does
not change, no matter what swirls around me. Can it be
that it is universal to all people, or does one's ancestry
have some part to play in forming that core or spine or
whatever one might call it? Having formed the question,
I decided to apply myself to pursuing the answer.

This entire book is my attempt to discover the answer. Most of it describes external happenings, with summary lacings of reflections. I see that interplay as my inner self always manages the effects of what goes on in life as it is lived. It does that, not by changing itself, but by sorting out life experiences in such a way that I know who I am. I am coming to the conclusion that I had little or nothing to do with shaping my inner core. I received it. Was it a direct gift from God? Did God make sure I was shaped that way through the influence of my ancestors? I think I am over my head here, but I would like to think about that.

Whatever it is, my inner self contains that most secret place where only two can enter, me and God. Because of what I know about God's love in Jesus, I am at rest there, for I have accepted that love as my very own. I also have a place a little larger but equally precious, where Anna Ruth and I share as one, with one another, and with our Lord. Our children are there, their spouses, our grandchildren, and great-grandchildren. This is a bower of precious relationships that exceed all price. I know who I am there, and I hope that all whom I touch there know how much I love them. Each significant life experience seems to speak meaningfully to my inner core.

As I think about it, even though I recognize that I have this inner core, that does not mean that it is the sum total of my identity. My daily life experiences provide color and texture. That is identity in human terms. I am gratified as I look around my office. On the wall are recognitions, B.A., M.A., Ph.D., Alumnus of the Year, Lifetime Achievement Award, honors degrees, plaques of appreciation for varieties of service, and so on. My shelf has a section containing books and articles I have written. Dominating it all is a large picture of our family on holiday at the beach.

As I review my life, I receive huge comfort from these reminders. Reminders of what? I am convinced that they are constant reminders of God's grace. I cannot figure it all out, but being a follower of Jesus makes an astounding difference about how I view my core and my life experiences. I am trying to see myself from God's point of view. It is all his doing. I am absolutely convinced that without Christ I can do nothing of worth, but with his power in my life almost anything is possible. I look at our family photo and then out the window where buds are bursting on the cherry tree. Spring is here. Who can restrain the spirit from singing a loud song of praise to God who made it possible? Not me.

Plenty to explore at 2118 Lyndell Drive, Lancaster PA

AFTERWORD

On that summer day when I, a 70-year-old man, ran my hand across the red oven brick, some deep stirrings in the depth of my being began to resonate in sympathy with a growing reality, partially tangible, partially imagined, but a reality nevertheless. I was holding not only a red oven brick but also a meaningful heritage. I was building a love bond between myself and Samuel and Susanna Blough, my great-grandparents, through whom I could look forward and backward.

A simple old brick can take on new meaning. That is what happens when people get passionate about something, and I was passionate about trying to find out what shaped my me.

I found myself imagining that the farm, now only a memory, was the epicenter of my heritage. I needed to do that to fill a void in my life. The "deep" in me needed to find an echo in the "deep" of my heritage. I either touched that "deep," or was very close to it, as I rummaged through the scattered bits and pieces of a house that was one day, in the distant past, buzzing with the activities of my own flesh and blood. It might have been long ago, but it was surprisingly real, touchable, and alive in heart and not just in memory. I was driven by an irresistible compulsion to go as deeply into my inner self as I could and make a real connection with someone I hoped I could relate to. For me, that was my great-grandfather, Samuel Blough, a Mennonite bishop like me.

I was born and raised a dozen or so miles from the now derelict Blough farm. My life's journey took me to the ends of the earth, literally, through decades of almost constant change, from continent to continent, culture to culture, tribe to tribe, decade after unfolding decade, through all seasons of life, from the vibrancy of infancy to the mellowness of old age.

The weight of that red oven brick in my hand was the weight of all that went into me, long before I was born and progressively ever after. It was a good brick—substantial, fairly symmetrical, flawed, purposeful, and strong. It obviously did what it was meant to do. It served as a red oven brick in my ancestral home. How about me? What am I making of my life, and who am I now?

As Twila and I walked away from what was left of the ancient Blough farm, I with my brick and she with the battered, blue, rusted porcelain bucket, we looked at each other and smiled. In her eyes I could see sadness and joy, pathos and hope. Or was I just seeing a reflection of what was in my own eyes, a glint of what stirred in my own heart?

Then we walked up the hill to the Robert Blough house where we found Robert working among his fabulously beautiful rhododendron plants. He offered Twila one of his best to plant in her own little garden. Into the car trunk it went. With deep appreciation, we thanked him and his wife for their kindness and drove off.

A few weeks later, I learned about a more immediate connection with my great-grandfather, more than a brick, even though that was good. It was a sheet of paper written in his own hand that he placed in the family Bible, ordering that the valued Bible should be given to his next ordained Mennonite descendant. After his death it went to his son, John Henry Blough, an ordained deacon whose tenure was cut short for some obscure reason. That meant that the next descendant of Bishop Samuel Blough to be ordained as a minister in the Mennonite church was, in fact, me.

I am heir to the priceless Froschauer Bible printed in Switzerland in 1536, brought to America by the Saylor family, one of whom married a Blough, and thus the misnomer "The Blough Family Bible." That note, written in a carefully crafted script, was a note to me. I was ecstatic, but I sensed that I would never possess that Bible as I had the red oven brick. Yet I grasped firmly the comfort that I had touched, in a tangible way, my ancestral home.

The Bible eventually found its home in one of the museums around Pittsburgh because the family could not decide who should have it. That decision was made before my time. In my imagination, I reverently held that heavy Bible, brought to this land by people who wanted to shape their lives in a new place, with their faith as the center point. In that instant, I was connected in another profound and moving way with my heritage. Through those immigrants I had a window through which I could view the world and myself.

In my life I see a melding of the spiritual and the historical, as though the vertical and the horizontal come together to form a cross of mercy and grace. As I ponder now who I am, I revel in a completeness that almost leaves me breathless. I am convinced that in my own life I see the love of God changing me, establishing me, and exciting me. The power of God's love is the wellspring of everything good. I understand only a little of that love, but I have experienced it mightily in my life. I am a debtor to God's love, now and forever. That is reason enough to set my face to the future, knowing that God's love knows no limits, in this life or in the glorious life to come.

ABOUT THE AUTHOR

Don and Anna Ruth Jacobs today live near Lancaster, Pennsylvania.